W9-BXB-613

GENERAL EDITORS
Gloria Bowles
Renate Klein
Janice Raymond

CONSULTING EDITOR
Dale Spender

The **Athene Series** assumes that those who formulate explanations of the way the world works need to know and appreciate the significance of basic feminist principles.

The growth of feminist research internationally has called into question almost all aspects of social organization in our culture. The **Athene Series** focuses on the construction of knowledge and the exclusion of women from the process—both as theorists and subjects of study—and offers innovative studies that challenge established theories and research.

ATHENE, the Olympian goddess of wisdom, was honored by the ancient Greeks as the patron of arts and sciences and guardian of cities. She represented both peace and war, the latter in its cognitive aspect. Her mother, Metis, was a Titan and presided over all knowledge. While pregnant with Athene, Metis was swallowed whole by Zeus. Some say this was his attempt to embody her supreme wisdom. The original Athene is thus twice born: once of her strong mother, Metis, and once more out of the head of Zeus. According to feminist myth, there is a "third birth" of Athene when she stops being an agent and mouthpiece of Zeus and male dominance, and returns to her original source: the wisdom of womankind.

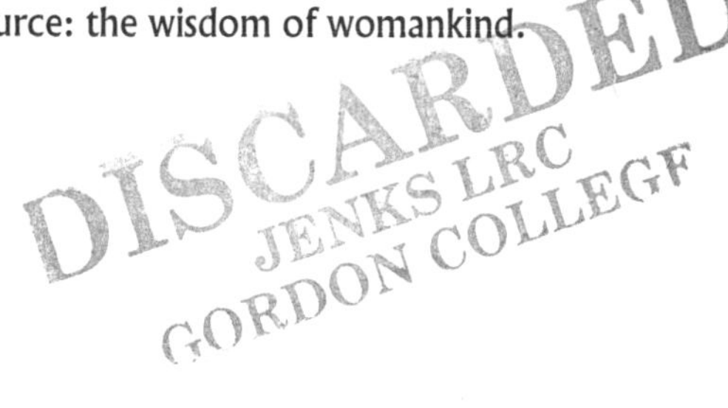
DISCARDED
JENKS LRC
GORDON COLLEGE

Teaching the Majority

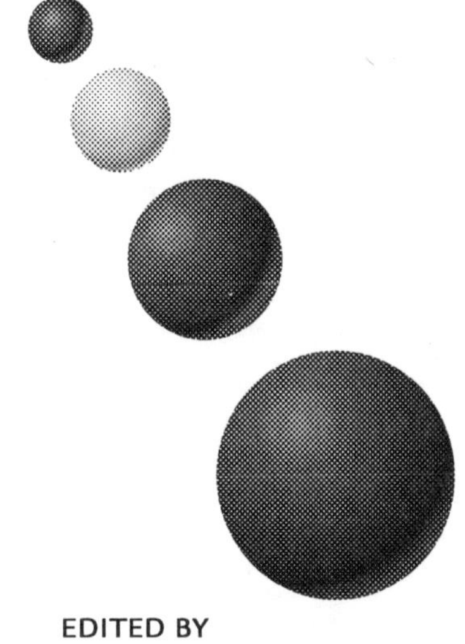

BREAKING THE GENDER BARRIER IN SCIENCE, MATHEMATICS, AND ENGINEERING

EDITED BY
Sue V. Rosser

JENKS L.R.C.
GORDON COLLEGE
255 GRAPEVINE RD.
WENHAM, MA 01984-1895

TEACHERS COLLEGE PRESS
Teachers College, Columbia University
New York and London

Q
181
.T3538
1995

Published by Teachers College Press, 1234 Amsterdam Avenue, New York, NY 10027

Copyright © 1995 by Sue V. Rosser

Chapter 2, copyright © 1995 by Karen Barad
Chapter 12, copyright © 1995 by H. Patricia Hynes

All rights reserved. No part of this publication may be reproduced or transmitted in any form or by any means, electronic or mechanical, including photocopy, or any information storage and retrieval system, without permission from the publisher.

Library of Congress Cataloging-in-Publication Data

Teaching the majority : breaking the gender barrier in science, mathematics, and engineering / edited by Sue V. Rosser.
p. cm. — (Athene series)
Includes bibliographical references and index.
ISBN 0-8077-6277-6. — ISBN 0-8077-6276-8 (pbk.)
1. Science—Study and teaching—Sex differences. 2. Mathematics—Study and teaching—Sex differences. 3. Engineering—Study and teaching—Sex differences. I. Rosser, Sue Vilhauer. II. Series.
Q181.T3538 1995
507.1—dc20 94-44738

ISBN 0-8077-6276-8 (paper)
ISBN 0-8077-6277-6 (cloth)

Printed on acid-free paper
Manufactured in the United States of America
01 00 99 98 97 96 95 94 8 7 6 5 4 3 2 1

Contents

Acknowledgments

As editor of this volume, I would like to acknowledge the expertise, commitment, and effort of each of the chapter authors. Their willingness to undertake new ventures, rewrite drafts, and meet short deadlines turned the vision for this project into a reality.

In addition to the individual authors, the editors and staff at Teachers College Press provided invaluable support for every phase of the book. I would like to thank Carole Saltz and Sarah Biondello for their general editorial insights in conceiving the book, and Cathy McClure and Carol Collins for their aid in their respective roles as developmental editor and in-house editor. The production and marketing staff also served as key players who ensured that the book reached the public in a timely manner.

Finally, I would like to acknowledge my own sources of support. My family, Charlotte, Meagan, and Caitlin, provided emotional encouragement as always. I am especially indebted to my administrative assistant Linda Lien, who worked very hard on all aspects of the book. She served as the communication link, connecting authors to me via letter and telephone. She also struggled with individual disks to link all the chapters into the consistent, sequential manuscript that became *Teaching the Majority*.

INTRODUCTION

Reaching the Majority

Retaining Women in the Pipeline

Sue V. Rosser

During the last two decades, women have entered the professions in record numbers. In recent years, women have received degrees in most fields in numbers approaching or exceeding their 51% of the American population. The physical sciences, mathematics, and engineering persist as the professional areas where women have not yet broken the gender barrier. Women constitute 45% of the employed labor force in the United States but only 16% of all employed scientists and engineers (National Science Foundation [NSF], 1992). A 1994 report from the National Research Council revealed that women constitute about 12% of the employed scientific and engineering labor force in industry. Of 1,647 living scientists elected to membership in the National Academy of Sciences, only 70 are women; in the 1992 election, 5 of the 59 honorees were women.

Women employed in science, mathematics, and engineering are concentrated in psychology and the life and social sciences, while male scientists and engineers are concentrated primarily in engineering (NSF, 1992). In 1988, women earned 32.9% of the doctorates and 44.0% of the bachelor's degrees in the life sciences. The physical and technological sciences continue to attract scant numbers of women: Women obtained only 16.8% of the PhDs and 29.7% of the bachelor's degrees in physical sciences; in engineering, women earned a scant 6.8% of the PhDs and 14.5% of the undergraduate degrees that year (NSF, 1990).

Increases in the numbers of women in the educational pipeline translate slowly into increased percentages of women in the overall science and engineering workforce. For example, in 1993, women made up only "1 percent of working environmental engineers, 2 percent of mechanical engineers, 3 percent of electrical engineers, 4 percent of medical school department directors, 5 percent of physics Ph.D.'s, 6 out of close to 300 tenured professors in the country's top 10 mathematics departments" (Holloway, 1993, p. 96). Although 41% of working life scientists and biologists and 17%

of the members of the American Chemical Society in 1991 were women, in the physical sciences such as physics, geology, and engineering, the percentage of women remains very low (Holloway, 1993).

With the exception of Asian Americans, underrepresentation of minorities in science and engineering also continues to be a serious problem. Although blacks and Hispanics constitute 10% and 7%, respectively, of the U.S. employed labor force, each represented only 3% of all employed scientists and engineers in 1988 (NSF, 1990). A large percentage (44%) of black scientists works in the life and social sciences, although a higher percentage of blacks (62%) than women works in engineering (Matyas & Malcolm, 1991). The small numbers of American Indians and difficulties in obtaining accurate reports of heritage on survey instruments have made statistics on this group problematic. Based on limited data, it appears that American Indians are underrepresented as scientists relative to their proportions in the overall population (NSF, 1992).

This dearth of women and minorities in these areas is unfortunate both for these people and for science and engineering. Demographers predict that nearly two thirds of new entrants into the workforce will be women (U.S. Department of Labor, 1987) and that between 80% and 90% of the workforce growth by the year 2000 will be women and minorities—the groups not traditionally attracted in large numbers to the physical sciences and engineering:

> There will be a larger segment of minorities and women: 23% more blacks, 70% more Asians and other races (American Indians, Alaska natives and Pacific Islanders), 74% more Hispanics and 25% more women, adding 3.6 million, 2.4 million, 6.0 million and 13.0 million more workers respectively. Altogether, the minorities and women will make up 90% of the work force growth and 23% of the new employees will be immigrants. (Thomas, 1989, p. 30)

The science and engineering professions typically offer relatively high paying, stable positions, which should be particularly appealing in an economy where unemployment and poverty are increasing for both women and people of color. Attracting more men of color and women to the physical sciences, mathematics, and engineering would provide career access for these individuals while filling the needs of our increasingly scientific and technological workforce.

Despite the relatively low percentages of women in most areas of science and engineering, until recently, few programs have directly targeted females. The results of a 1991 study by Matyas and Malcolm, which included surveys of the presidents and chancellors of 276 colleges and universities and the directors of nearly 400 recruitment and retention programs, revealed that less than 10% of the programs included in the study were specifically focused on the recruitment and retention of women in science or engineering. This study confirmed similar findings from previous studies that virtually no programs directly target female students or faculty.

A growing body of research documents the need to change the way science is taught in order to appeal to women. Women's studies scholars have explored the ways in which science as it is currently taught and practiced may reflect a masculine approach to the world that tends to exclude women (S. Harding, 1986; Keller, 1985). This critique has been developed most extensively for biology (Birke, 1986; Bleier, 1984; Fausto-Sterling, 1992; Hubbard, 1990; Rosser, 1986, 1990), leading scholars to examine curricular content and pedagogy in that discipline.

Based on these investigations, faculty have evolved new approaches to teaching traditional material that is more "female-friendly" (Rosser, 1990, 1993). In two previous volumes in the Athene Series, I explored revisions of biology and health curricular content and syllabi (Rosser, 1986) and pedagogical techniques (Rosser, 1990) to include women. After reading these books or hearing me speak about them, people frequently request similar information for the physical sciences, mathematics, and engineering.

This volume is an attempt to fill that request. Knowing that such curricular and pedagogical innovations had to be developed by individuals who teach the subjects, I agreed to edit the volume with chapters contributed by mathematicians, engineers, physicists, chemists, computer scientists, and geologists who teach in colleges and universities throughout the United States. *Teaching the Majority* includes descriptions of changed teaching techniques, course content, syllabi, laboratory exercises, and problem sets demonstrated to attract and retain women. Each chapter is written by a faculty member who has successfully transformed his or her science, mathematics, or engineering course to appeal to women students in particular, while retaining its appeal for male students.

Although it would be desirable to include a course description and syllabus, examples of laboratory exercises and problem sets, and specific pedagogical techniques for each discipline within the physical sciences and engineering, the cutting-edge nature of this volume makes that impossible. A few faculty members in the physical sciences and engineering have only recently begun to consider the impact of gender and the application of the new scholarship on women in their classrooms. It is not surprising that one faculty member working in isolation—not only alone in her or his department and institution but also unsupported by a national professional organization or project—may make a considerable contribution to the field by describing a new pedagogical technique or transformed curricular content of one subsection of a traditional syllabus. The uneven extent of the transformation for the different disciplines is inevitable in this cutting-edge work.

Twenty-five years of women's studies scholarship and experience with curriculum transformation projects have enabled faculty to develop models that chart the phases through which changes occur in a variety of disciplines in diverse institutions (McIntosh, 1984; Schuster & Van Dyne, 1984; Tetreault, 1985). Building upon these models for other disciplines, I developed similar phase models and pedagogical techniques for the sciences (Rosser, 1990, 1993). The phases of curriculum transformation may be visualized as a continuous spiral with overlapping components rather than as discrete stages; many of the pedagogical techniques are appropriate to accompany multiple stages of the curriculum. A six-phase model for curricular and pedagogical transformations provides a framework to explore contributions by the authors of *Teaching the Majority*.

PHASE MODEL

Phase I: Absence of Women Is Not Noted

Most physical science, mathematics, and engineering curricula throughout the country are in phase I. In this phase, faculty and students are not aware of the absence of women scientists in the theoretical and decision-making positions in the scientific establishment nor of the absence of and focus on women in the curriculum. They assume that since science is "objective," gender does not influence either who becomes a scientist or the science produced by those scientists. Many scientists would suggest that science is "manless" as well as "womanless"; they are unaware of or would openly reject the notion that gender might influence the theories, data collection, subjects chosen for experimentation, or questions asked. Authors contributing to this volume have moved beyond this stage to acknowledge the influence of gender and to evolve positive strategies to incorporate it in appropriate ways in their classrooms.

Phase II: Recognition That Most Scientists Are Male and That Science May Reflect a Masculine Perspective

Recent publicity from the federal government and various professional societies has made most scientists aware that women are underrepresented in all natural science fields, particularly in the theoretical and decision-making levels of the profession. Some scientists, influenced by scholarship in women's studies, the philosophy and history of science, and psychology, have begun to recognize that gender may influence science. Kuhn (1970) and his followers suggested that all scientific theories are the products of individuals living in a particular historical and social milieu. As such, they are biased by the perspective and paradigms of those individuals. Fee (1982) and Keller (1982) suggested that the absence of women from the decision-making levels of science has produced a science that views the world from a male perspective and is, therefore, womanless. The failure of scientists to recognize this bias has perpetuated the idea of the "objectivity" of science. In her chapter called "A Feminist Approach to Teaching Quantum Physics," Barad describes this masculine approach to physics as personified by Richard Feynman and explores alternative explanations that open new ways of teaching the subject that reach more students. Hynes, in "No Classroom Is an Island," examines the destructive effects that the masculine approach to environmental science and public policy may have had on women, third world populations, and the environment.

Because scientific theories, practices, and approaches may reflect a masculine approach to the natural physical world, the teaching of science in the lecture hall, classrooom, and laboratory may also reflect that perspective. The following pedagogical techniques may serve as correctives to teaching techniques that represent a masculine approach. They may be useful in attracting individuals, such as women and men of color, whose experiences and perspectives differ from those of the white male scientist.

Undertake fewer experiments likely to have applications of direct benefit to the military and propose more experiments to explore problems of social concern. Most women are more likely to understand and be interested in solving problems and learning techniques that do not involve guns, violence, and war. Much of this lack of interest is undoubtedly linked with sex-role socialization. Until very recently (Browne, 1994), much research in basic science has been funded by or linked with the military. As Hynes, Webb, Nair, and Majetich all suggest in their chapters, some women wish to avoid science, technology, and mathematics because they are disturbed by the destructive ways technology has been used in our society against the environment and human beings. Most girls and young women are neither adamant nor articulate in voicing their feelings about the uses of science and the resulting avoidance of science. However, many are uncomfortable engaging in experiments that appear to hurt animals for no reason at all (Halpin, 1989) or that seem useful only for calculating a rocket or bomb trajectory.

Faculty may confront this issue rather than assume that the "objectivity" of science protects the scientist from the social concerns about applications of theory and basic research. Numerous studies have documented the attraction of science for females when they can perceive its social usefulness for human beings (J. Harding, 1985; Kahle, 1985; Rosser, 1993). As both Hynes and Webb indicate in describing their approaches to teaching environmental science, a strong argument for convincing females that they should become scientists is that they can have more direct influence over policies and decisions controlling the uses of technology. Avoiding science and not acquiring the mathematical and scientific skills to understand complex decisions surrounding the use of technology ensure the exclusion of women from the decision-making process.

Include problems that have not been considered worthy of scientific investigation because of the field with which they have traditionally been associated. In seeking out methods to teach problem-solving skills, it may be advisable to search for examples and problems from more traditionally female-dominated fields such as home economics or nursing. Although these fields have been defined as "nonscience," primarily because they are dominated by women (Ehrenreich & English, 1978; Hynes, 1984), many of the approaches are scientific. In their chapter "Toward a Feminist Algebra," Campbell and Campbell-Wright develop word problems in which nutrition, purchasing clothes, and body weight become the central focus. Using familiar terminology, equipment, and subjects allows the student to concentrate on what the problem really asks rather than being put off because she or he does not know what a transformer or trajectory is.

Undertake the investigation of problems with a more holistic, global scope and use interactive methods to approach them rather than the more reduced and limited scale problems traditionally considered. The work of Gilligan (1982) suggests that adolescent girls approach problem solving from the perspective of interdependence and relationship rather than from the hierarchical, reductionistic viewpoint favored by most adolescent boys. In addition, the average female first-year college student of traditional age scores higher on the Perry scale (Perry, 1970) of student development than the average 18-year-old male. This means that she is better able to deal with complex problems and ambiguity, while he is more comfortable dealing with dualisms and problems that have one correct or concrete answer. Thus, females are more likely to feel comfortable in approaching problems and laboratory experiments if they understand the relationship of the particular problem or experiment to the broader context of the bigger problem of which this solution may be a small part. The high attrition rate of women from science majors after their first course despite good grades (Matyas, 1985) may be explained partially by the fact that introductory courses may be pitched more toward the limited one-correct-answer approach, which favors traditional-aged male college freshmen.

In the teaching of science, most instructors underline the importance of the scientist's objectivity in approaching the subject of study. This is thought to be necessary to establish scientific rigor and to school students in the difference between approaches used in the sciences and those used in the humanities and social sciences. Feminist critics (Haraway, 1978; Keller, 1982) as well as practicing scientists (Bleier, 1984; Hubbard, 1990) have pointed out that the portrayal of the scientist as distant from the object of study masks the creative, interactive relationship many scientists have with their experimental subjects. Barad considers successful strategies for overcoming this distance in her chapter on physics; in "Female-Friendly Geoscience: Eight Techniques for Reaching the Majority," Richardson, Sutton, and Cercone explain techniques they use in geology that help students feel connected with what they are studying.

Phase III: Identification of Barriers That Prevent Women From Entering Science

Acceptance of the possibility that a preponderance of male scientists may have led to the production of a science that reflects a masculine approach to the world constitutes the first step toward recognizing that there are barriers to women's becoming scientists. An aspect of phase III shows up in the studies of attempts to attract more women into science and math, the traditionally "male" disciplines. Virtually every federal funding agency (NSF, 1992; Pinn & LaRosa, 1992), professional society, and foundation (American Chemical Society [ACS], 1983; National Research Council [NRC], 1991; Vetter, 1992) involved with science and science funding has issued studies and reports documenting the lack of women in science and the possible barriers that have led to this dearth. In their chapters in this volume, Harris, Nair and Majetich, Kelly, Bohonak, and Eastman discuss barriers to women in their respective disciplines of chemistry, engineering and physics, mathematics, and computer sciences, along with strategies they have found to be successful in lowering the barriers.

These barriers for women and people of color are likely to begin in the home and early years of school and be continually reinforced in secondary school and the surrounding society. Methods applied at the college level to overcome these barriers must include attention to social factors (Kahle, 1988) that affect the student both inside and outside the classroom, since women's higher grade point averages cannot explain their deterrence from science.

Expand the kinds of observations beyond those traditionally carried out in scientific research. Frequently the expectations of faculty, reinforced by experiments and problems, convince female students that they are not scientific because they do not see or are not interested in observing the "right things" for the experiment. This lack of interest or feeling of inferiority may come from the fact that most scientific investigations have traditionally been undertaken by males who determined what was interesting and important to study.

Accurate perceptions of reality are more likely to come from scientists with diverse backgrounds and expectations observing a phenomenon. Because women's expectations may be different from those of men, women may note different factors in their observations. This example may explain why female primatologists (Fossey, 1983; Goodall, 1971; Hrdy, 1977, 1979, 1984) saw "new" data such as female-female interaction when observing primate behaviors. Including these data, which had not been previously considered, led to substantial changes in the theories of subordinance and domination as the major interactive modes of primate behavior. Women students may see new data that could make valuable contributions to scientific experiments. Barad discusses an approach to a laboratory in quantum physics that opens the possibility for different interpretations of spin angular momentum of electrons and differs substantially from the traditional way that laboratory is taught. Richardson, Sutton, and Cercone emphasize alternative interpretations for experiments in geosciences.

Increase the numbers of observations and remain longer in the observational stage of the scientific method. Data from the National Assessment of Educational Progress (NAEP) indicate that females at ages 9, 13, and 17 have significantly fewer science experiences than boys of comparable ages (Educational Testing Service, 1988). This disparity in the use of scientific equipment and work with experimental materials, the lower achievement rate on standardized tests, and the less positive attitude of girls toward science persist despite enrollment patterns in high school science classes (Kahle, Parker, Rennie, & Riley, 1993). The achievement rate may be directly related to participation in fewer science activities outside the classroom (Kahle & Lakes, 1983). Girls and young women who lack hands-on experience with laboratory equipment are apt to feel apprehensive about using equipment and instruments in data gathering. Some research on the decreasing numbers of women majoring in computer science (Gries & Marsh, 1992) suggests that this may be occurring in part because women dislike spending so much time with computer hardware. Kelly's Four-Component System (Chapter 5) for teaching mathematics may be especially successful for females because it includes strategies that reduce student anxiety about the concept being introduced.

Because of time constraints, the observational stage of an experiment is frequently shortened, and students are simply given the data for analysis. This practice is particularly detrimental to females, who have fewer extracurricular opportunities for hands-on experiences. Nair and Majetich suggest ways to include extra opportunities for women to work with the equipment in physics and engineering. Considerable research documents that programs that are successful in attracting and retaining women in equipment-oriented nontraditional fields, such as engineering, often have a special component for remedial hands-on experience (Daniels & LeBold, 1982).

Making young women feel more comfortable and successful in the laboratory can be accomplished by providing more hands-on experience during an increased observational stage of data gathering. In a coeducational environment, it is essential that females be paired with females as laboratory partners. Male-female partnerships frequently result in the male working with the equipment while the female writes down the observations. Her clerical skills are improved, but she has gained no more experience with equipment for her next course in science, mathematics, or engineering. Sanders and Eastman, in their respective chapters on computer science in the precollege and undergraduate levels, emphasize the importance of insisting that females work with computer hardware.

Incorporate and validate women's personal experiences as part of class discussions or laboratory exercises. Most learners, regardless of their learning style, are interested in phenomena and situations with which they have had personal experience. Research on science anxiety suggests that experience with an instrument and familiarity with a task ameliorate anxiety (Malcolm, 1983). Beginning a course or an individual lesson with examples and equipment that women are more likely to be familiar with may reduce their anxiety. Often the context of a problem can be switched from one that is male gender-role stereotyped to one this is female gender-role typed or gender neutral. Campbell and Campbell-Wright have evolved algebra problems that not only come from experiences common to females but also break stereotypes regarding race, class, and sexual orientation. Richardson, Sutton, and Cercone provide similar specific examples for both undergraduate majors and nonmajors in the geosciences.

Phase IV: Search for Women Scientists and Their Unique Contributions

Although we sometimes labor under the false impression that women have become scientists only in the latter half of the twentieth century, early works by Christine de Pizan (1405/1982), Giovanni Boccaccio (1355–1359/1963), and H. J. Mozans (1913/1974) recorded past achievements of women in science. Their works underscore the fact that women have always been in science. The recovery of the names and contributions of the lost women of science has been invaluable research provided by historians of science who were spurred by the work of feminists in history. There are several classic examples of the loss of the names of women scientists and the value of their work. Rosalind Franklin's fundamental work on the x-ray crystallography of DNA, which led to the theoretical speculation of the double helical nature of the molecule by Watson and Crick, continues to be brushed aside and undervalued (Watson, 1969; Sayre, 1975). The groundbreaking work of Ellen Swallow in water, air, and food purity, sanitation, and industrial waste disposal, which began the science of ecology, was reclassified as home economics primarily because the work was done by a woman (Hynes, 1984, 1989). Swallow is thus honored as the founder of home economics rather than as the founder of ecology. Using the history of science to demonstrate that women have been successful in traditional science is important in that it documents the fact that despite extreme barriers and obstacles, women have done excellent science.

Include the names of women scientists who have made important discoveries. Teaching methods must be modified to include work done by women in the discussion of important scientific experiments. It can be rewarding for students to learn about the nine women who succeeded in the traditional scientific establishment and won the Nobel Prize. In some cases, just mentioning the first name of the experimenters, for example, Alfred Hershey and Martha Chase when discussing the experiments determining that DNA was the genetic component in bacteriophage (Taylor, 1965), will break the documented stereotype held by students that scientists are males (Chambers, 1983; Kahle, 1990). Eastman discusses the points she makes regarding women in the history of computer science in her classes.

It may be crucial to convey to students that although the scientific hierarchy is set up so that often only one man wins the prize or heads the laboratory, much of the actual work leading to the important discovery is done by teams of people, many of whom are women. Rossiter's (1982) *Women Scientists in America: Struggles and Strategies to 1940* is a groundbreaking work that examines how the work of ordinary women scientists suffers from underrecognition due to the application of double standards and other social barriers inherent in the structure of the scientific community. Schiebinger's (1989) work on the role of women in Europe during the formulation of modern science documents a lengthy tradition for less famous women scientists. Emphasizing the lives of ordinary women scientists who have not won prizes or achieved fame may be particularly significant in building the confidence of young women. Some recent research (American Women in Science [AWIS], 1993) suggests that they may feel inadequate to become scientists when confronted with role models of only famous historical or current women scientists.

Use less competitive models and more interdisciplinary methods to teach science. Research by Horner (1969) and Shaver (1976) indicates that women learn more easily when cooperative rather than competitive pedagogical methods are used. Although male students may thrive on competing to see who can finish the problem first, females prefer and perform better in situations in which everyone wins. Emphasizing cooperative methods in the classroom and the laboratory, which has become increasingly popular with mainstream scientists (Treisman, 1992), makes mathematics and science more attractive to females. Kelly's Four-Component System for teaching mathematics includes a cooperative component.

Changing the teaching of first-year courses from the "weed-out" model to one that lays a foundation for further science courses has proved successful in retaining more students in chemistry (Mills, 1993) and mathematics (Davis, 1993). "Weeding out" teaching styles are less likely to appeal to even the best female students because women in our society suffer from lower self-esteem, which decreases while they are in college (Astin & Astin, 1993). Their lower self-esteem, coupled with their tendency to attribute failure to self and success to luck, may explain why more females drop out of science and math courses despite their superior grades, in comparison to the males who remain (Kahle, 1988). As Kelly suggests in her chapter, tutoring by peers or collaborative work may be more effective than weed-out lectures for retaining females in mathematics. Females, who tend to be well socialized to heed overt and covert messages suggesting that they are not welcome (Kahle, 1988), may respond particularly well to foundation-building rather than weeding-out approaches. Nair and Majetich consider the cooperative measures they have instituted to help retain women in engineering and physics at Carnegie-Mellon.

Because of their interest in relationships and interdependence, female students are more attracted to science and its methods when they perceive its usefulness in other disciplines. Mills College, a small liberal arts college for women, capitalized on this idea by offering interdisciplinary courses stressing the applications of mathematics in courses such as sociology, economics, and chemistry (Blum & Givant, 1982). The college also developed a five-year dual degree engineering program that permits students to receive bachelor's degrees in both liberal arts and engineering (Blum & Givant, 1982). The chapters in this volume by Hynes and Webb underline the interdisciplinary nature of environmental science. Richardson, Sutton, and Cercone also indicate that interdisciplinary approaches attract women to the geosciences.

Discuss the role of scientist as only one facet that must be smoothly integrated with other aspects of students' lives. A major issue concerning most females is the possibility and difficulty of combining a scientific career with marriage, family, or both. Arnold (1987), Matyas (1985), and Gardner (1986) found that women's decisions to switch majors to nonscience fields were related to issues surrounding marriage and family. It is clear that the issue of the compatibility of a career and family life must be addressed in order for larger numbers of young women to be attracted to science. Role models of successful and ordinary women scientists from a variety of backgrounds who exhibit diverse lifestyles can best address this issue (AWIS, 1993). Including these female role models as part of the curricular content, for example, having them present seminars on their research, suggests to both male and female students that women scientists exist and exhibit a variety of ages, sizes, races, and lifestyles. Harris, Bohonak, and Nair and Majetich discuss in their chapters how they have used role models in their courses and programs to retain women in their respective fields of chemistry, computer sciences, and engineering.

Put increased effort into strategies such as teaching and communicating with nonscientists to break down barriers between science and the layperson. Scientific, mathematical, and medical terminologies are frightening and inaccessible to many people in our society, particularly females (Bentley, 1985). This terminology proliferates as scientific investigation into an area becomes increasingly sophisticated and as its accompanying technology becomes more complex. The combination of these factors makes many students, particularly females, fear and desire to avoid science and mathematics. In her chapter "Culturally Inclusive Chemistry," Middlecamp explores how the language and technology of chemistry have created a culture unique to chemistry. This culture makes it difficult for individuals outside that culture, such as those from other countries and from our country who approach things differently, to fail to be intimidated by the somewhat male and objective world of chemistry.

Research (Hall & Sandler, 1982; Tannen, 1990) indicates that females face the additional barrier of having their answers and theories about science devalued because of their speech patterns and other verbal and nonverbal methods of communication. New approaches for communicating scientific information may aid in attracting women to science while opening the door for a new appreciation and valuing of their ideas in science. Hynes and Webb develop such approaches in their environmental science courses.

It may become necessary to restructure the science curriculum to include more information on communication skills and ethics. A survey of engineering seniors conducted at Purdue University (Daniels & LeBold, 1982) discovered that female students were more apt than males to place greater importance on educational goals stressing general education, communication skills, and the development of high ethical standards. "However, they were similar to the men in their perception that such goals were not achieved very well" (Daniels & LeBold, 1982, p. 157). Nair and Majetich also find that women appreciate a more holistic approach in their engineering courses.

Discuss the practical uses to which scientific discoveries are put to help students see science in its social context. A persuasive argument to attract women to science is the tremendous usefulness it has for improving people's lives. The positive social benefits of science and technology seem to be overwhelmingly important to females. The research of Jan Harding (1985) shows that females who choose to study science do so because of the important social implications of the problems science can solve. When asked to solve a particular mechanical problem, boys and girls take different approaches: Boys view the problem as revolving around the technicalities of producing an apparatus; girls describe the problem in its social context or environment, developing a technology to solve a difficulty faced by an elderly person, for example (Grant, 1982).

In a study of differential attitudes between boys and girls toward physics, Lie and Bryhni (1983) gave the following summary of their results:

> Taken together we may say that the girls' interests are characterized by a close connection of science to the human being, to society, and to ethic and aesthetic aspects. Boys more than girls are particularly interested in the technical aspects of science. (p. 209)

Campbell and Campbell-Wright, Webb, Hynes, Nair and Majetich, and Richardson, Sutton, and Cercone all describe how important practical application is for attracting and retaining women in their diverse disciplines in science, mathematics, and engineering.

Phase V: Science Done by Feminists and Women

Uncovering women scientists and their contributions provides an opportunity to examine differences beween their work and that of men scientists. Because of the scarcity of women scientists and the fact that the value of their work must conform to standards set largely by their peer group of male scientists, few studies have contrasted the work of women and men scientists (S. Harding, 1991; Morell, 1993). Examples of recent work suggest that there may be differences between males and females in the distance between scientist and subject of study and in the effect of language in conceptualizing theories.

Barbara McClintock was an achieving scientist who was not a feminist. However, in her approach toward studying maize, she indicated a shortening of the distance between the observer and the object being studied and a consideration of the complex interaction between the organism and its environment. Her statement upon receiving the Nobel Prize was that "it might seem unfair to reward a person for having so much pleasure over the years, asking the maize plant to solve specific problems and then watching its responses" (Lewin, 1983, p. 402). This statement suggests a closer, more intimate relationship with the subject of her research than is typically expressed by the male "objective" scientist. One does not normally associate words such as "a feeling for the organism" (Keller, 1983) with the rational, masculine approach to science. McClintock also did not accept the predominant hierarchical theory of genetic DNA as the "master molecule" that controls gene action but focused on the interaction between the organism and its environment as the locus of control. In her chapter "A Feminist Approach to Teaching Quantum Physics," Barad suggests that female students in particular may desire and profit from a more intimate understanding of the theoretical concepts rather than simple manipulation of the numbers.

As more women have entered primate research, they have begun to challenge the language used to describe primate behavior and the patriarchal assumptions inherent in searches for dominance hierarchies in primates. Lancaster (1975) describes a single-male troop of animals as follows:

> For a female, males are a resource in her environment which she may use to further the survival of herself and her offspring. If environmental conditions are such that the male role can be minimal, a one-male group is likely. Only one male is necessary for a group of females if his only role is to impregnate them. (p. 34)

Her work points out the androcentric bias of primate behavior theories, which would describe the above group as a "harem" and consider dominance and subordination in the description of behavior. Describing the same situation using a gynocentric term such as "stud" reveals the importance of using more gender-neutral language such "one male" and "a group of females" as suggested by Lancaster to remove bias. As Richardson, Sutton, and Cercone suggest, using gender-neutral language in all areas, including the geosciences, helps make women feel included.

Use precise, gender-neutral language in describing data and presenting theories. Although adult women have learned that they are supposed to be included in generic language, some studies (Tannen, 1990; Thorne, 1979) indicate that women feel excluded when such language is used. Hall and Sandler (1982) documented the negative effects sexist language has on females in the classroom. In her chapter, Sanders points out the negative effects of some of the sexist jokes commonly found on computer boards for females interested in computer science.

Because most scientists in our culture are male, science tends to be perceived as a nontraditional area for women. It may be necessary to move beyond the absence of sexism and make particular efforts to correct stereotypes in students' minds and to emphasize female scientists and their contributions. Campbell and Campbell-Wright provide examples of algebra problems useful in correcting stereotypes.

Encourage development of theories and hypotheses that are relational, interdependent, and multicausal rather than hierarchical, reductionistic, and dualistic. Laboratories in science classes tend to be excessively simplistic and reductionistic. In an attempt to provide clear demonstrations and explanations in a limited span of time, instructors and laboratory manuals avoid experiments focusing on relationships among multiple factors. Well-controlled experiments in a laboratory environment may provide results that have little application to the multivariate problems confronted by scientists outside the classroom and by students in their daily lives in the real world.

Building on the theory of Chodorow (1978) and the research of Gilligan (1982) and Belenky, Clinchy, Goldberger, and Tarule (1986), instructors can capitalize on females' interest in relationships and interaction among factors when introducing and discussing concepts and experiments. Females are likely to be eager to learn how the specific bit of information provided by a particular experiment or data is likely to influence and be influenced by other related factors; in contrast, males, with their more technical orientation (J. Harding, 1985), may be content to examine the bit of information out of context. Hynes discusses the importance of providing complex contexts for studying problems in environmental science, not only to make the problems more attractive to females but also to provide a more realistic picture of how science influences and is influenced by other parameters.

Use a combination of qualitative and quantitative methods in data gathering. Some females have suggested that their lack of interest in science comes in part from their perception that the quantitative methods of science do not allow them to report their nonquantitative observations, thereby restricting the questions asked to those that they find less interesting. These perceptions are reinforced by textbooks, laboratory exercises, and views of scientific research propagated by the media. In their efforts to teach the objectivity of science and the steps of the scientific method, very few instructors and curricular materials manage to convey the creative and intuitive insights that are a crucial part of most scientific discoveries. Hynes and Webb illustrate strategies that they have found successful for combining qualitative and quantitative methods in projects in environmental science.

Encourage the uncovering of biases such as those of race, class, sexual orientation, and religious affiliation, as well as gender, which may permeate theories and conclusions drawn from experimental observation. Removing sexism from the classroom and providing an awareness of the feminist critique of science are not sufficient to attract the diversity of individuals needed to correct the bias within science. Science in the United States (and in the Western world) suffers from bias and lack of diversity in other areas besides gender. In addition to being largely a masculine province, it is also primarily a white (except for the recent addition of Asian Americans) and middle- to upper-class province (NSF, 1992). This relatively homogeneous group results in a restricted diversity of scientists compared with the general population. Restricted diversity may lead to excessive similarity in approaches to problem solving and interpretation of data, thereby limiting creativity and introducing bias. Middlecamp explores the culture of chemistry and the extent to which it may reflect white and Western, as well as male, influences.

Data collected from programs attempting to recruit and retain minorities in science have been interpreted to show that minorities of both sexes may fail to be attracted to science for some of the same reasons that white women are not attracted (George, 1982; Matyas & Malcolm, 1991). In addition, racism among scientists—both overt and covert—and the use of scientific theories to justify racism are powerful deterrents. The changes made in mathematics problems by Campbell and Campbell-Wright indicate the sort of covert racism that may be reflected in traditional algebra problems.

Women of color face double barriers posed by racism and sexism. More research needs to be done to elucidate particular curricular and pedagogical techniques that might help attract and retain minority women, including complex analyses recognizing the intersection of class, race, and gender as factors affecting each individual in the classroom. Sensitivity of instructors to these interlocking phenomena in women's lives is a first step toward attracting a diverse population to science.

Phase VI: Science Redefined and Reconstructed to Include Us All

The ultimate goal of the methods and curricular changes suggested in phases I–V is the production of a curriculum and pedagogy that includes women and people of color and therefore attracts individuals from those groups to become scientists. Obviously, this curriculum and these methods have not been fully developed yet. *Teaching the Majority* represents pioneering work in teaching by scientists, mathematicians, and engineers to attract and retain women. The examples the contributing authors give in the following chapters of transformed curricula, expanded problem sets and laboratory exercises, and successful pedagogical techniques will aid others in breaking the gender barrier in science and technology.

REFERENCES

American Chemical Society. (1983). Medalist's study charts women chemists' role. *Chemistry and Engineering, 14*, 53.

American Women in Science. (1993). *A hand up: Women mentoring women in science* (Deborah Fort, Ed.). Washington, DC: Author.

Arnold, Karen. (1987). *Retaining high achieving women in science and engineering*. Paper presented at Women in Science and Engineering: Changing Vision to Reality Conference, University of Michigan, Ann Arbor, sponsored by the American Association for the Advancement of Science.

Astin, Alexander, & Astin, Helen S. (1993). *Undergraduate science education:The impact of different college environments on the educational pipeline in the sciences*. Los Angeles: Higher Education Research Institute, University of California.

Belenky, Mary Field, Clinchy, Blythe McVicker, Goldberger, Nancy Rule, & Tarule, Jill Mattuck. (1986). *Women's ways of knowing*. New York: Basic Books.

Bentley, Diana. (1985). Men may understand the words, but do they know the music? Some cries de coeur in science education. *Supplementary Contributions to the Third GASAT Conference* (pp. 160–168). London: Chelsea College, University of London.

Birke, Lynda. (1986). *Women, feminism, and biology: The feminist challenge*. New York: Methuen.

Bleier, Ruth. (1984). *Science and gender: A critique of biology and its theories on women*. Elmsford, NY: Pergamon Press.

Bleier, Ruth. (1986). *Feminist approaches to science*. Elmsford, NY: Pergamon Press.

Blum, Lenore, & Givant, Steven. (1982). Increasing the participation of college women in mathematics-related fields. In Sheila Humphreys (Ed.), *Women and*

minorities in science (pp. 119–137). AAAS Selected Symposia Series. Boulder, CO: Westview.
Boccaccio, Giovanni. (1963). *De Clairis Mulieribus* [Concerning famous women] (Guedo A. Guardno, Trans.). New Brunswick, NJ: Rutgers University Press. (Original work published 1355–1359)
Browne, Malcolm W. (1994, February 20). Cold war's end clouds research as openings in science dwindle. *The New York Times*, pp. A-l, A-11.
Chambers, Diane. (1983). Stereotypic images of the scientist: The draw-a-scientist test. *Science Education, 76*, 475–476.
Chodorow, Nancy. (1978). *The reproduction of mothering: Psychoanalysis and the sociology of gender*. Berkeley, CA: University of California Press.
Daniels, Jane, & LeBold, William. (1982). Women in engineering: A dynamic approach. In S. Humphreys (Ed.), *Women and minorities in science* (pp. 139–163). AAAS Selected Symposia Series. Boulder, CO: Westview.
Davis, Cinda Sue. (1993, April 16). Stepping beyond the campus. *Science, 260*, 414.
de Pizan, Christine. (1982). *The book of the city of ladies* (Earl Jeffrey Richards, Trans.). New York: Persea. (Slightly modified from the translation by Earl Jeffrey Richards; original work published 1405)
Educational Testing Service. (1988). *The science report card: Elements of risk and recovery, trends, and achievement based on the 1986 national assessment* (Report No. 17-S-01). Princeton, NJ: Author.
Ehrenreich, Barbara, & English, Deirdre. (1978). *For her own good: 150 years of the experts' advice to women*. Garden City, NY: Anchor.
Fausto-Sterling, Anne. (1992). *Myths of gender*. New York: Basic Books.
Fee, Elizabeth. (1982). A feminist critique of scientific objectivity. *Science for the People, 14*(4), 8.
Fossey, Dian. (1983). *Gorillas in the mist*. Boston: Houghton Mifflin.
Gardner, A. L. (1986). *Effectiveness of strategies to encourage participation and retention of precollege and college women in science*. Unpublished doctoral dissertation, Purdue University, West Lafayette, IN.
George, Yolanda. (1982). Affirmative action programs that work. In S. Humphreys (Ed.), *Women and minorities in science* (pp. 87–98). AAAS Selected Symposia Series. Boulder, CO: Westview.
Gilligan, Carol. (1982). *In a different voice: Psychological theory and women's development*. Cambridge, MA: Harvard University Press.
Goodall, Jane. (1971). *In the shadow of man*. Boston: Houghton Mifflin.
Grant, Marcia. (1982). Prized projects. *Studies in Design, Education, Craft and Technology, 15*, 1.
Gries, David, & Marsh, Dorothy. (1992, January). The 1989–90 Taulbee survey. *Communications of the ACM, 35*(1), 133–143.
Hall, Roberta, & Sandler, Bernice. (1982). *The classroom climate: A chilly one for women*. Washington, DC: Project on the Status and Education of Women, Association of American Colleges.
Halpin, Zuleyma. (1989). Scientific objectivity and the concept of "the other." *Women's Studies International Forum, 12*, 285–294.

Haraway, Donna. (1978). Animal sociology and a natural economy of the body politic. *Signs, 4*(1), 21–60.
Harding, Jan. (1985). Values, cognitive style and the curriculum. *Contributions to the Third Girls and Science and Technology Conference* (pp. 159–166). London: Chelsea College, University of London.
Harding, Sandra. (1986). *The science question in feminism*. Ithaca, NY: Cornell University Press.
Harding, Sandra. (1991). *Whose science? Whose knowledge?* Ithaca, NY: Cornell University Press.
Holloway, Marguerite. (1993). A lab of her own. *Scientific American, 269*(5), 94–103.
Horner, Matina. (1969). Fail: Bright women. *Psychology Today, 3*, 36–38.
Hrdy, Sarah B. (1977). *The langurs of Abu: Female and male strategies of reproduction*. Cambridge, MA: Harvard University Press.
Hrdy, Sarah B. (1979). Infanticide among animals: A review, classification and examination of the implications for the reproductive strategies of females. *Ethology and Sociobiology, 1*, 3–40.
Hrdy, Sarah B. (1984). Introduction: Female reproductive strategies. In M. Small (Ed.), *Female primates: Studies by women primatologists* (pp. 103–109). New York: Alan Liss.
Hubbard, Ruth. (1990). *The politics of women's biology*. New Brunswick, NJ: Rutgers University Press.
Hynes, Patricia. (1984, November/December). Women working: A field report. *Technology Review, 38*, 37–38, 47.
Hynes, Patricia. (1989). *The recurring silent spring*. Elmsford, NY: Pergamon Press.
Kahle, Jane B. (1985). *Women in science*. Philadelphia: Falmer Press.
Kahle, Jane B. (1988). Recruitment and retention of women in college science majors. *Journal of College Science Teaching, 27*(5).
Kahle, Jane B. (1990). [Draw a mathematician test]. Unpublished raw data.
Kahle, Jane B., & Lakes, Marsha. (1983). The myth of equality in science classrooms. *Journal of Research in Science Teaching, 20*, 131–140.
Kahle, Jane B., Parker, L., Rennie, L. J., & Riley, D. (1993). Gender differences in science education: Building a model. *Educational Psychologist, 28*(4), 379–404.
Keller, Evelyn F. (1982). Feminism and science. *Signs, 7*(3), 589–602.
Keller, Evelyn F. (1983). *A feeling for the organism*. San Francisco: Freeman.
Keller, Evelyn F. (1985). *Reflections on gender and science*. New Haven, CT: Yale University Press.
Kuhn, Thomas. (1970). *The structure of scientific revolutions* (2nd ed.). Chicago: University of Chicago Press.
Lancaster, Jane. (1975). *Primate behavior and the emergence of human culture*. New York: Holt, Rinehart and Winston.
Lewin, Roger. (1983). A naturalist of the genome. *Science, 222*, 402–405.
Lie, Svein, & Bryhni, Eva. (1983). Girls and physics: Attitudes, experiences and underachievement. *Contributions to the Second GASAT Conference* (pp. 202–211). London: Chelsea College, University of London.
Malcolm, Shirley M. (1983). *An assessment of programs that facilitate increased access*

and achievement of females and minorities in K–12 mathematics and science education. Washington, DC: American Association for the Advancement of Science, Office of Opportunities in Science.

Matyas, Marsha L. (1985). Factors affecting female achievement and interest in science and scientific careers. In Kahle, Jane B. (Ed.), *Women in science: A report from the field* (pp. 27–48). Philadelphia: Falmer Press.

Matyas, Marsha, & Malcolm, Shirley. (1991). *Investing in human potential: Science and engineering at the crossroads*. Washington, DC: American Association for the Advancement of Science.

McIntosh, Peggy. (1984). The study of women: Processes of personal and curricular re-vision. *Forum for Liberal Education, 6*(5), 2–4.

Mills, James. (1993, April 16). Shedding chemistry's uncool image. *Science, 260*, 413.

Morell, Virginia. (1993, April 16). Called "trimates," three bold women shaped their field. *Science, 260*, 420–425.

Mozans, H. J. (1974). *Women in science*. Cambridge, MA: MIT Press. (Original work published 1913)

National Research Council. (1991). *Women in science and engineering: Increasing their numbers in the 1990's: A statement on policy and strategy*. Washington, DC: Author.

National Research Council. (1994). *Women scientists and engineers employed in industry: Why so few?* Washington, DC: Author.

National Science Foundation. (1990). *Women and minorities in science and engineering* (NSF 90–301). Washington, DC: Author.

National Science Foundation. (1992). *Women and minorities in science and engineering: An update* (NSF 92–303). Washington, DC: Author.

Perry, William. (1970). *Forms of intellectual and ethical development in the college years*. New York: Holt, Rinehart and Winston.

Pinn, Vivian, & LaRosa, Judith. (1992). Overview: Office of research on women's health. *National Institutes of Health*, 1–10.

Rosser, Sue V. (1986). *Teaching science and health from a feminist perspective: A practical guide*. Elmsford, NY: Pergamon Press.

Rosser, Sue V. (1990). *Female-friendly science*. Elmsford, NY: Pergamon Press.

Rosser, Sue. V. (1993). Female friendly science: Including women in curricular content and pedagogy in science. *The Journal of General Education, 42*(3), 191–220.

Rossiter, Margaret. (1982). *Women scientists in America: Struggles and strategies to 1940*. Baltimore: Johns Hopkins University Press.

Sayre, Anne. (1975). *Rosalind Franklin and DNA: A vivid view of what it is like to be a gifted woman in an especially male profession*. New York: Norton.

Schiebinger, Londa. (1989). *The mind has no sex? Women in the origins of modern science*. Cambridge, MA: Harvard University Press.

Schuster, Marilyn, & Van Dyne, Susan. (1984). Placing women in the liberal arts: Stages of curriculum transformation. *Harvard Educational Review, 54*(4), 413–428.

Shaver, Phillip. (1976). Questions concerning fear of success and its conceptual relatives. *Sex Roles, 2*, 305–320.

Tannen, Deborah. (1990). *You just don't understand*. New York: Ballantine.

Taylor, John. (1965). *Selected papers on molecular genetics*. New York: Academic Press.

Tetreault, Mary Kay. (1985). Stages of thinking about women: An experience-derived evaluation model. *Journal of Higher Education, 5*, 368–384.

Thomas, Valerie. (1989). Black women engineers and technologists. *Sage, 4*(2), 24–32.

Thorne, Barrie. (1979, September 12). *Claiming verbal space: Women, speech and language in college classrooms*. Paper presented at the Research Conference on Educational Environments and the Undergraduate Woman, Wellesley College, Wellesley, MA.

Treisman, Philip Uri. (1992). Studying students studying calculus: A look at the lives of minority mathematics students in college. *The College Mathematics Journal, 23*(5), 362–372.

U.S. Department of Labor. (1987). *Workforce 2000*. Washington, DC: U.S. Government Printing Office.

Vetter, Betty M. (1992). *What is holding up the glass ceiling? Barriers to women in the science and engineering workforce* (Occasional Paper 92-3). Washington, DC: Commission on Professionals in Science and Technology.

Watson, James D. (1969). *The double helix*. New York: Atheneum.

PART I

PHYSICS AND ENGINEERING

CHAPTER 1
Physics and Engineering in the Classroom

Indira Nair
Sara Majetich

Physics and engineering are the two areas where the participation of women is the lowest, in the workforce as well as in academia. Among the natural sciences, physics has the lowest percentage of women, with only 15% of the bachelor's degrees and 9% of the PhDs. In engineering, the percentage of bachelor's degrees awarded to women has hovered around 14% since the mid-1980s, despite concentrated efforts to recruit and retain more women and the institution of "women in engineering" programs in several schools (National Science Foundation [NSF], 1993; Women in Engineering Program Advocates Network [WEPAN], 1990, 1991, 1992, 1993). The situation is even worse for minority students.

In this chapter we describe some of the causes of this disparity and suggest solutions that can benefit physics and engineering instruction on the whole and these populations in particular. The emphasis is on early (first- and second-year) college courses in physics and engineering. These courses are intended to cater to a large and diverse group of students, but the greatest losses of potential physicists and engineers occur here. We focus on how these courses contribute to students leaving science and engineering, even after they have persisted through high school physics and mathematics, and what can be done to avoid this. The underlying issues are social and psychological as well as educational. It is useful to explore these issues first, to provide a context for the classroom strategies discussed later.

In designing classroom instruction, we need to recognize and correct the factors that lead large numbers of students, especially women and minorities, to turn away from the subject. We cannot afford to wait until there are enough female and underrepresented minority role models; the efforts of white and Asian males are essential. We support a more inclusive approach to teaching as a means of tapping into America's entire talent pool. This does not imply reduced standards but rather a way to avoid shunting aside capable and interested students of all types. Not only in the interest of equity, but also in the interest of competitiveness in the next century, we can afford to do no less.

BACKGROUND

Although from the practitioner's viewpoint, physics and engineering are very different in perspective, practice, and product, they are quite similar in classroom teaching methods and in both philosophy and intellectual context. The relevance of physics, or the view of physics as a means of understanding everyday fundamental phenomena, is lost in most classrooms. Most courses present physics as an application of mathematics rather than using mathematics as a convenient language to describe physics. Despite the prevalence of technology in their lives, or perhaps because of it, many students do not perceive engineering as an adventure in "how things work" but as abstract and abstruse.

Even at the early stages of education, science is presented falsely. Rather than emphasizing observations of objects and phenomena and the use of trial and error, teachers present science as an existing structure largely dependent on a dry process of "hypothesis testing." This attitude drives students away before they have even had a chance to engage in it. Early childhood education has begun to correct some of this by emphasizing "hands-on" science, but teacher education and most classroom practices are still far behind. The small amount of science required by teacher education curricula produces many teachers who lack a sense of mastery or a feeling of excitement about science, and they unconsciously convey this to their students.

Most students rarely glimpse the excitement of science, nor do they see scientists as people they could grow up to be. This is especially true for girls and minority children. This is also evident in studies in which students are asked to name a "real-life" scientist or engineer and cannot. When asked to draw a scientist, the scientists pictured are "mostly benevolent, male and white" (Hesse, 1989; Keeton, 1991).

A number of existing programs seek to make chemistry and physics more accessible and relevant to students, among them the American Chemical Society's ChemCom (Chemistry in the Community) and the American Physical Society's more recent Active Physics. They are still in the early stages of diffusion into mainstream education (American Chemical Society, 1988; Khoury & Kirwan, 1993). The American Chemical Society is in the process of field-testing a parallel college course, Chemistry in Context. Engineering remains largely unknown in precollege education. Technology education has recently begun to be introduced into the precollege curriculum in the United States, and a science-technology-society curriculum in the United Kingdom has begun to gain success in turning children on to science through a large-scale effort called the Salter's Program (Fensham, 1992).

At the college level, physics and engineering, more than other disciplines, present an overwhelmingly monolithic, immutable countenance to students. They disenfranchise bright, intellectually curious students who have not had experience with the subjects, such as a physicist or engineer parent or an unusual educational program, of their original impression that physics and engineering offer exciting intellectual adventures. In discussing this phenomenon, Tobias (1990) maintains that the "top" (or first-tier) students in physics and engineering classrooms persist and excel because their parents or teachers have set them on the right track and serve as intellectual and professional role models. Layzer (1992) thinks that these students are often autodidacts and, more important, have *discovered* physics early in their lives. This discovery has "insulated them from the deadening impact of a standard American education in math and science" (p. 69). The approach to teaching introductory physics and engineering courses makes a great difference in the retention of those from nontraditional backgrounds. Since it does not harm those who thrive under the current system, it is worth exploring in more detail.

MODEL OF FACTORS THAT ARE IMPORTANT FOR LEARNING

Betz (1990) applied a model of perceived self-efficacy first developed by Albert Bandura of Stanford University to study gender differences in educational and career decisions. Many of the factors are applicable here, so we briefly discuss this model, drawing heavily from Betz's presentation.

Perceptions of self-efficacy are developed through success in accomplishments, through observing others like ourselves perform and succeed, through freedom from anxiety with respect to the area in question, and through persuasion and support from others (Figure 1.1). Based on this model, what are some of the experiences that can affect a student's choice and performance in physics and engineering? Doing well in high school physics or being selected for special precollege programs in physics or engineering can affect a student's sense of accomplishment. Knowing an engineer or a physicist—either a parent or another adult she knows well—can help with modeling or vicarious learning, as can precollege programs. In high school and particularly in the early years of college, freedom from anxiety can be provided by a supportive learning environment. Peer men-

FIGURE 1.1. Modified representation of Bandura's model of self-efficacy.

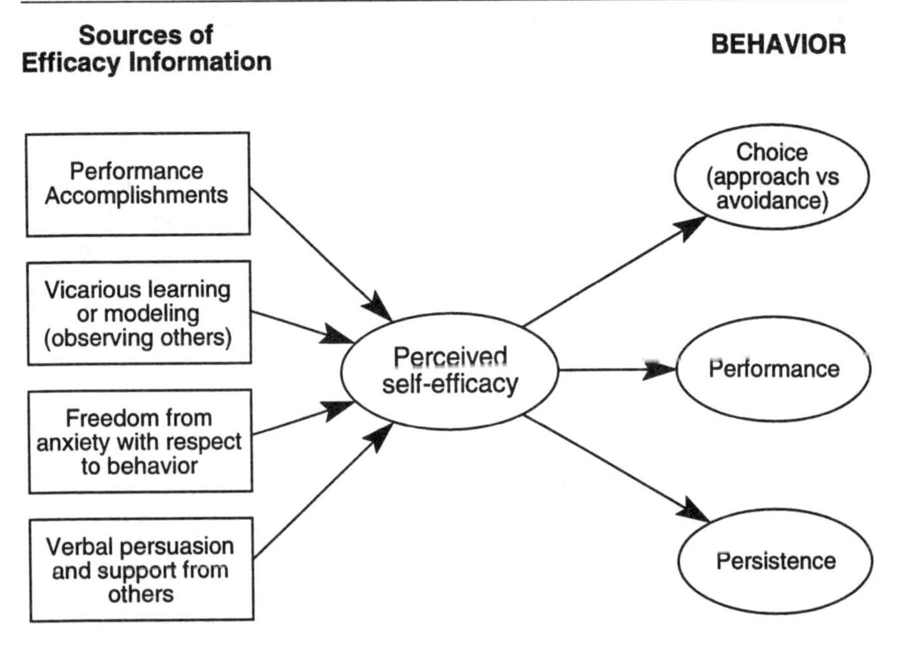

tors, readily available tutoring, and an encouraging classroom atmosphere can contribute to a student's self-efficacy.

Feelings of self-efficacy, in turn, affect the physics or engineering student's choice of major, performance, and persistence. In a series of studies, Betz and Hackett (1983) showed that college-age women had significantly lower efficacy expectations with respect to science and math career fields in comparison with equally able men. The model says that these women with lower expectations will opt out of these fields. When this model is applied to teaching introductory physics and engineering courses, the major barriers can be categorized as follows:

1. Ignoring students' motivation for taking the course
2. Unequal background preparation
3. Subject-centered course content
4. Teaching methods
5. Teaching style
6. Lack of role models

In the remainder of this chapter, we discuss each of the major barriers and offer possible solutions.

Students' Motivation

The first barrier to learning concerns the difference between students' reasons for taking introductory physics and engineering courses and the role of these courses in the departmental curriculum. Beginning physics courses serve three distinct types of audiences: students who take physics for science literacy (most often as a distribution requirement), students who take physics for required background knowledge (engineers, chemists, and biologists), and students who may decide (or have decided) to major in physics. The last group is the smallest, yet most physics faculties tailor the courses to those who do not question the importance of learning physics. "Teaching to the major" is one of the most serious problems in early physics and engineering courses. Most of the students in beginning engineering courses are indeed engineering majors but have had no previous exposure to the subject. Many students look to an entry-level course as a way to affirm their interest and to understand the nature of their prospective field. Referring again to the Bandura model in Figure 1.1, this course can provide all the factors that contribute to a sense of self-efficacy. A method of teaching that ignores these motives leads to the loss of many students from physics and engineering programs. As discussed later, this may be particularly true of women and minority students, who have no role models to encourage persistence in these areas. In teaching to the major (which is often seen as teaching to the first tier), the educational objectives relevant to the other groups are often lost. A truly inclusive method of teaching can avoid this and, in fact, may be better for students already committed to the major.

The approach to teaching introductory physics and engineering courses shows a very different motivation. By teaching to the top of the class rather than to the average student, these courses help identify those students who will be the future physicists and engineers and "call to the priesthood those ordained to be physicists." There is an emphasis on "native ability" rather than achievement through sincere effort, and the assessment of this ability often ignores the difference in students' preparation. This would be less of a problem if all the students in the course wanted to become professors in these fields, but there are many nonspecialists who want or need to know something about physics. Here the teaching style serves only to prove to the students that they are not fit to be physicists. They either won't learn the material well or won't know what to do with it if they do. In the long term, we may be better off with fewer highly trained physicists but a large number of people with a general technical background, and the teaching style in introductory courses should be adjusted accordingly.

Teaching physics as a venture into the unknown is not a new idea, although this approach is seldom followed. Sharing the excitement we have for our fields is a way to motivate students' interest. Indeed, Richard Feynman (Feynman, Leighton, & Sands, 1963), master teacher and Nobel laureate, notes in his introductory physics volume that it is important to "develop a 'feel' for the subject" (p. 1-1), that "everything we know is only some kind of approximation" (p. 1-1), and that imagination is central in theoretical physics. Feynman introduces basic physics in this way:

> the complicated array of moving things which constitutes "the world" is something like a great chess game being played by the gods, and we are observers of the game . . . all we are allowed to do is *watch* the playing . . . if we watch long enough, we may eventually catch on to a few of the rules. *The rules of the game* are what we mean by *fundamental physics*. (p. 2-1)

Every once in a while, he says, something goes on that we do not understand. How often is this sense of adventure and uncertainty conveyed in basic physics courses? Instead, physics and engineering are often presented simply as arenas for the practice and manipulation of mathematical formulas.

Background Preparation

Once a student has decided to enroll in a physics or engineering course, the first difficulties often arise due to poor background preparation. The disparity of the students' preparation is greatest in these entry-level courses. However, the students judge their aptitude for physics or engineering based on their performance in these courses, without recognizing the advantage of having seen the material before. Whether real or perceived, this lack of preparation leads to anxiety and often reduces students' persistence in the field.

Capable students from nontraditional backgrounds do not need further discouragement if they wish to study physics or engineering; society provides more than enough. Often these students have received less preparation or have weaker study skills when they enter their first college-level technical courses. In these introductory courses, it is easy to mistake poor performance for lower ability. This is not to say that standards should be compromised but rather that every effort should be made to get all students up to speed as early as possible. A student who cannot be trained to a certain level of competence does not deserve admission. Other than in traditionally black colleges and single-sex institutions, it is all too common for a student with potential to be accepted but not to be shown how to develop that competence.

Mathematics is the language of physics and engineering. Weak preparation in mathematics is often a detriment to students. This inadequacy stems from poor teaching methods in the early grades and a prevailing attitude that mathematics is hard and irrelevant. This perception of irrelevance continues even in college students. Teaching the subject in context and developing mathematical methods and other skills as the course progresses would be an encouragement to all students. An approach that starts with phenomena also has the practical advantage of getting students to review or learn the mathematics as needed. An emphasis on science and engineering as the core, and on mathematics as a tool, allows students with some form of "math anxiety" to anticipate needs and improve their performance.

Some current trends in engineering education are attempting to reverse the usual sequence, which starts with introductory mathematics and science and then approaches engineering as applied math and science. This curricular movement seeks to introduce engineering first as design and provides students with mathematics "just in time" for them to use it (Samaras, 1991). This movement has not been around long enough to evaluate its impact on engineering education. Similarly, teaching physics from an experiential base is gaining popularity in some schools (Sherwood & Chabay, 1992). When trying to differentiate the factors related to continuation in university-level physics, a study by the American Institute of Physics (Fehrs & Czujko, 1992) found the greatest gender difference not in mathematical aptitude but in whether the students had ever tried to fix something.

The introductory engineering program at Purdue University is a prime example of what can be done. Realizing that many prospective female engineers felt less capable because they perceived themselves to be less mechanical, a Tools and Engines course for first-year students was introduced to provide experience taking things apart and seeing how they worked (Daniels, 1990). Not only was this course successful in increasing the self-confidence of female students, but many male students thought that they benefited as well. The proportion of women in the Purdue undergraduate engineering program is now far above the national average. These approaches can help minimize or reduce any gap that exists in the background preparation of students, while giving them an understanding of the math and science in context.

Other institutions have tried segregating women or minority students into certain sections of large undergraduate physics and engineering courses in order to monitor their progress more carefully. Women in engineering programs generally work on the principles of Figure 1.1 by providing encouragement and acknowledgment of accomplishments, other forms of learning and verbal support, and role models. It is likely that most students would choose the increased attention available in these programs if they had that option.

Equalizing student backgrounds after they have entered college with unequal preparation can also be facilitated by the virtual laboratory concept (V. Stonick, personal communication, October 1993). The virtual laboratory concept is implemented by using a consistent core of laboratory equipment comprised of low-cost, commercially available hardware and software. These labs, built around simulation programs on a PC, provide the student with a "laboratory environment" that is accessible from virtually anywhere, at all times. Students can gain practice outside laboratory sessions using these programs (Electrical and Computer Engineering [ECE], 1991).

Curriculum Content

The content of traditional physics and engineering courses can be a barrier to students because this approach is subject centered and treats the subjects in isolation, with little attention to their place in society. This results in many of the students questioning the value of these endeavors in their lives and dropping out of the classes if they have a choice or are doing badly. In addition, this method hinders the objective of scientific and technological literacy, which is why most of the students are taking the courses.

The subject matter of both physics and engineering, especially at the early course level, is based on empirical observations. However, the majority of physics and engineering courses do not adopt either a historical or an empirical approach to teaching. Many exciting adventures can be found in the study of the historical development of these fields. The intellectual (and sociopolitical) history of physics and engineering not only is enlightening but also helps students follow a similar path in building and revising their concepts. This process, in addition to making the subject interesting, can give students a unique sense of ownership, comfort, and attainability as they learn how ideas that once held sway have had to be revised or replaced.

An explanation of the work by the scientist who did it provides context and clarity. There is no parallel to the description of Maxwell's equations as done by Maxwell (1954), or to Millikan's (1924) description of all his experiments on measuring the charge on an electron, or to the explanation of the spectral line notation by Sommerfield (1934). Discussions of the roots of engineering in Florman's (1976) *Existential Pleasures of Engineering* or in Petroski's (1985) *To Engineer Is Human*, interspersed in engineering courses, could open the world of engineering to students in a way that no other introduction can. These are examples of "real" physics and engineering explained by masters of the fields, yet our students rarely get to know them.

The very exploration of the roots of the words *physics*, *engineering*, and *technology* brings a perspective that draws students in. *Physics* is the "nature of things"; *ingenieure* is "to contrive or to use ingenuity"; and *techne* is "art" in the original sense of being artful or clever about finding solutions. All these terms have human dimensions as their basis, a fact that can be central to helping students set them in context.

Inclusion of readings on the history, sociology, or philosophy of science does not mean that the dimension of rigor is lost from the teaching of the subject matter. However, it reveals additional dimensions of the subjects—as human endeavors in which we learn from observation and error, and indeed as forms of the highest intellectual creativity. This approach invites student participation in the adventure called physics or engineering. Teaching from the historical and empirical perspective also reverses the traditional order of presentation of these subjects—as problems in applied mathematics and as immutable maxims. It presents physics and engineering as human observations, as practice, as attempts to find elegant and unifying principles in the working of nature, and, in turn, trying to apply these for the benefit of humankind.

Physics and engineering are in phase III of the sociological developmental stage in Rosser's (1990) model of the inclusion of women. This is a stage characterized by a gender-stratified labor market and the beginning of identification of factors that prevent women from entering. At this point, women are still an anomaly in these fields.

All fields of science and engineering are growing at exponential rates, and there is a tendency to try to teach a little of everything. Although it seems arbitrary to select a few topics, if they illustrate the basic principles of the field and hold together as a group, it will be easier to teach them well. The perspective of the department determines what it means to teach well. Although the course should represent the field adequately, the real goal is to transmit basic knowledge to the students in an understandable form. With the continued expansion of physics and engineering, the distinction between encyclopedias and introductory textbooks is blurring. It is desirable to have a text with a wide range of material, but a professor should not be constrained to present it all in a single course.

Several strategies may be pursued to avoid this problem. An additional introductory course on physics or engineering can be taught that focuses on the history and philosophy of these subjects, with subject matter being introduced as appropriate. If that is not possible, short readings and writing exercises can become a routine part of homework assignments, with a portion of every class (or recitation) being spent discussing these assignments. We have also used a scheme in which a short amount of class time is set aside for students to take turns reporting on new science (or engineering) items they have read in *Science News* or any other easily understood and accurate source of new scientific information.

Teaching Methods

Introductory courses in physics and engineering are typically held in large lecture halls, where a professor presents the material and students take notes without asking too many questions. Teaching methods that concentrate on the "foreign language" of mathematics and that ignore students' experiences and the way they assimilate new information are a barrier to understanding.

The teaching of physics and engineering in college as a mastery of jargon and formulas further distances some students from these subjects. They opt out, causing another leak in the "educational pipeline" (Widnall, 1988). Naples (1993) likened opting out to the reaction of some upon entering a foreign culture and not understanding the language. Some retreat, finding a group of people like themselves, minimizing the need to speak the foreign language. In the language analogy, however, we do not have the embedded belief that the "foreign language" is unconquerable, a feeling that is often conveyed in classes obscured with technical jargon. Although many students experience this "culture shock," there are special implications for those who lack the acculturation to engineering or physics that comes from tinkering with mechanical things, a situation far more common among women than men.

Because mathematics is used so much in science and engineering, students often perceive little difference between the fields. Practicing physicists and engineers appreciate that mathematics is an extremely efficient way of conveying ideas and understand that mathematics must be mastered. Beginning students often get lost when confronted simultaneously with mathematics and physics, neither of which they understand. Frustrated students are likely to lose interest if they think that physics is merely integrals and differential equations rather than a way of describing nature.

White male students on the whole seem less bothered by a mathematical approach to science, in which the justification for the effort need not be tangible. Female students, however, frequently mention lack of relevance as their reason for not choosing careers in physics or engineering. There is also a perspective conveyed in the classroom that there is a "right" solution that can be constructed in isolation rather than a range of solutions having various trade-offs. This perspective "is comfortable and intuitive to only a narrow set of self-selected individuals" (Tobias, 1992, p. 9).

There are numerous solutions to this dilemma that enable the same material to be taught with greater effectiveness by changing the order or the emphasis. Using the "just in time" teaching style (Samaras, 1991), a professor can pose a significant problem that a professional in the field might have to solve. After discussing strategies with the students and breaking the problem down into smaller steps, the professor can justify the need to know how to calculate a flow rate or a volume expansion. This approach may seem at first to be a less elegant way of ordering a syllabus, but the problem-solving skills taught are the most valuable asset our students gain. A problem-oriented approach integrates individual topics in physics or engineering and provides a more realistic idea of what it's like to be a physicist or engineer.

Students bring with them a variety of experiences and everyday wisdom. They have also developed their own mental models of everyday processes. The term *mental model* has many definitions. These models have been described as a picture in one's mind of how a system operates, essentially a qualitative simulation of that system (de Kleer, 1990). It has been suggested that people use these models to understand the world by "running" them in their heads. This also means that students have their own models of physical phenomena, based on a partial and sometimes erroneous set of concepts. To what extent do we address these "naive models" in drawing examples or developing the patterns that we call "laws of physics"? We assume in teaching that the knowledge we impart is "objective truth" and that all students receive and process it in more or less the same way. Experiments in cognitive psychology show that new ideas are assimilated into the student's existing mental model, and this process may result in a set of misperceptions that are nevertheless coherent in fitting together to form a self-consistent structure (Bostrom, Fischhoff, & Morgan, 1992; Gentner & Stevens, 1983). There is a vast literature on mental models, including work on students' understanding of physical principles and of complicated phenomena such as global warming (Atman & Nair, 1992; Hesse, 1989). The approach of understanding a learner's mental model before designing instructional material has been used successfully in physics instruction as well as in the design of public information material on technological risks such as radon in homes, electric and magnetic fields, and AIDS (Bostrom et al., 1992; McDermott, 1991).

Kuhn (1974) said that the dominant paradigms of the time, rather than some objective scale, determine scientifically valid theories. Thus, there is at least an element of subjectivity in science, and the dominant paradigm is determined by the dominant authors of the science. This means that the prevalent approach to science teaching may be unsuited to those people who have historically been omitted from science. Examples drawn from predominantly male sports and from weapon deployment dominate mechanics courses and ignore the backgrounds of female students as they attempt to understand or visualize situations.

These observations call for a constructivist approach to curriculum and instruction. Constructivism is based on the premise that a learner actively constructs his or her internal understanding of the experienced world (Hewson & Hewson, 1988). A study of first-year engineering students found that only 12% were able to identify the forces acting on a coin tossed in the air. For two groups of students who had taken a mechanics course, this percentage was raised to only 28% for one group and 30% for the other (Clement, 1982). A constructivist rather than objectivist model of teaching includes the student's mental model (Driver & Oldham, 1986; Tobias, 1992). The constructivist approach views the curriculum "not as a body of knowledge or skills, but the program of activities from which such knowledge or skills can possibly be acquired or constructed, . . . the selection of possible learning experiences is guided by the knowledge of experts" (Cheek, 1992, p. 139). The ideal approach to classroom instruction would be one in which the teacher helps students move through a process of conceptual change from a "naive" model to the accepted scientific models. Although individual teachers cannot fully exploit this scheme for course design, the recognition of student experience as a foundation for learning should gradually lead to a modification of materials, including examples and classroom methods that emphasize active participation by students in examining conflicts between their existing mental models and the models taught in the course. The work of Halloun and Hestenes (1985) demonstrated the persistence of naive conceptions in students and has led to several projects in reforming college physics. In addition to getting the material across better, such an approach can also give students a sense of ownership about their knowledge. This can result in increased self-efficacy according to the Betz model discussed earlier and encourage students—particularly women—to persist in the study of science and engineering.

Course material designed on the basis of a constructivist approach may be fruitful in addressing some of the cognitive discomfort and possible misinterpretations that students face in the traditional material of physics and engineering courses. Intuition gained from everyday experience is often of little help in introductory courses that start with idealized physics. It is easy in a beginning mechanics course to believe that physicists concern themselves only with blocks sliding down a frictionless inclined plane or with springs that never lose their elasticity from overextension.

Students often have difficulty working problems because they lack good physical intuition, but introductory courses rarely do enough to develop intuition. Quantitative problem solving with idealized conditions is favored over hands-on experience with real physical problems. This is not to say that the reduced friction of an air track isn't useful for demonstrating momentum conservation, or that experience with mathematical methods isn't essential for higher-level studies. However, qualitative physics is far more useful in teaching physical intuition and scientific reasoning, and it helps boost students' interest and confidence about their ability in the area. A qualitative course in physical mechanics can be at least as challenging as a quantitative one. When confronted with qualitative questions, students often balk at first because it is easier to plug into an equation. Despite this, they gain more understanding by learning to apply the scientific method than by blindly substituting numbers into equations. With greater emphasis on qualitative reasoning, students can develop their intuition and gain motivation to work on the more quantitative problems.

Teaching Style

Many subtle factors involving professors' teaching styles can significantly affect the learning environment in physics or engineering classrooms. The impersonal approach to teaching typified by introductory physics courses encourages students to feel anonymous. Often it is impossible for a professor to learn all 300 of the students' names in a single term. Departments choose to teach this way because it frees up other faculty to offer higher-level courses on special topics. However, it is not necessarily the best way to teach introductory physics.

The large lecture style encourages passive behavior at a time when students should be learning to aggressively challenge assumptions. This is a particular problem for women students, who have been conditioned to be passive. In high school, it was easier for students to be successful because someone knew their names and how they were doing. They could get feedback about their work and approach the teacher if they were having difficulty. It is easy in a large lecture course to take notes without questioning the material as it is presented. Often by the time the student looks at the notes and cannot make sense of them, he or she feels reluctant to ask questions. It is also easy to skip class in a large lecture when students believe they won't be missed. This is especially true for textbook-based courses in physics and engineering. All the equations they need are in the book, and it is easy for students to convince themselves that reading the book is sufficient to master the material. This may be feasible for a few top students, but the vast majority benefit from a combination of approaches.

It is not always feasible to break up large lectures into smaller groups, but there are some partial solutions. The major goals are to make individual contact with students and to encourage them to be active participants. Whatever efforts are necessary to learn students' names should be made; students respond to a professor who knows who they are, how they've been doing, and whether they attend class regularly. Although students dislike being put on the spot to answer questions, they respond favorably if they are called by name when they raise questions. It is useful to point out to the rest of the class when a good point has been made by a student, particularly a female or minority student or someone who rarely speaks up.

In order to keep students actively involved, it helps to get them accustomed to responding to questions. In a traditional physics or engineering course, a student who is asked to give the correct answer to a question is put under considerable pressure. A less stressful but equally useful approach is to present several possible solutions and ask students to discuss them and vote for the one they believe is correct. This dilutes the pressure and encourages students not merely to guess at the answer but to think through the problem and be willing to defend their approach. After background material has been presented, it is helpful for students to work a problem or two in class, either alone or in small groups. These problems don't always have to be graded, but they force students to apply the material and help them see whether they've mastered it. To ensure that students make an effort, these problems can be collected and graded occasionally, or students can be required to volunteer several times during the term to explain a problem to the class.

Many courses have individual sections with teaching assistants (TA's), but interaction with TA's doesn't substitute for time with a faculty member. There is often considerably reduced attendance at sections taught by TA's, and there is a perception that the sections aren't synchronized with the lectures. In addition, women and minority students experience more problems in sections taught by TA's. This may be due to inexperience on the part of the TA's or to cultural differences, which are common, since many graduate students in physics and engineering come from parts of the world where women and minorities have low status. TA training is essential to minimize these problems, and it is accomplished most easily when graduate students first arrive. There is far more leverage available when requiring TA's to meet certain standards than there is for tenured faculty, and these students haven't had time to get used to bad habits.

The way a course is taught implicitly demonstrates how much students are valued. Students often give the benefit of the doubt to a less talented teacher who is clearly trying and genuinely likes teaching. As universities endeavor to maximize the faculty effort while minimizing the costs of educating students, this issue should not be ignored.

Often both professors and TA's are overworked, and this shows up in the quality of teaching. It also affects the amount of time faculty have to spend helping students outside of class, which must be balanced with time spent writing grant proposals and papers, supervising research, and giving talks at meetings and other universities. This differentially harms female students, who are socialized to refrain from burdening others, even if this interferes with their education. Without clear evidence that extra effort in teaching is rewarded as much as extra production in research, teaching activities will continue to have second-class status at major research universities. Despite the professed value of teaching, it is unheard of for a major university to lure a professor away from a competitor for his or her teaching ability.

Although parts of this problem can be solved only by high-level changes, there are small but significant modifications that can be made at the classroom level. Even the most harried professor has time to show respect for his or her students. Students need encouragement and support when they ask questions or approach a faculty member during office hours. In the classroom, this can be particularly important when other students show disapproval of questions raised by women or minorities. For better or worse, a professor has considerable power to determine what is acceptable behavior and what is not tolerated. In addition to teaching physics or engineering, the style the professor uses to teach conveys the standards of professionalism in the field. Professors should use their authority to step in and comment on the disrespect of others when it occurs.

Role Models

The importance of role models should not be discounted, since a large proportion of women and minorities in science or engineering today have a parent or close relative who works in a technical field (Layzer, 1992). Students without such a parental role model often look to a teacher who can provide guidance, support, and a model to emulate. As noted earlier, children view scientists as white and male, and this makes it more difficult for women and minorities to model themselves after scientists. Since only about 2% of the faculty in physics and engineering are women, and an even smaller percentage are black or Hispanic, the professor is unlikely to be a role model for students from nontraditional backgrounds. Institutions with members of underrepresented groups often overburden them with extra mentoring duties without acknowledging the amount of time and effort involved.

There are several possible solutions to these problems. Faculty members who devote considerable time to encouraging women and minority students in physics or engineering should be given a formal title, and this service to the university should be treated as a committee assignment. In the absence of female or minority faculty in a physics or engineering department, it should be remembered that graduate or upperclass undergraduate students, faculty from closely related departments, and professionals from outside the university are often interested in helping others like themselves to succeed. Although white male faculty are less-than-perfect role models for some students, they have many opportunities to improve the learning environment and to act as mentors for members of any group.

CONCLUSIONS

We have explored the dimensions of learning and teaching that can enhance the quality of the environment for everyone, but particularly for nontraditional students. The recent concern about teaching has brought forth a spate of books on teaching techniques (Davidson & Ambrose, 1994; Wankat, 1993). In addition, women in science and women in engineering programs address some of the needs described above. Early introduction of engineering courses, teaching science and engineering in context, and providing opportunities to gain experiences that would bring students up to speed can all help address the problems discussed. An important requisite, however, is that colleges and universities provide rewards and opportunities for faculty to engage in innovative teaching techniques and to move toward a student-centered learning environment.

REFERENCES

American Chemical Society. (1988). *ChemCom: Chemistry in the community.* Dubuque, IA: Kendall/Hunt.

Atman, Cynthia J., & Nair, Indira. (1992). Constructivism: Appropriate for engineering education? *American Society for Engineering Education Annual Conference Proceedings* (pp. 1310–1312).

Betz, Nancy. (1990). What stops women and minorities from choosing and completing majors in science and engineering? Science and Public Policy Seminar presented by the Federation of Behavioral, Psychological and Cognitive Science, Washington, DC.

Betz, Nancy, & Hackett, Gail. (1983). The relationship of mathematics self-efficacy expectations to the selection of science-based college majors. *Journal of Vocational Behavior, 23,* 329–345.

Bostrom, Ann, Fischhoff, Baruch, & Morgan, M. Granger. (1992). Characterizing mental models of hazardous processes: A methodology and an application to radon. *Journal of Social Issues, 48*(4), 85–100.

Cheek, Dennis. (1992). *Thinking constructively about science, technology and society education.* Albany, NY: State University of New York Press.

Clement, John. (1982). Students' perceptions in introductory mechanics. *American Journal of Physics, 50,* 66–71.

Daniels, Jane. (1990). *The nuts & bolts of program planning: Recruitment programs.* Proceedings of Women in Engineering Conference. Washington, DC: WEPAN.

Davidson, Cliff, & Ambrose, Susan. (1994). *The new professors handbook: An introduction to teaching and research in engineering and science.* Bolton, MA: Anker.

de Kleer, Johan. (1990). *Readings in qualitative reasoning about physical systems.* San Mateo, CA: Morgan Kaufman.

Driver, Rosalind H., & Oldham, Valerie. (1986). A constructivist approach to curriculum development in science. *Studies in Science Education, 13,* 105–122.

Electrical and Computer Engineering. (1991). *A new ECE curriculum for Carnegie Mellon.* Pittsburgh, PA: Carnegie Mellon University.

Fehrs, Mary, & Czujko, Roman. (1992). Women in physics: Reversing the exclusion. *Physics Today, 45,* 33–40.

Fensham, Peter J. (1992). Science and technology. In Phillip W. Jackson (Ed.), *Handbook of research on curriculum* (pp. 83–115). New York: Macmillan.

Feynman, Richard P., Leighton, Robert B., & Sands, Matthew. (1963). *The Feynman lectures on physics: Vol. 1. Mainly mechanics, radiation and heat.* Palo Alto, CA: Addison-Wesley.

Florman, Samuel. (1976). *Existential pleasures of engineering.* New York: St. Martin's Press.

Gentner, Deidre, & Stevens, Albert L. (Eds.). (1983). *Mental Models.* Hillsdale, NJ: Erlbaum.

Halloun, Ibrahim A., & Hestenes, David. (1985). The initial knowledge state of college physics students. Common sense concepts about motion. *American Journal of Physics, 53,* 1055.

Hesse, Joseph. (1989, September). From naive to knowledgeable. *The Science Teacher,* 55–58.

Hewson, Paul, & Hewson, Mary G. (1988). An appropriate conception of teaching science: A view from studies of science learning. *Science Education, 72,* 597–614.

Keeton, Kimberly. (1991). *Students' images of scientists and engineers.* Unpublished undergraduate research paper, Carnegie Mellon University, Pittsburgh, PA.

Khoury, Bernard V., & Kirwan, Donald F. (1993). *Active physics project.* College Park, MD: American Association of Physics Teachers.

Kuhn, Thomas S. (1974). *The structure of scientific revolutions.* Chicago: University of Chicago Press.

Layzer, David. (1992). Why women (and men) give up in science. In H. Ausell & J. Wilkinson (Eds.), *On teaching and learning* (Vol. 4, pp. 36–47). Cambridge, MA: Derek Bok Center for Teaching and Learning, Harvard University.

Maxwell, James C. (1954). *A treatise on electricity and magnetism.* New York: Dover.

McDermott, Lillian C. (1991). Millikan lecture 1990: What we teach and what is learnt—closing the gap. *American Journal of Physics, 59*, 301–315.

Millikan, Robert A. (1924). *Electron: Its isolation and measurement and the determination of some of its properties.* Chicago: University of Chicago Press.

Naples, Larisa. (1993). *A study of the parallels between expatriate culture shock and the reactions of students entering the scientific community.* Unpublished master's thesis, State University of New York, Brockport.

National Science Foundation. (1993). *Indications of science and mathematics education 1992.* Washington, DC: Author.

Petroski, Henry. (1985). *To engineer is human: The role of failure in success fuel design.* New York: St. Martin's Press.

Rosser, Sue. (1990). *Female-friendly science: Applying women's studies methods and theories to attract students.* Elmsford, NY: Pergamon Press.

Samaras, Patricia W. (1991, November). Integrating the first two years. ASEE *Prism*, 16–19.

Sherwood, Bruce, & Chabay, Ruth. (1992). *Qualitative reasoning in electricity* (Working Paper). Pittsburgh, PA: Carnegie Mellon University.

Sommerfield, Arnold. (1934). *Atomic structure and spectral lines.* London: Methuen.

Tobias, Sheila. (1990). *They're not dumb, they're different.* Tucson, AZ: Research Corporation.

Tobias, Sheila. (1992). Reforming college physics: Attending to cognitive issues. In S. Tobias (Ed.), *Revitalizing undergraduate science: Why some things work and most don't* (pp. 96–113). Tucson, AZ: Research Corporation.

Wankat, Phillip C. (1993). *Teaching engineering.* New York: McGraw-Hill.

Widnall, Sheila. (1988). AAAS presidential lecture: Voices from the pipeline. *Science, 241*, 1740–1745.

Women in Engineering Program Advocates Network. (1990, 1991, 1992, 1993). *Women in engineering conference proceedings.* Washington, DC: Author.

CHAPTER 2
A Feminist Approach to Teaching Quantum Physics

Karen Barad

> On the other hand, I think I can safely say that nobody understands quantum mechanics. So do not take the lecture too seriously, feeling that you really have to understand in terms of some model what I am going to describe, but just relax and enjoy it. I am going to tell you what nature behaves like. If you simply admit that maybe she does behave like this, you will find her a delightful, entrancing thing. Do not keep saying to yourself, if you can possibly avoid it, "But how can it be like that?" Because you will get "down the drain," into a blind alley from which nobody has escaped. (Feynman, 1965, p. 129)

> And Von Neumann gave me an interesting idea; that you don't have to be responsible for the world that you're in. So I have developed a very powerful sense of social irresponsibility. . . . It's made me a very happy man ever since.
> —Feynman speaking of advice given to him by the mathematician John von Neumann while they were working together at Los Alamos on the atomic bomb (Schweber, 1986, p. 467)

In the physics community, Richard Feynman is a hero. In different ways, the quotes above speak of a yearning for innocence, a boyish playfulness that won't quit even in the face of life's most serious moments. Feynman, the self-proclaimed *enfant terrible*, portrayed himself as a fun-loving kind of guy, thumbing his nose at responsibility and taking advantage of every opportunity to persuade Nature herself to yield to his charms. Richard Feynman was not your stereotypical physicist. He was the non-quiche-eating real man of the physics community: a kind of James Dean, John Wayne, and John Travolta hybrid. His rebel-without-a-cause, rugged-individual, cool-and-unpretentious-New Yorker-womanizing personality stood in stark contrast to the asexual, nerdy, last-pick-for-the-ball-team stereotype. Central to his personality was a need to impress others with his cleverness. But underneath it all, he cared deeply about understanding quantum mechanics, if not the fate of the world.

My purpose here is not to speculate about, psychologize, or debate the nuances of Feynman's personality. My interest is not in Feynman the man but in Feynman as a symbol of the dominant culture of U.S. post-*Sputnik* physics. In particular, I think it is important to ask why Feynman is a hero of inordinate proportions. That is, what, aside from genius, makes Feynman a superhero in the eyes of the contemporary physics community? Which aspects of the Feynman legacy have been appropriated and integrated into the culture of U.S. physics, and which have not? How is this culture perpetuated in the classroom, and what does it mean for students?

"Whatever else Dick Feynman may have joked about, his love for physics approached reverence" (L. Brown, cited in Lubkin, 1989, p. 23). Anyone who has watched the "Nova" interview, "The Pleasure of Finding Things Out," will testify to the sheer delight this remarkable scientist found in doing physics. His energy, enthusiasm, and love for physics have endeared him to students and colleagues alike. Dick Feynman epitomized the "Physics is Phun" pedagogical approach of post-*Sputnik* science in the United States—what I like to call the "Boys Just Wanna Have Fu-un" (a gender-reversed appropriation of Cyndi Lauper's hit tune) approach. This approach may have worked well for the particular purposes the physics community had in mind in the period immediately following the success of *Sputnik*, but its flaws have been more than evident in the post-*Challenger* period in which we now live. The contrast between the 1950s *Sputnik* success and the 1980s *Challenger* disaster serves as an interesting metaphor for what can happen when pedagogy becomes inflexible in the face of rapidly changing demographics.[1]

For more than two decades, feminist science studies scholars have been offering increasingly complex and sophisticated accounts of the role of gender, race, sexuality, and class ideologies in the production of scientific knowledge. As testimony to the depth and effectiveness of these critiques, it is important to note that feminist studies of biology and primatology have already led to marked changes in the actual content of these natural sciences (see, e.g., Bleier, 1984; Fausto-Sterling, 1985, 1987; Haraway, 1986, 1989; Hrdy, 1986; Hubbard, 1990; Longino & Doell, 1983). However, few analyses have focused on the physical sciences. Does the scientific method simply "work better" when the subject matter is the physical world rather than the biological or social ones, or are the issues simply less obvious? It would be ironic to find that the physical sciences, those sciences that have traditionally been most exclusive of women and people of color, are unmarked by the politics of race, ethnicity, class, gender, sexuality, and other critical social variables.

The analysis I present in this chapter relies on a feminist reading of Niels Bohr's philosophy of physics, the details of which I present in a companion paper focusing largely on the epistemological issues (see Barad, in press). This chapter focuses on pedagogical issues, outlining an alternative to the "you don't have to be responsible," "just relax and enjoy it," "Physics is Phun" approach to teaching. Recognizing the diverse population of students that will become future scientists and their serious concerns about the complex world for which they must share responsibility, we must clearly try different approaches. Although there are models available to reform introductory science courses, most of these approaches leave the remainder of the curriculum intact. The entire curriculum must be transformed; it is not sufficient to put all our efforts into the introductory courses and then go on with business as usual. I therefore use an advanced physics course for junior and senior majors as an example here. Although a course on quantum physics relies on a certain level of mathematical sophistication, I have tried to make the ideas presented here accessible to the uninitiated. I hope that this example will inspire a multitude of other efforts needed to transform entire science curricula.

NEWTONIAN FRAMEWORK: REFLECTIONS ON MIRRORING THEORIES

> It was quite clear to me that the religious paradise of youth, which was thus lost, was a first attempt to free myself from the chains of the "merely personal," from an existence which is dominated by wishes, hopes and primitive feelings. Out yonder there was this huge world, which exists independently of us human beings and which stands before us like a great, eternal riddle, at least partially accessible to our inspection and thinking. The contemplation of this world beckoned like a liberation, and I soon noticed that many a man whom I had learned to esteem and to admire had found inner freedom and security in devoted occupation with it. The mental grasp of this extrapersonal world within the frame of the given possibilities swam before my mind's eye.
> —Albert Einstein speaking of choosing a career in physics (Schilpp, 1970, p. 5)

> When someone with the authority of a teacher, say, describes the world and you are not in it, there is a moment of psychic disequilibrium, as if you looked into a mirror and saw nothing.
> —Adrienne Rich, from her essay "Invisibility in Academe" (Rich, 1986, p. 198)

There is more to sparking student interest in physics than warming the "chilly climate" of science classrooms. Contemporary physics curricula in the United States reflect what Traweek (1988) calls "an extreme culture of objectivity: a culture of no culture, which longs passionately for a world without loose ends, without temperament, gender, nationalism, or other sources of disorder—for a world outside human space and time" (p. 162). Newtonian physics is consonant with such a vision of the world.

The Newtonian worldview is compatible with an objectivist epistemology, in which the well-prepared mind is able to produce a privileged mental mirroring of the world as it exists independently of us human beings (see Rorty, 1979). That is, what is "discovered" is presumed to be unmarked by its "discoverer." The claim is that the scientist can read the universal equations of nature that are inscribed on G-d's blackboard: Nature has spoken. Paradoxically, the objects being studied are given all the agency, even and most especially when they are seen as passive, inert objects moving aimlessly in the void. That is, these cultureless agents, existing outside of human space-time, are thought to reveal their secrets to patient observers watching and listening through benignly obtrusive instruments. Notice that agency is not attributed to human beings; once all subjective contaminants have been removed by the scientific method, scientists simply collect the pure distillate of truth.[2]

The Newtonian worldview is still so much a part of contemporary physics culture that it infects the teaching of post-Newtonian physics as well. That is, the stakes are so high in maintaining the mirroring view of scientific knowledge that quantum physics is presented as mysticism. Take the example of a photon being emitted from a light source. Students are told that according to quantum mechanics, the photon does not have a polarization until it is measured. This goes against classical intuition, since it seems that the polarization that is measured must be the one the photon had when it was emitted. The curious student wants to know how it can possibly be otherwise: How can the photon have traveled through space without a polarization? The physics professor smiles one of those smiles and "explains": "That's just the way it is. This is what quantum mechanics predicts, and this is what we find in the lab."

The unabashedly persistent student asks, "If the photon does not have a polarization until it is measured, then how are the fields aligned before it reaches the detector? How does the detector give the photon a polarization? What is the mechanism at work?" The professor smiles again and answers: "These are questions of philosophy. We don't care about whether falling trees make noises in forests when no one is there to hear them. The point is that quantum mechanics is the most precise theory we have. Using this theory we can calculate the outcomes and successfully predict an incredible range of phenomena that can be verified experimentally." Eventually, even the most tenacious student will give in to the mysticism, or leave.

Can a more satisfying explanation of polarization be given? I believe that Niels Bohr's interpretation of quantum theory provides a rich, complex, and intelligible explanation, but it is seldom taught in spite of the fact that an overwhelming majority of physicists claim an allegiance to Bohr's interpretation of quantum theory, the so-called Copenhagen interpretation.[3] In fact, few physicists can articulate Bohr's position. Of course, my point here is not to chastise individual instructors; the point is that this learned ignorance is part of the culture of extreme objectivity in physics. After I outline Bohr's interpretation of quantum physics, I present a Bohrian explanation of photon polarization and I consider an explanation for the constructed irrelevancy of Bohr's interpretation of quantum theory to physics.

A BOHRIAN APPROACH TO QUANTUM PHYSICS

The uncertainty principle, students are told, is the foundation of quantum physics. Yet it is given scarce attention in textbooks on quantum mechanics. Typically, physics instructors also spend very little time discussing this pivotal point. Furthermore, many quantum physics texts give inadequate or even misleading accounts of the uncertainty principle. The following assertions are common: The uncertainty principle states that we cannot simultaneously know both the position and the momentum of an object; or, the uncertainty principle states that the very act of observation disturbs the way the object would have been had it not been observed.[4] In the following discussion, I explain why these articulations are problematic.

A thorough discussion of the uncertainty principle is a critical starting point for a quantum mechanics course. Most students have already had some exposure to the uncertainty principle in a sophomore-level modern physics class; however, this principle is particularly subtle, requiring repeated and increasingly sophisticated treatments. Furthermore, a substantive discussion brings to the fore important historical and philosophical issues, shows disagreement and misunderstanding on the part of physicists, and emphasizes the importance of bringing critical and metacritical perspectives to bear on science.

Warm-up for the Uncertainty Principle: Heisenberg's Microscope With Crucial Insights From Bohr

MAIN POINTS:

1. Discontinuity is not sufficient; indeterminateness must be considered in deriving the uncertainty principle
2. Object-instrument distinction is arbitrary

According to Newtonian physics, if we know the "initial conditions," that is, if we know the object's position and momentum at a given time, then the entire trajectory (past and future motion) of the particle can be calculated (Newton's second law). The idea then is to perform a measurement to determine an object's initial conditions.

A rather intuitive approach to determining the initial conditions is to use the "time of flight" technique. The strategy involved is to measure the object's position at two closely separated moments in time and then calculate the momentum from the measurements of the object's successive positions.

The following experimental setup can be used to perform this measurement: a dark laboratory (since light carries momentum and we want to disturb the object as little as possible), a long sheet of film with fine rulings nailed to the laboratory wall (for measuring position), a light source (for illuminating the object, i.e., taking its picture, during position measurements), and a clock (to determine the time at which the position measurements are made). The measurement is performed by taking two pictures closely separated in time. From this information, the velocity can be calculated by finding out how far the object has moved in a given amount of time. The momentum is then obtained by multiplying the velocity of the object by the value of its mass. In the limit in which the time interval between photographs approaches zero, a determination of the position and momentum of the object at one given time, that is, the initial conditions, would be accomplished.

There are several important features of time of flight measurements that we need to consider. First, it is important to emphasize that the film must remain fixed in the laboratory. This is necessary so that we know what we mean by "position." Second, we need to work in a dark room in order to make a precise measurement; since light has its own momentum, the act of shining light on an object changes the momentum that we assume the object had before the measurement. Since we don't want to disturb the object unnecessarily, we illuminate the object with a flash of light only when we are measuring its position. But that means that the time of flight measurement requires us to disturb the object twice—once for each position measurement. Finally, notice that this method is based on the seemingly innocent assumption that objects have a definite trajectory, that is, a precise value of position and momentum at each moment in time.

Figure 2.1 illustrates the time of flight measurement. Assume that the object has momentum $\mathbf{p}_0$ and position $\mathbf{x}_0$ at some time t_0 before the measurement. (Vector quantities are denoted in boldface.) The first flash of light rebounds off the object and produces a mark on the film, which we record to be position $\mathbf{x}_1$ at time t_1. After the initial illumination, the momentum of

FIGURE 2.1. Schematic illustration of a time of flight measurement.

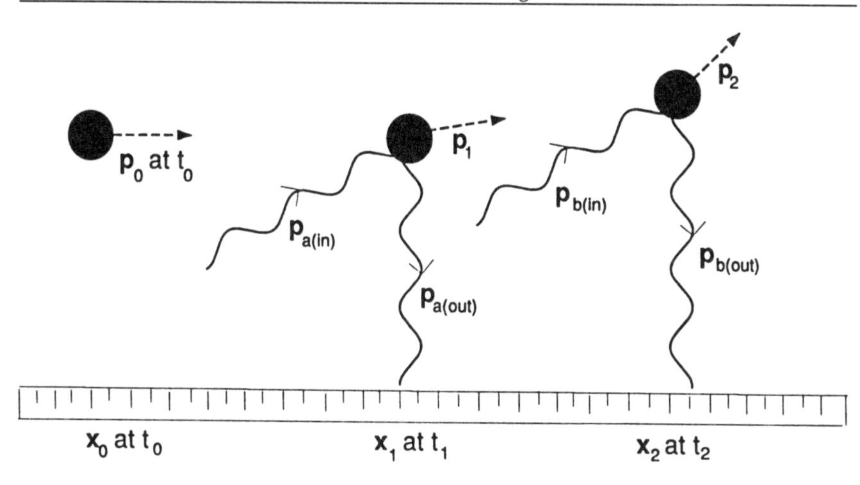

the object will generally be a new value, $\mathbf{p}_1$. According to the conservation of momentum (equating the total momentum before the interaction with the total momentum after), the momentum of the object before it is illuminated, $\mathbf{p}_0$, plus the momentum of the first incoming photon ("photon" refers to the particlelike behavior of light), $\mathbf{p}_{a(in)}$, is equal to the momentum of the object after collision with the first photon, $\mathbf{p}_1$, plus the momentum of the first outgoing photon, $\mathbf{p}_{a(out)}$:

$$\mathbf{p}_0 + \mathbf{p}_{a(in)} = \mathbf{p}_1 + \mathbf{p}_{a(out)}.$$

Similarly, the second flash of light rebounds off the object and produces a mark on the film, which we record to be position x_2 at time t_2. The momentum of the object after the second illumination we designate $\mathbf{p}_2$. The conservation of momentum can be applied to this second interaction as well: The momentum of the object before it is illuminated a second time, $\mathbf{p}_1$, plus the momentum of the second incoming photon, $\mathbf{p}_{b(in)}$, is equal to the momentum of the object after measurement, $\mathbf{p}_2$, plus the momentum of the second outgoing photon, $\mathbf{p}_{b(out)}$:

$$\mathbf{p}_1 + \mathbf{p}_{b(in)} = \mathbf{p}_2 + \mathbf{p}_{b(out)}.$$

The idea behind the time of flight method is that it is possible to calculate momentum using successive position measurements. The momentum is calculated by multiplying the mass of the object, m, times the distance traveled, Δx, during the time interval in question, Δt, and taking the limit of these values as the time interval gets immeasurably small:

$$\mathbf{p} = \lim_{\Delta t \to 0} m \frac{\Delta x}{\Delta t} = \lim_{\Delta t \to 0} m \frac{x_2 - x_1}{t_2 - t_1}.$$

But which momentum is this? Unfortunately, the momentum that we calculate, $\mathbf{p}_1$, is neither the value of the momentum of the object before the measurement, $\mathbf{p}_0$ (the value that we set out to determine and which we assume represents the observer-independent value of the object's momentum), nor even the value it has after we finish the measurement, $\mathbf{p}_2$. Rather, the momentum that we calculate is an abstraction: the value that the object has during the measurement process. Niels Bohr explains this as follows:

> Indeed, the position of an individual at two given moments can be measured with any desired degree of accuracy; but if, from such measurements, we would calculate the velocity of the individual in the ordinary way, it must be clearly realized that we are dealing with an abstraction, from which no unambiguous information concerning the previous or future behavior of the individual can be obtained. (Bohr, 1963a, p. 66)

According to classical physics, there is nothing to worry about, since we can determine the position and momentum that the object would have had if we had not performed the measurement by one of two methods: (1) choosing a measurement process that involves negligible interaction with the object being measured, or (2) determining the size of the measurement interaction and subtracting its effects. Let's consider each strategy in turn.

The first strategy, reducing the magnitude of the interaction to the point where the disturbance is negligible, is perhaps the most obvious. In fact, our everyday experiences with macroscopic objects are of this kind. Macroscopic objects are so large that we are unable to notice any disturbances caused by light hitting an object when a lamp is suddenly turned on. However, the effect on a microscopic object is pronounced. Our classical intuition would suggest decreasing the disturbance by using a lamp with less intensity. Ultimately, however, this method would fail, due to the quantum postulate.

The quantum postulate is based on the empirical finding that there is a discontinuity in our interactions within nature. One pronounced manifestation of this discontinuity is that in certain experimental situations, including the one we have been discussing, light behaves as particles, called photons. And here's the rub: To record the position of an object requires at least one photon, one quantum of light, to make a mark on the film—but even one photon is sufficient to disturb the object. (Technically speaking, this interaction is an example of Compton scattering.) The discontinuous nature of the interaction means that it is not possible to reduce the interaction any further; according to quantum theory, one has reached a fundamental limit. Notice that a solution to this dilemma cannot be found by using a low-energy photon that produces only a mild disturbance of the object, since an accurate position measurement requires short wavelength light, which means a high-energy photon. This paragraph summarizes the essence of Heisenberg's derivation of the uncertainty principle. Bohr argued that this analysis is incomplete and that the indeterminate nature of observational interactions is a crucial ingredient in a proper derivation of the uncertainty principle (see Bohr, 1963a, pp. 63, 67).

Now that I have shown why, according to quantum theory, it is not possible to reduce the observation interaction to the point where it is negligible, let's consider the second strategy: determining the actual disturbance involved and subtracting it, leaving the desired preobservation values of the variables. In theory, this can be accomplished by using the conservation of momentum: The total momentum before the interaction equals the total momentum after. So to determine $\mathbf{p}_0$ from $\mathbf{p}_1$ we would subtract the disturbance due to the photon:

$$\mathbf{p}_0 + \mathbf{p}_{a(in)} = \mathbf{p}_1 + \mathbf{p}_{a(out)}$$

or

$$\mathbf{p}_0 = \mathbf{p}_1 - [\mathbf{p}_{a(in)} - \mathbf{p}_{a(out)}].$$

That is, it would be possible to determine $\mathbf{p}_0$ from the value of $\mathbf{p}_1$ if we knew the momentum of the photon before and after the interaction.

Now the focus turns to measuring the photon momenta. One method would be to employ a direct approach. To measure momentum directly, however, requires an apparatus with movable parts. This is necessary so that we know what we mean by "momentum."[5] But as noted earlier, the film that absorbs the photon must be fixed, not movable, to serve the complementary purpose of recording the position. The fact that *mutually exclusive* experimental arrangements are required for defining position and momentum, *and* that it is *necessary* to assign values to both variables simultaneously in specifying the initial conditions, is an example of Bohr's principle of complementarity. (Complementarity is seen by Bohr as an alternative to the classical notion of description. For more details, see Barad, in press.)

What about using indirect methods, such as the time of flight approach discussed above, for determining the momenta of the photon? Here the difficulty lies in the fact that part of the measuring instrument (the photon) has now become part of the object being measured. In other words, the disturbance can be determined only if the measuring device is treated as an object, thereby defeating its purpose as a measuring instrument. Hence, observation is possible on the condition that the disturbance is indeterminable. (The term *disturbance* has been used in this analysis because it follows the Newtonian assumption that objects exist in definite states that are subsequently disturbed in the process of measurement. This terminology is misleading, however. Later discussion makes this point clear.)

A crucial consequence of this analysis is that we see that due to the discontinuous nature of the interaction, any distinction drawn between objects of investigation and the agencies of observation is necessarily *constructed*.[6] This is in sharp contrast to the Newtonian belief that objects are unambiguously defined: that a natural boundary, sometimes called a "Cartesian cut," exists, delineating object from instrument. As Bohr emphasized, quantum theory demands "the recognition that no sharp separation can be made between an independent behaviour of the objects and their interaction with the measuring instruments which define the reference frame" (Bohr, 1949, p. 224). That is, a discontinuous, indeterminable interaction implies that we must *choose* between an experimental setup that includes the photon as an object being measured and one in which the photon is part of the apparatus used to perform the measurement. The point is that a discontinuous, indeterminable interaction implies that we must choose between an experimental setup that enables us to know what we mean by "momentum" (film on a movable platform, photon as object) and an incompatible experimental setup that allows us know what we mean by "position" (fixed film, photon as apparatus). If, as Bohr says, "the finite magnitude of the quantum of action prevents altogether a sharp distinction being made between [an object] and the agency by which it is observed, a distinction which underlies the customary concept of observation" (Bohr, 1963a, p. 11), what then do we mean by such fundamental concepts in science as "object," "objective," and "observation" when we take quantum theory into account? These questions cut at the very core of our understanding of "science."

In summary, the time of flight measurement is a sound method for determining the initial conditions only from the perspective of classical physics. The reason is that classical physics is premised on the assumption that observation interactions are continuous and determinable. Quantum theory is based on the fact that interactions are discontinuous and indeterminable. Therefore, it is not possible to determine the initial conditions using time of flight measurements, or any other method for that matter. The question is, Why?

The Indefiniteness (or Ambiguity) Principle (commonly referred to as The Uncertainty Principle)

MAIN POINTS:

1. Wave-particle duality is the starting point
2. Limitation of classical descriptions
3. Properties are not intrinsic

> The uncertainty principle, as Heisenberg first formulated it, is an epistemic principle: it lays down the limits to what we can know; it is not an ontic principle, circumscribing the physical properties which objects may substantiate. On this view quantum mechanics is an indeterministic theory simply because the data required for deterministic predictions of the sort that classical mechanics provides are unobtainable. (Murdoch, 1987, p. 47).

Bohr was very critical of Heisenberg's derivation and interpretation of the uncertainty principle. Heisenberg's derivation is based on a discontinuous disturbance (think of the "Heisenberg microscope" analysis, which shares essential features with the time of flight approach discussed above). Bohr's derivation is based on wave-particle duality. That is, Bohr insisted that discontinuity alone was not enough; what was at issue was the indeterminateness of the discontinuous measurement process. (In fact, the divergence between the interpretations of Bohr and Heisenberg becomes more evident in Bohr's later writings, where he moves away from any reference to *disturbance* whatsoever, since the term disturbance connotes the existence of some undisturbed, well-defined, observer-independent classical state. Instead, Bohr emphasized the unanalyzable wholeness between the "object" and the "agencies of observation." For more information, see Barad, in press.) Consequently, Bohr could not accept an epistemic interpretation of the uncertainty principle.

Let's look at Bohr's argument (see Bohr, 1963a, pp. 57–68). The famous debates about the nature of light, which in part spawned the development of quantum theory, are summarized in the wave-particle duality relations.[7] Wave-particle duality is expressed mathematically as a precise relationship between particle variables (momentum p and energy E) and wave variables (wavelength λ and frequency f):

$$\lambda = h/p \qquad \text{and} \qquad f = h/E.$$

In each equation, the wave characteristics are on the left side of the equation, and particle characteristics are on the right side. In each case, wave characteristics are related to particle characteristics through Planck's constant h, the fundamental constant of quantum physics.

Now according to quantum theory, localized objects (particles) are represented by wave packets.[8] Wave packets are composed of a superposition of a large number of waves, each of a different yet well-defined wavelength (Figure 2.2). The more wave components (of different wavelengths) that go into making a given wave packet, the more narrow the wave packet is, and the more well-defined the notion of "position" becomes (Figures 2.3 and 2.4). From this we see that there is a complementary rela-

FIGURE 2.2. Two component waves of different wavelengths.

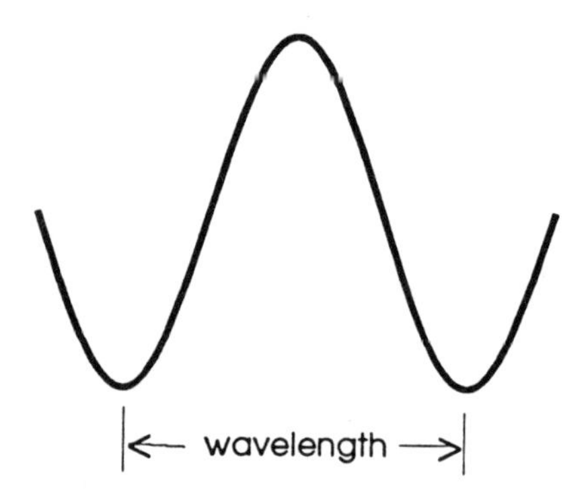

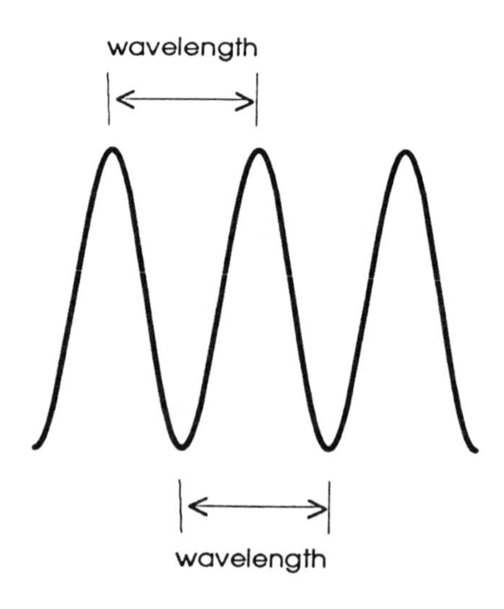

FIGURE 2.3. Example showing the construction of a wave packet by the superposition of two component waves.

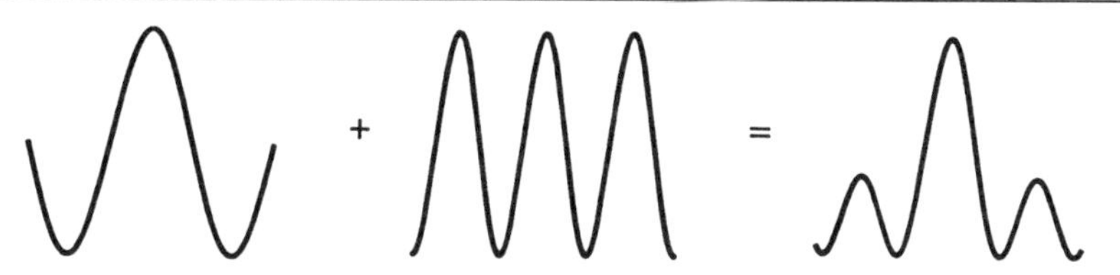

tionship between position and wavelength: A narrow wave packet represents a particle with a fairly well-defined position, but this requires including so many different component waves, each with a different wavelength, that it is not possible to associate meaningfully a given well-defined wavelength to the overall wave packet; alternatively, a broad wave packet includes few component waves so that it is still possible to associate meaningfully a fairly well-defined wavelength to the wave packet, but this wave packet cannot represent an object with a well-defined position (Figure 2.5).[9]

The inverse relationship between the definability of wavelength and the definability of position can be translated into an inverse relationship between the definability of momentum and the definability of position by invoking wave-particle duality. The precise mathematical relationship

$$\Delta x \, \Delta p \geq h/4\pi$$

expresses the fact that it is not possible to simultaneously *define* both the position and the momentum of an object; the definability of position and the definability of momentum stand in reciprocal relationship because it

FIGURE 2.4. The construction of a localized wave packet requires the superposition of many component waves.

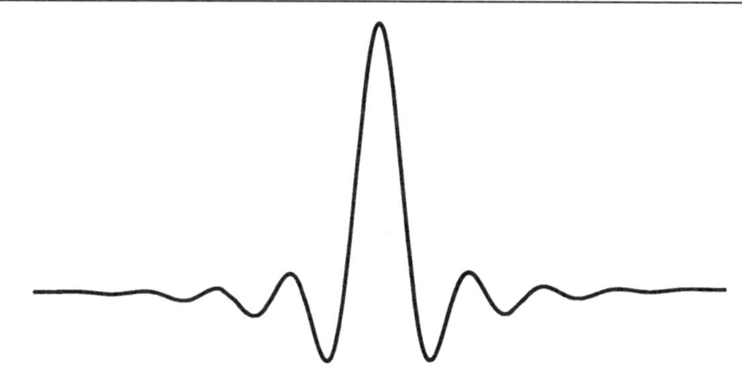

FIGURE 2.5. The top wave packet represents a particle with a fairly well-defined position. It is composed of a large number of different wavelengths; consequently, it is not clear how to define a wavelength for the wave packet. In contrast, the bottom wave packet includes very few different component waves. This wave packet has a fairly well-defined wavelength, but it is not clear how to define its position.

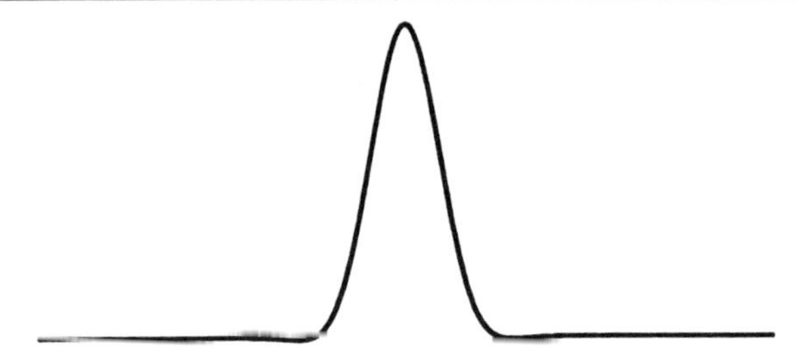

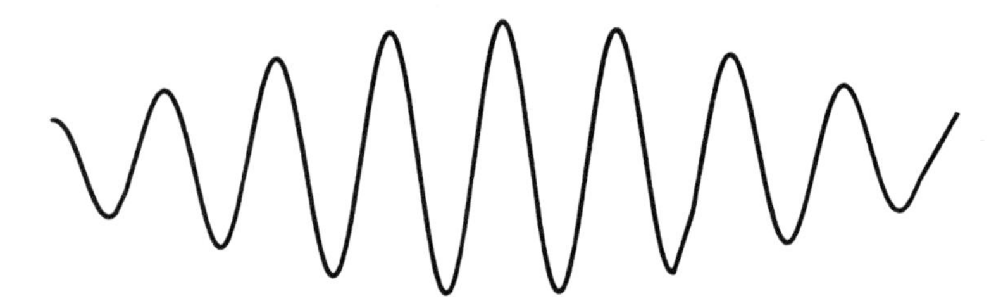

is necessary to simultaneously take account of mutually exclusive descriptions encountered in the theory of particles on the one hand and the theory of waves on the other.[10] This is the essence of Bohr's derivation of the Heisenberg uncertainty principle, which Bohr saw as a "simple symbolic expression" of the more general notion of complementarity (Bohr, 1963a, p. 60).

This argument clearly shows that Heisenberg's epistemic interpretation is not tenable. If objects actually possessed well-defined properties, such as position and momentum, at any given moment in time, then it would be sensible to talk about disturbances that occur during the process of measurement. However, Bohr's derivation shows that objects do *not* possess definite values of position and momentum. After a few weeks of intensive discussion, Heisenberg finally acquiesced to Bohr's point of view and added a postscript to his article on the uncertainty principle in which he stated:

> In this connection Bohr pointed out to me that I have overlooked essential points in some of the discussions in this work. Above all the uncertainty in the observation does not depend exclusively on the occurrence of discontinuities, but is directly connected with the necessity of doing justice simultaneously to the different experimental data which are expressed in the corpuscular theory on the one hand, and the wave theory on the other [i.e., wave-particle duality]. (quoted in Murdoch, 1987, p. 51)

In the decades following Bohr's death, empirical evidence was gathered that directly supports his claim.[11]

This brings new understanding to the mathematical expression

$$\Delta x \, \Delta p \geq h/4\pi.$$

Students are usually told that Δx represents the uncertainty in position. This is particularly misleading, given the analysis presented above, since the word *uncertainty* has the connotation that an object possesses definite properties but we're just not certain what they are (as in the incorrect epistemic interpretation of Heisenberg). According to Bohr, Δx represents the limit of the applicability of classical description based on the concept "position." Perhaps a better term would therefore be the *indefiniteness principle* or the *ambiguity principle*, as a reminder that the concepts we use are constructs that are definite or unambiguous only in particular contexts, where a well-defined cut is constructed for each situation, delineating the objects of investigation from the agencies of observation.[12]

Notice that particular experimental arrangements can be used to give more or less definite meaning to each of the complementary variables, but due to the lack of object-instrument distinction (see Warm-up for the Uncertainty Principle, above) it is not possible to assign the value obtained to the object itself. The "property" being measured in a particular experimental context is therefore not "objective" (that is, a property of the object as it exists independently of all human interventions), but neither is it created by the act of measurement (which would belie any sensible meaning of the word *measurement*). Bohr speaks of this "interaction" between "object" and "instrument" as a "phenomenon." The properties then are properties of phenomena. That is, within a given context, classical descriptive concepts can be used to describe phenomena, our intra-actions within nature. (I use the term *intra-action* to emphasize the lack of a natural object-instrument distinction, in contrast to *interaction*, which implies that there are two separate entities; that is, the latter reinscribes the contested dichotomy.) Readers familiar with contemporary feminist theories will recognize Bohr's "phenomenon" as a sign of the impossibility of a fixed, acontextual, simplistic, or final resolution. That is, the ambiguity between object and instrument is only temporarily, contextually decided; therefore, our characterizations do not signify properties of objects but rather describe the intra-action as it is marked by a particular constructed cut chosen by the experimenter (see Barad, in press, for more details).

The notion of "observation" then takes on a whole new meaning according to Bohr: "[B]y an experiment we simply understand an event about which we are able in an unambiguous way to state the conditions necessary for the reproduction of the phenomena" (quoted in Folse, 1985, p. 124). According to the analysis of the previous section, this is possible because, in performing each measurement, the experimenter intervenes by introducing a constructed distinction between the "object" and the "measuring device" (e.g., deciding whether the photon is part of the object or the instrument). The claim is that unambiguous, reproducible measurements are possible through the introduction of constructed cuts. Notice that "[n]o explicit reference is made to any individual observer" (Bohr, 1963c, p. 3): Different observers will get the same data set in observing any given phenomenon. Therefore, reproducibility, not some Newtonian notion of objectivity denoting observer independence, is the cornerstone of this new framework for understanding science.

For Bohr, the uncertainty principle is a matter of the inadequacy of classical description. Unlike the "mirroring" representationalism inherent in the Newtonian-Cartesian-Enlightenment framework of science, scientific concepts are not to be understood as describing some independent reality. A post-Newtonian framework sees these constructs as useful (i.e., potentially reproducible) descriptions of the entire intra-action process (the phenomenon, which is context dependent by definition), not of an isolated object. The implications of this finding are profound. In Bohr's own words:

> The extension of physical experience in our days has . . . necessitated a radical revision of the foundation for the unambiguous use of elementary concepts, and has changed our attitude to the aim of physical science. Indeed, from our present standpoint, physics is to be regarded not so much as the study of something a priori given, but rather as the development of methods for ordering and surveying human experience. (Bohr, 1963c, p. 10)

In other words:

> These facts not only set a limit to the extent of the information obtainable by measurements, but they also set a limit on the meaning which we may at-

> tribute to such information. We meet here in a new light the old truth that in our description of nature the purpose is not to disclose the real essence of [physical objects] but only to track down, so far as it is possible, relations between the manifold aspects of our experience. (Bohr, 1963a, p. 18)

Applications: Bringing the Point Home

EXAMPLES:

1. Photon polarization
2. The nature of light
3. Superpositions represent indefiniteness

I have found that a thorough discussion of the uncertainty principle produces a much more coherent understanding of quantum theory. In this section, I briefly discuss a few examples.

What does Bohr have to say about the photon's polarization? According to Bohr, "polarization" is a classical concept that has its origins in experiences with the macroscopic world, that is, the world of everyday experiences. This classical concept is an abstract idealization, a construct of the human mind, that can be usefully applied, even in the microscopic realm, under particular experimental circumstances where the notion of polarization can be unambiguously defined. Outside of this context, polarization does not have meaning. Within the particular context, polarization has meaning but cannot be identified with an observer-independent property of some independently existing object, such as a photon. Neither is polarization some subjective artifact imposed by the observational process, since this would belie any meaningful sense of "experiment" or "observation." The distribution of measured values can in fact be reproduced, even though what has been measured is not a mirror image of independently existing reality. Polarization can be used to characterize particular phenomena, that is, the intra-action of the object of investigation (matter) and the agencies of observation (a particular conceptual scheme as represented by a given experimental apparatus). Therefore, it becomes clear that classical descriptions, which presume to describe the world as it exists independent of our observations of it, rely on classical epistemological and ontological assumptions.

Typical discussions of the dual nature of light are confusing at best. Students are correctly bewildered by statements that light behaves sometimes like a particle and sometimes like a wave. A student who is trying to come to terms with the subject matter (rather than submitting to some form of brainwashing) wants to know what light really is. Is it neither a particle nor a wave? Is it both (as in the unfortunate term *wavicle*)? Are all objects in physics actually particles, and are waves only representations of the probability distributions? What is the nature of light? After a thorough discussion of the indefiniteness or ambiguity principle, students are relieved to hear a refreshingly cogent explanation from Bohr (1963a): "the two views of the nature of light are rather to be considered as different attempts at an interpretation of the experimental evidence in which the limitation of classical concepts is expressed in complementary [that is, both necessary and mutually exclusive] ways" (p. 56). That is, light-as-a-wave represents a different phenomenon than light-as-a-particle. Although Bohr's explanation is not as simplistic and easy an answer as one might like, complexity cannot be avoided at all costs and can even be illuminating.

The third example concerns the nature of the superposition of states in quantum theory. This is another fundamental issue in quantum physics that is much more understandable when viewed from the perspective of Bohr's crucial insights. The superposition of states is discussed here using three thought experiments involving the Stern-Gerlach (SG) apparatus.[13]

An SG apparatus is purported to measure the value of the spin angular momentum of electrons. Classically, angular momentum is a vector quantity having projections along the x, y, and z axes. A classical physicist would determine the angular momentum vector by finding the values of all three components of angular momentum. The SG apparatus could be oriented first along the x-axis, then along the y-axis, and finally along the z-axis, gathering information about each component. In actual experiments, an SG apparatus oriented along any particular axis separates electrons into two beams: Each electron is deflected either upward or downward, presumably revealing the appropriate component of its spin. Electrons deflected upward are sometimes called "spin up electrons," and those deflected downward are called "spin down electrons."

Experiment 1. Suppose we first shoot a beam of electrons through an SG device oriented along the z-axis, SG_z for short. If the beam is unpolarized (i.e., nothing has been done to select out one particular value of spin in the z-direction from the other), we expect half the electrons to be deflected up and half down. If we block the downward-deflected beam of electrons and pass the up beam through yet another SG_z device, we find that all the electrons are deflected upward. Classically, we would explain this result by saying that the electrons that are deflected upward after passing through the first SG_z device have a value of spin up in the z-direction, that is, S_z = up. The second SG_z device then amounts to a consistency check, since clearly all S_z = up particles will be deflected upward by the second SG_z device (Figure 2.6).

FIGURE 2.6. Schematic of Experiment 1.

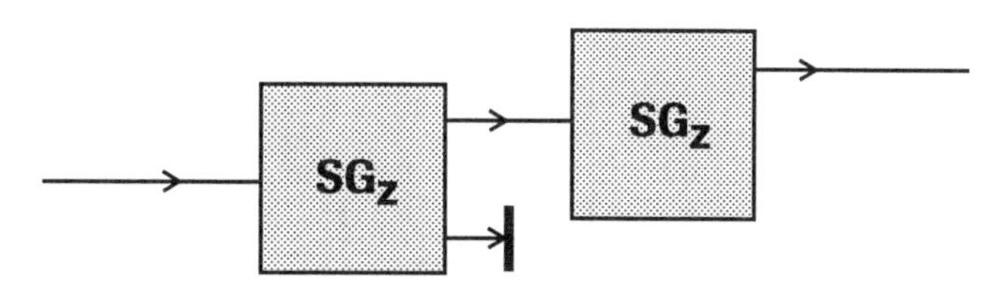

Experiment 2. Suppose that the second SG_z device in the previous experiment is replaced with an SG_x device. That is, first an unpolarized beam of electrons is shot at an SG_z device. Half the electrons are deflected upward, half downward. The downward-deflected beam is blocked, and the upward-deflected beam then encounters an SG_x device. In this case, we find that half the electrons are deflected upward and half are deflected downward. Classically, we would explain this result by saying that the first SG_z device separates S_z = up from S_z = down electrons. The S_z = up electrons then go through an SG_x device. Since half go up and half go down, the electrons deflected upward have S_z = up and S_x = up, and the electrons deflected downward have S_z = up and S_x = down. Everything seems just fine so far (Figure 2.7).

Experiment 3. Suppose that we now take the apparatus of Experiment 2 and add another SG_z device that receives only the beam that is deflected upward after passing through the SG_x device (the beam that is deflected downward through this second device is blocked). The result is that half the electrons are deflected upward and half downward after passing through the third device. This is bizarre from a classical perspective, since the electrons directed into the third device are thought to have S_z = up and S_x = up, according to the preceding classical analysis. But, if this is true, how can half of these electrons be deflected downward by the third device (Figure 2.8)?

FIGURE 2.7. Schematic of Experiment 2.

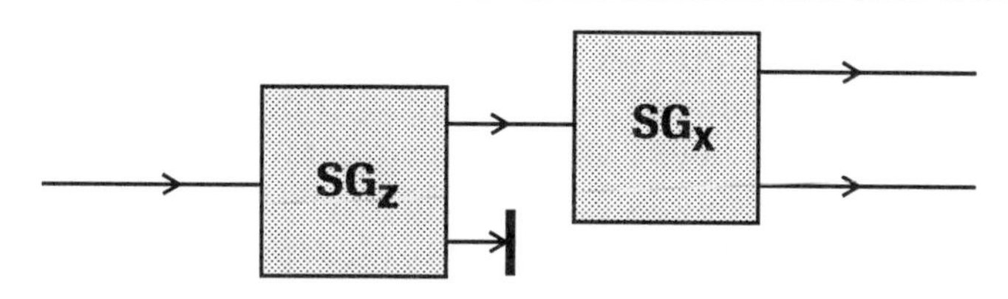

FIGURE 2.8. Schematic of Experiment 3.

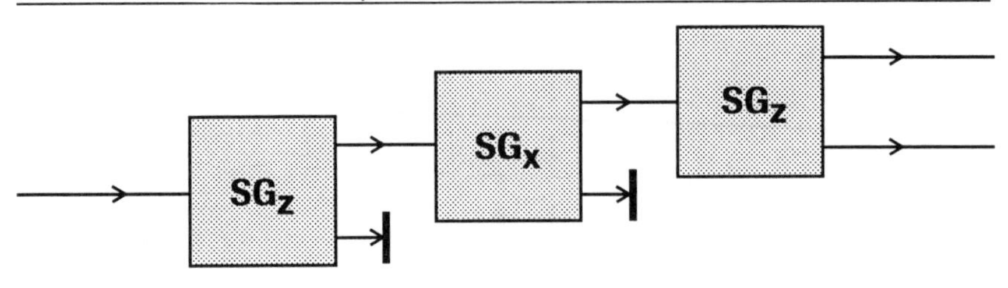

This result is disturbing to our classical sensibilities, but we have an explanation. From our previous discussion of the indefiniteness or ambiguity principle, we learned that we are not measuring objective properties of electrons as they exist independently of any given experimental context, that is, attributes that these electrons possess before any measurement is performed. The spin angular momentum vector is a human construct used here to describe the phenomena we are observing. Properties of phenomena are reproducible, but not observer-independent.

What we have encountered here is a version of the indefiniteness or ambiguity principle: We cannot unambiguously define two components of spin angular momentum simultaneously. We can choose an experimental context in which we can define one given component at a time (using a particular SG device), but then the other components are necessarily indefinite.

This explanation leads to a cogent understanding of superposition of states. Let's carefully analyze Experiment 3. Passing an unpolarized beam of electrons through the first SG_z device results in half the electrons being deflected upward and half downward. The upward-deflected electrons have one definite value of S_z, and the downward-deflected electrons have a different definite value of S_z. That is, *in this particular experimental context*, we can define the z-component of spin, S_z. Of course, S_z is a property of this *phenomenon* and not of electrons. We then block the downward-deflected beam and pass the upward-deflected beam through an SG_x device. *In this experimental context*, the x-component of spin, S_x, is definite; however, we no longer know what we mean by S_z: S_z is not unambiguously defined—it is indefinite. This accounts for the fact that when the upward-deflected beam emerging from the SG_x device is directed at another SG_z device we get a beam deflected in both directions.

Now suppose we represent a phenomenon with a definite value of S_z as $|up\rangle_z$ if we are talking about the upward-deflected beam that just passed through an SG_z device, and as $|down\rangle_z$ if we are talking about the downward-deflected beam. Similarly, a phenomenon with a definite value of S_x is represented as either $|up\rangle_x$ or $|down\rangle_x$ depending on whether the beam that just passed through an SG_x device is deflected up or down, respectively. A phenomenon with a definite S_x value can be represented as a linear combination of phenomena with definite S_z values.[14] Therefore, the last stage of Experiment 3 can be represented as

$$|\text{up}\rangle_x = c_u\ |\text{up}\rangle_z + c_d\ |\text{down}\rangle_z, \text{ with } c_u \neq 0 \text{ and } c_d \neq 0.$$

That is, whereas the phenomenon associated with the upward-deflected beam emerging from the SG_x device had a definite value of S_x, represented by $|\text{up}\rangle_x$, in passing this beam through the next device, SG_z, we find both $|\text{up}\rangle_z$ phenomena and $|\text{down}\rangle_z$ phenomena emerging.[15] This statement is once again just a reflection of the indefiniteness principle: When an SG_x measuring device is used S_x is unambiguously defined and S_z is indefinite.

If we follow Bohr, the meaning of superpositions is clear. If we fill students' heads with the rhetoric of uncertainties and disturbances, they will be mystified by the notion of superposition. What do you say to your students when they ask questions like: Does a superposition represent our ignorance? Are electrons placed in a superposition of states as a result of a measurement, or can unmeasured electrons exist in superpositions as well? Does a superposition of states mean that an electron shares its time between one state and another? Does the disturbance cause some kind of oscillation between these states? How does it avoid spending some of its time in between these states?

"AGENTIAL REALISM" AND THE CULTURE OF PHYSICS

It was during his years at Los Alamos, working on the Manhattan project, that Feynman said that he learned that: "If you have a problem, the real test of everything—you can't leave [it] alone—you've got to get the numbers out; if you don't get down to earth with it, it really isn't much. . . . [the] perpetual attitude [is] to use the theory—to see how it really works is to really use it" (quoted in Schweber, 1986, p. 466). At a time when meaning would seem to matter most, when accountability would seem inescapable, cracking nature open and exposing her secrets was the shared obsession. According to physicist Silvan Schweber (1986):

> Feynman's love for solving problems—his father's nurturing brought to full bloom—is quintessentially Feynman: part of it is a passionate need to "undo" what is "secret" to demystify, part of it is a need to constantly prove to himself that he is as good as anyone else, part of it is a fiercely competitive nature which converts challenges into creative opportunities. (p. 466)

"Getting the numbers out," the defining feature of contemporary physics culture, is an ideal attributed to a uniquely American style of doing physics. Coinciding with the development of the quantum theory, theoretical physics gained professional status in the United States during the late 1920s, early 1930s. As the center of physics shifted westward across the Atlantic, the disciplinary boundaries shifted as well: Meaning, interpretation, and critical reflection were banished from the domain of physics. In the aftermath of World War II, this approach to doing physics became hegemonic worldwide.

Students are well aware of the fact that there was a time when the subject of physics legitimately included questions about meaning and interpretation. They know this because physics professors often try to entice students into physics by telling them romantic tales: passing around samplers of luscious anecdotes from the famous Bohr-Einstein debates during their classes. As students become acculturated, they accept the fact that the main course of calculational techniques is the only thing on the menu; that they will never be served the full richness of the quantum theory.[16] The students who do not drop out of physics are those that can accept the fact that they will have to curtail any desire to *really* understand quantum theory.

Students are taught almost nothing about Bohr's ideas, even though, as Feynman put it: "Even to the big shots, Bohr was a great God" (quoted in Schweber, 1986, p. 467). The physicist Abraham Pais (1991) wrote in his biography of Bohr:

> What did Bohr really do? How could it happen that two generations would accord Bohr's influence the highest praise while the next one hardly knew why he was a figure of great significance? Also, why is it that complementarity . . . which Bohr himself considered to be his main contribution, is not mentioned in some of the finest textbooks on physics, such as the one on quantum mechanics by Paul Dirac, the historically oriented quantum mechanics text by Sin-itiro Tomonaga, or the lectures of Richard Feynman? It has taken me the writing of this biography to give, to the best of my ability, the answers to such central questions. (p. 14)

> I can now answer [this] question . . . Why do some textbooks not mention complementarity? Because it will not help in quantum mechanical calculations or in setting up experiments. Bohr's considerations are extremely relevant, however, to the scientist who occasionally likes to reflect on the meaning of what she or he is doing. (p. 23)

Bohr viewed the question of the meaning of quantum theory to be part of physics, not philosophy. That Bohr's message did not get transmitted to subsequent generations is evident in most textbooks on quantum theory. The rhetoric that is used, the words that are routinely assigned to go with mathematical expressions continue to support a Newtonian perspective of science. The fact is that many physicists continue to use phrases that imply that properties are observer-independent attributes of objects—even in texts on quantum mechanics. The continued unqualified use of Newtonian language makes the quantum world "oh so bizarre," but the message transmitted is that the mathematical formalism produces experimentally verified results, so don't despair. After a while, students become complacent about their inability to understand. Eventually they come to expect that they are to "just relax and enjoy it," that they are not to understand. Indeed, lack of understanding becomes the norm. Although our students are taught to be good calculators, this is clearly not sufficient.

Feynman was aware of the fact that psychological perspectives influence individual and group approaches to physics research:

> Theories of the known, which are described by different physical ideas may be equivalent in all their predictions and are hence scientifically indistinguishable. However, they are not psychologically identical when trying to move from that base into the unknown. For different views suggest different kinds of modifications which might be made . . . I, therefore, think that a good theoretical physicist today might find it useful to have a wide range of physical viewpoints and mathematical expressions of the same theory . . . available to him [*sic*]. This may be asking too much of one man [*sic*]. Then new students should as a class have this. If every individual student follows the same current fashion in expressing and thinking about [the generally understood areas], then the variety of hypotheses being generated to understand [the still open problems] is limited. Perhaps rightly so, for possibly the chance is high that the truth lies in the fashionable direction. But [if] it is in another direction . . . who will find it? (quoted in Schwinger, 1989, p. 48)

Feminist science scholars have been dismissed for making similar arguments on behalf of diversity and differences. This quotation implores us to ask: What are the consequences for physics research of training young scientists in a culture that values fun and irresponsibility over meaning and understanding?

On the first day of quantum mechanics class, I give my students a quiz, asking them to explain the meaning of some very basic equations and concepts of quantum theory with which they should be familiar from their exposure to these topics in a sophomore-level modern physics course. The results so far indicate to me that students have heeded Feynman's warning to stay away from the interstitial spaces, where meaning resides, in order to avoid going down the drain; they sleepwalk through their undergraduate physics careers, staring anxiously at the ground, avoiding cracks and crevices along the way, paying little attention to where they are going. (I am not blaming individual students; I am commenting about the culture and its pedagogical consequences.) Calculating is one aspect of being able to apply the theory to the world, and it is important. But it is also vital to understand what the theory means, what the implications are, what a socially responsible position is in the face of the power that science holds in our society. We send messages to our students not only by what we say but also by what we don't bother saying.

As I mentioned earlier, many quantum physics courses cover the so-called uncertainty principle, following Heisenberg's conceptually inadequate analysis, in one lecture or a portion of one lecture. The profound historical debates and philosophical consequences are never mentioned.[17] If any history is given, it is a retrospective reconstruction that makes progress in physics seem linear and the work of smart white men. Philosophy is quickly differentiated from physics, and professors generally show only minimal tolerance for students' philosophical questions that are sure to come up when discussing quantum theory. Often, Bohr's principle of complementarity is not even mentioned. The mathematical formalism is immediately introduced, and away we go. Calculation becomes the be-all and end-all. Using this approach, even the most exciting professors who desperately want to communicate their love and enthusiasm for physics to their students may fail to convince these students that physics is the most important, most pressing issue of their time and that they should dedicate themselves to it.

Features of this shared culture of physics are transmitted to students in subtle and surreptitious ways during the course of their science education. Starting with introductory physics, students garner the following "philosophy of science": The professor tells the students that we use a particular theory because it works; as more and more successful examples are laid out, students get the message that the theory must be right, since the universe is so complex that it would be too coincidental if this theory just happened to account for things so well. Using these simple theoretical concepts, one is able to understand so many different aspects of the universe that the implication is that these concepts have been cleverly discovered in studies of complex interactions and that these concepts represent actual attributes of independent physical reality. The scientific method is hailed triumphant. It is as if we are to believe that the scientific method serves as a giant distillation column, removing all biases, allowing patient practitioners to collect the pure distillate of truth. There is no agent in this view of theory construction: Knower and known are distinct—nature has spoken.

Knowledgeable readers will recognize that the above "philosophy" is an incoherent mixture, a pastiche of many different philosophical issues and conflicting stances. Notice how easily the currently more palatable instrumentalism slides into realism. The blurring of interpretative and epistemological elements serves to erase the role of the scientist in knowledge production: It is made to seem that Nature writes science, not scientists. I would now like to contrast this covert "philosophy" that holds calculations in a privileged position, as the arbitrator of truth (see Schweber, 1986, p. 504), with one that I think is consistent with changes in the framework of science that Bohr was suggesting. In my article "Meeting the Universe Halfway" (Barad, in press), I proposed a post-Newtonian framework, inspired by Bohr's work on quantum theory, that shares epistemological and ontological concerns with contemporary feminist theories. I outline some of these ideas below.

Bohr's philosophy of physics involves a kind of realism in the sense that scientific knowledge is clearly constrained, although not determined, by "what is out there," since it is not separate from us; and given a particular set of constructed cuts, certain descriptive concepts of science are well-defined and can be used to achieve reproducible results. However, these results cannot be decontextualized. Scientific theories do not tell us about objects as they exist independently of us human beings; they are partial and located knowledges. Scientific concepts are not simple namings of discoveries of objective attributes of an independent Nature with inherent demarcations. Scientific concepts are not innocent or unique. They are constructs that can be used to describe "the between" rather than some independent reality. (Why would we be interested in such a thing as an independent reality anyway? We don't live in such a world.) Consideration of mutually exclusive sets of concepts produces crucial tensions and ironies, underlining a critical point about scientific knowledge: It is the fact that scientific knowledge is socially constructed that leads to reliable knowledges about "the between"—which is just what we are interested in.[18] This shifting of boundaries deconstructs the whole notion of identity: Science can no longer be seen as the end result of a thorough distillation of culture. There is an author who marks off the boundaries and who is similarly marked by the cultural specificities of race, history, gender, language, class, politics, and other important social variables. Reproducibility is not a filter for shared biases. In stark contrast to the objectivist representationalism that is usually transmitted to students, the new framework inspired by Bohr's philosophy of physics is robust and intricate. In particular, there is an explicit sense of agency and therefore accountability. And so I refer to this Bohr-inspired framework, which shares much in common with central concerns in contemporary feminist theories, as "agential realism."

I teach my quantum mechanics class in a way that emphasizes that agential realism provides a way to understand quantum mechanics. Calculations are easier and more meaningful if students know what they are doing and why. A deep new sense of relevance comes to the fore, since agential realism gives us a way to understand the role of human concepts in knowledge production.[19] Descriptive concepts cannot be attributed to objects of an investigation; they characterize the intra-action itself and therefore have no meaning outside the chosen context.

In fact, agential realism offers a way to interrogate not just classical notions of realism versus instrumentalism, objectivity versus subjectivity, absolutism versus relativism, or nature versus culture in science but also dualistic and fixed notions of race, class, gender, and sexuality in the realm of social dynamics. For example, according to agential realism, "gender," "race," "class," and "sexuality" refer to specific social dynamics, not to properties attributable to a particular person. These terms are historically, geographically, and politically situated.[20] Agency is involved in using these categories. People use these terms for specific purposes. Realism is involved because, in a power-imbalanced society, sexism, racism, classism, and heterosexism have real material consequences, even though the concepts are socially constructed.

Dualisms, binary oppositions, dichotomies, and other demarcations are not secured with "natural" status as Cartesian cuts, which form the foundation of all knowledge—not even (and the point here is that perhaps especially not) in physics. What I am suggesting is that the "Physics is Phun" approach is not working, and new approaches are needed that directly address the implications of the subject under study and see the relevance for the pressing issues of our time.[21] As feminist scientists, we must teach our students that science is not a way to free oneself from "the chains of the merely personal, from an existence which is dominated by wishes, hopes, and primitive feelings," as Einstein saw it, but rather that science is about our intra-actions within nature and that we must act accordingly (quoted in Schilpp, 1970, p. 5).

AGENTIAL REALISM AND CRITICAL PERSPECTIVES

It surprised me to read that Pais had to write a biography on Bohr before he came to terms with the most obvious answer to Bohr's displacement and consequent invisibility: that Bohr's framework is not necessary for purposes of calculation. I believe that this answer is insufficient to account for the extent of Bohr's erasure, which becomes more conspicuous when considering the following supplement to Pais's list of questions: How is it possible that the majority of physicists abide by Bohr's Copenhagen interpretation of quantum theory, although they cannot precisely articulate its tenets? How is it that many physicists believe that there is *a* Copenhagen interpretation, based on the understandings of Bohr and Heisenberg, when these two physicists had profoundly different philosophical perspectives and therefore disagreed about many of the essential issues? How is it possible that professors teaching quantum physics can incorrectly claim that all philosophical and foundational issues in quantum theory were ultimately answered by Bohr, and furthermore use this claim to argue that students need not concern themselves with the larger questions? Why have foundational questions in quantum theory been left primarily to philosophers? Why are physicists not concerned that philosophers have unveiled a wealth of quantum quandaries that were not resolved by Bohr? Why are students and the public more familiar with Bohr's colleagues than with Bohr? Does the physics community prefer that its heroes champion Enlightenment-Newtonian-Cartesian perspectives, like Einstein with his commitment to objectivism and nostalgia for Newton,[22] or like the seemingly benign positivistic leanings of Werner Heisenberg? Why has debate over the interpretation of quantum theory all but stopped within the physics community, though it is far from resolved?[23] How is it that Bohr's interpretation has been labeled as mystical, when physicists seem to be saying that they would prefer to have their students accept quantum theory as bizarre rather than study the role of descriptive concepts in scientific knowledge construction? How can physicists claim to strive for an understanding of the nature of reality while ignoring the meaning of one of its fundamental theories? Why would the physics community embrace an acritical-anticritical pedagogy in teaching quantum theory, when it clearly goes against the grain of critical and inquisitive approaches that we expect from other disciplines?

The social construction of knowledge is inevitably accompanied by the construction of ignorance, and important insights can be gained by considering the topography of each domain. The fact that the community that relies on Bohr's considerations for the interpretation of quantum theory is grossly ignorant of these foundational issues requires a more extensive explanation than the simple assertion that calculation is possible without understanding, because it leaves unanswered the question about the high value accorded to calculation over understanding (for more details, see Barad, forthcoming). What does it mean that Bohr's attempt to interject a discourse on science into scientific discourse is widely ignored by the physics community? I assert that only a community with an acritical view of science could have decided that Bohr's interpretation of quantum theory was beside the point.

In this post-Kuhnian era, it is common to characterize the shift from the centuries-old Newtonian paradigm to the new quantum paradigm as a scientific revolution. This paradigm shift is explained as a response to a perceived crisis regarding the adequacy of the paradigm that had guided "normal science." After the revolution, when the smoke has cleared, "normal science" resumes, guided by the new paradigm. And so, quantum formalism replaces Newtonian formalism, and science goes on with business as usual. This is a popular account of the quantum story.

I have been trying to tell a different story. There was something profoundly different about Bohr's response to the crisis of Newtonian physics. Bohr, who won a Nobel Prize for his crucial role in the development of the quantum theory, did more than advance a new paradigm. His primary response was to see the crisis as a crisis of science itself, not of a particular scientific theory. Bohr used this historical moment to try to interject a critical perspective into scientific discourse. During the quantum crisis, Bohr challenged the traditional views of the nature of scientific description (see Folse, 1985; Honner, 1987) rather than acting on the traditional impulse to project the crisis onto a given description of Nature.

Unlike practitioners of most other academic disciplines, scientists continue to try to immunize themselves against the burden of critical examination of their endeavors by invoking the Cartesian division between the discourse of science and any discourse about science, which, by definition, is seen as extraneous. Most scientists shake their heads at their diseased nonscientific colleagues stricken with hermeneutic hemorrhages and metastasized multiculturalisms, feeling secure that the inoculation of the scientific method has saved them from such ugly fates. It is against this extreme culture of objectivity that we must measure the radical nature of Bohr's interpretation. Only then does it become clear that both Bohr and contemporary feminist science scholars commit nothing less than blasphemy in insisting that science is not immune from the rational imperative of the incorporation of critical discourse as part of all human endeavors.

Feminist and other science scholars have offered compelling analyses revealing various ways in which the sciences are marked by the cultural and ideological specificities (e.g., political, historical, linguistic, racial, religious) of their creators. As I have argued here, reproducibility, not some abstract notion of objectivity, characterizes a post-Newtonian understanding of Western science. Reproducibility of phenomena assures the usefulness of constructed scientific conceptual schema. According to agential realism, it is the very fact that scientific knowledge is socially constructed that leads to reliable knowledge about "the between," our intra-actions within nature, which is just what we are interested in. That is, the usefulness of science is parasitic on the intra-actions of science and society, contrary to the Enlightenment insistence that its justification and reliability depend precisely on a strict division between the two. Reproducibility is not a filter for shared biases.[24] Scientific methodologies can offer empirically adequate theories of the physical world even though the theories are methodologically, conceptually, and institutionally allied with specific social and political agendas.

Physics is not immune to feminist analysis simply because electrons are not obviously gendered. The issues at stake are subtle yet far-reaching. With a sense of human agency incorporated into scientific theories, perhaps physicists will no longer find it necessary to speak of elementary particles having attributes such as charm, beauty, and strangeness, or to give seminars with topless, naked bottom, and exotic hermaphrodite states in the titles. Of course, feminist scientists realize that the suggestion of human characteristics is seen as playful—a humorous, innocent distraction from serious concerns about the nature of the universe. After all, boys just wanna have phu-un.

NOTES

1. Recall that during congressional hearings on the *Challenger* disaster, Feynman, in typically dramatic fashion, nonchalantly dipped an O-ring into a drinking cup filled with ice water and proceeded to reveal, before Congress's very eyes, the fact that the accident had probably been caused by cold weather conditions that led to a rigid O-ring's inadequate performance. Feynman had apparently been tipped off by an engineer who wanted to expose this crucial piece of information without exposing himself. Feynman had a healthy disrespect for authority. Like many scientists, he saw himself as a champion of the Truth and quite above the minutiae of politics.

2. Alexandre Koyré (1965) contends that Newton was responsible for splitting the world into quantity and quality, the latter of which was ignored for its subjective character.

3. No defense of Bohr's interpretation is provided here. My focus on Bohr's interpretation is not based on any claim of the superiority of Bohr's interpretation over other interpretations, rather it is based on the fact that most physicists claim to embrace it.

4. Sloppy articulations have led many people to think that this principle is obvious: as in, of course people will behave differently if you watch them. For example, consider the following statement heard on National Public Radio on October 6, 1993: "Corporate executives are like subatomic particles, their behavior changes when you observe them." Of course, my main concern here is misconceptions held by physics students and not those of the general public, although, sadly, there often is overlap.

5. As an example, think of the act of catching. A person catching an object gains a qualitative sense of the momentum of the object coming at her or him. If the person's arm swings back far upon impact, it is because the momentum of the

object is large. If the person's arm does not swing back far, then the momentum of the object is small.

6. Bohr uses the term *arbitrary*, but it is misleading because the cut is not totally arbitrary: The cut must be made in such a way that the measuring device is defined as macroscopic (see Murdoch, 1987, for example, as well as more detailed discussions in Barad, in press); hereafter, the term *constructed* is used in contrast to the inherent, fixed, universal, Cartesian cut, which is assumed in classical physics.

7. To follow the discussion here, readers unfamiliar with the debates about the nature of light in the early twentieth century need only know that there was seemingly contradictory evidence that light behaved as a wave under certain experimental conditions and as a particle under different experimental conditions. Since a particle is a localized object and a wave is extended in space, these findings seemed to be inconsistent. Physicists tied to Enlightenment assumptions that scientific concepts characterize an independent reality wanted to know whether light was really a wave or really a particle. Bohr wrestled with the paradox for years, and his resolution is presented later in this chapter.

8. The superposition principle enables us to identify wave packets with particles because, as shown by de Broglie, the group velocity of the wave packet can be identified with the translational velocity of the particle associated with the wave packet.

9. I present only a qualitative argument here so that the discussion is accessible to a broader audience. Instructors may want to go over the mathematical details; see references to Bohr's argument.

10. $\Delta x = 0$ corresponds to a situation in which the position is defined exactly. Similarly, $\Delta p = 0$ corresponds to a situation in which the momentum is defined exactly. For both position and momentum to be defined exactly, both Δx and Δp would have to equal zero, but then so would their product. However, a zero on the left side is in violation of the inequality: Zero is not greater than or equal to some positive number.

11. Experiments confirming the fact that objects do not possess definite properties are based on Bell's inequality. A readable conceptual treatment of Bell's inequality and experiments that test it can be found in Mermin (1985). For a more technical treatment, see Townsend (1992, Ch. 5).

12. Indeterminacy principle doesn't work either, since the emphasis seems to be on the fact that we can't determine the *disturbance*.

13. See Townsend (1992) for an approach to quantum theory motivated by Stern-Gerlach experiments.

14. By virtue of the fact that up and down states form a complete basis (i.e., exhaust all possibilities).

15. Physicists will realize that what I am motivating here is the mathematical apparatus of abstract vector spaces in quantum mechanics using the bra-ket formalism. I encourage instructors to build the entire framework by proceeding with this line of argument.

16. At this point the more reflective student will often become disillusioned and leave physics. Perhaps it is due to the fact that women students, students of

color, and other marginalized students are more likely to be reflective, since their survival depends upon it, that contributes to their higher attrition rates.

17. I should point out that many of the issues I have presented here are not well known to many physicists, primarily because of the culture in which they received their training. Admittedly, it is not easy to read Bohr, but one must begin by trying.

18. The seemingly paradoxical nature of this statement is revealed as a holdover of classical representationalism, insisting that the reliability of scientific theories is contingent upon objective discoveries of an independent reality.

19. Although it is a step forward, students are often not taken in by approaches that append selected applications to an existing theory-based course agenda in an attempt to show the relevance of physics to their lives, when the culture of U.S. physics insists on a pure versus applied distinction, clearly valuing the former over the latter. A pedagogical approach based on agential realism shows relevance at the level of theoretical concerns as well, while simultaneously calling into question the pure versus applied dichotomy itself.

20. For example, race is not biological (i.e., a property of individual human beings); it is a construct introduced by particular people for particular purposes. Race is historically, geographically, and politically situated. Consider the fact that Jews were defined as a distinct, specifically non-Aryan race in Nazi Germany, but they are not so classified by the majority culture in the United States today. See also discussions on the social construction of race by Omi and Winant (1986) and Frankenberg (1993).

21. Students who have access to few of society's privileges (including race, gender, class, and heterosexual privileges) are likely to insist on relevance in selecting classes and majors. (How do students from working-class backgrounds justify indulging in the luxury of spending their lives studying an esoteric subject like particle physics, when their families and communities are focused on issues of survival?) I am currently designing a community-based physics course that will be offered through the Pitzer College Annex Program (which is committed to open-enrollment courses offered not in elite and Anglo Claremont but in working-class, non-Anglo Pomona, California). The idea behind the course is to take the material from real-life situations and show the relevance of physics to the issues. (Urban environmental pollution is just one example that I have discussed with community activists.) Notice the contrast between this approach and physics courses that are motivated by a desire to transmit a particular set of knowledge to students and at best attempt to draw connections between certain topics and real-life situations.

What I am proposing here is a two-pronged approach. On the one hand, it is vital that students see the relevance of the academic curriculum to their lives (as in this feminist approach to teaching quantum physics). On the other hand, curricula must embrace issues of relevance to the majority of the world's populations, taking into account the specificities of each situation (see Harding, 1991).

22. Einstein is quoted as saying: "May the spirit of Newton's method give us the power to restore unison between physical reality and the profoundest characteristic of Newton's teaching—strict causality" (Honner, 1987, p. 59).

23. See, for example, Albert (1992), Bell (1987), Cushing and McMullin (1989), and Wheeler and Zurek (1983) for contemporary discussions, conducted primarily by philosophers, about the interpretation of quantum theory and the measurement problem. See Keller (1985, Ch. 7) for a gender analysis of physicists' unwillingness as a whole to deal with the foundational issues of their field.

24. See Barad (1988, 1989) for earlier discussions of this point. See also Hubbard (1990, p. 67) for clarification of feminist concerns about subjectivity in science.

REFERENCES

Albert, David Z. (1992). *Quantum mechanics and experience.* Cambridge, MA: Harvard University Press.

Barad, Karen. (1988, Spring). A quantum epistemology and its impact on our understanding of scientific process. *The Barnard Occasional Papers,* vol. 3, no. 1.

Barad, Karen. (1989). Complementarity: Dichotomies in perspective. *The Barnard Occasional Papers,* vol. 4, no. 1.

Barad, Karen. (in press). Meeting the universe halfway: Ambiguities, discontinuities, quantum subjects and multiple positionings in feminism and physics. In Lynn Hankinson Nelson and Jack Nelson (Eds.), *Feminism, science, and the philosophy of science: A dialogue.* Boston: Kluwer Press. Expected date of publication is 1995.

Barad, Karen. (forthcoming). Physics American style: Discontinuous transitions, shifting centers, and the problematics of pragmatism. Manuscript in preparation.

Bell, John S. (1987). *Speakable and unspeakable in quantum mechanics.* Cambridge: Cambridge University Press.

Bleier, Ruth. (1984). *Science and gender: A critique of biology and its theories on women.* New York: Pergamon Press.

Bohr, Niels. (1949). Discussion with Einstein on epistemological problems in atomic physics. In Paul Arthur Schilpp (Ed.), *Albert Einstein: Philosopher-scientist* (pp. 199–241). London: Cambridge University Press.

Bohr, Niels. (1963a). *The philosophical writings of Niels Bohr: Vol. 1. Atomic theory and the description of nature.* Woodbridge, CT: Ox Bow Press.

Bohr, Niels. (1963b). *The philosophical writings of Niels Bohr: Vol. 2. Essays 1932–1957 on atomic physics and human knowledge.* Woodbridge, CT: Ox Bow Press.

Bohr, Niels. (1963c). *The philosophical writings of Niels Bohr: Vol. 3. Essays 1958–1962 on atomic physics and human knowledge.* Woodbridge, CT: Ox Bow Press.

Cushing, James T., & McMullin, Ernan. (Eds.). (1989). *Philosophical consequences of quantum theory.* Notre Dame, IN: Notre Dame Press.

Fausto-Sterling, Anne. (1985). *Myths of gender.* New York: Basic Books.

Fausto-Sterling, Anne. (1987). Society writes biology/biology constructs gender. *Daedalus, 116*(4), 61–76.

Feynman, Richard. (1965). *The character of physical law.* Cambridge, MA: MIT Press.

Folse, Henry. (1985). *The philosophy of Niels Bohr: The framework of complementarity.* New York: North-Holland.

Frankenberg, Ruth. (1993). *White women, race matters: The social construction of whiteness.* Minneapolis: University of Minnesota Press.

Haraway, Donna. (1986). Primatology is politics by other means. In Ruth Bleier (Ed.), *Feminist approaches to science* (pp. 77–118). New York: Pergamon Press.

Haraway, Donna. (1989). *Primate visions: Gender, race, and nature in the world of modern science.* New York: Routledge.

Harding, Sandra. (1991). *Whose science? Whose knowledge? Thinking from women's lives.* Ithaca, NY: Cornell University Press.

Honner, John. (1987). *The description of nature: Niels Bohr and the philosophy of quantum physics.* Oxford: Clarendon Press.

Hrdy, Sarah Blaffer. (1986). Empathy, polyandry, and the myth of the coy female. In Ruth Bleier (Ed.), *Feminist approaches to science* (pp. 119–146). New York: Pergamon Press.

Hubbard, Ruth. (1990). *The politics of women's biology.* New Brunswick, NJ: Rutgers University Press.

Keller, Evelyn Fox. (1985). *Reflections on gender and science.* New Haven, CT: Yale University Press.

Koyré, Alexandre. (1965). *Newtonian studies.* Chicago: University of Chicago Press.

Longino, Helen, & Doell, Ruth. (1983). Body, bias, and behavior: A comparative analysis of reasoning in two areas of biological science. *Signs, 9*(2), 206–227.

Lubkin, Gloria B. (1989, February). Special issue: Richard Feynman. *Physics Today.*

Mermin, David N. (1985, April). Is the moon there when nobody looks? Reality and the quantum theory. *Physics Today, 38*(4), 38–49.

Murdoch, Dugald. (1987). *Niels Bohr's philosophy of physics.* New York: Cambridge University Press.

Omi, Michael, & Winant, Howard. (1986). *Racial formation in the U.S.: From the 1960s to the 1980s.* New York: Routledge.

Pais, Abraham. (1991). *Niels Bohr's times in physics, philosophy, and polity.* New York: Oxford University Press.

Rich, Adrienne. (1986). *Blood, bread, and poetry: Selected Prose 1979–1986.* New York: Norton.

Rorty, Richard. (1979). *Philosophy and the mirror of nature.* Princeton: Princeton University Press.

Schilpp, Paul Arthur (Ed.). (1970). *Albert Einstein: Philosopher-scientist.* London: Cambridge University Press.

Schweber, Silvan. (1986). Feynman and the visualization of space-time processes. *Reviews of Modern Physics, 58*, 449–508.

Schwinger, Julian. (1989, February). A path to quantum electrodynamics. *Physics Today, 42*(2), 42–49.

Traweek, Sharon. (1988). *Beamtimes and lifetimes: The world of high energy physicists.* Cambridge, MA: Harvard University Press.

Townsend, John. (1992). *A modern approach to quantum mechanics.* New York: McGraw-Hill.

Wheeler, J. A., & Zurek, W. H. (Eds.). (1983). *Quantum theory and measurement.* Princeton: Princeton University Press.

PART II

CHEMISTRY

CHAPTER 3
Culturally Inclusive Chemistry

Catherine Hurt Middlecamp

It was the first day of class. Sixteen of us had gathered for a new seminar course entitled Culturally Inclusive Chemistry[1] (Middlecamp & Moore, 1994). As we moved our chairs into a semicircle facing the chalkboard, I began with the usual words of welcome. However, when it came time to introduce ourselves, I headed off in a new direction.

"As we start off the course," I announced, "we probably should find out some things about each other." I walked over to the board and began writing at the far left edge:

credit	*undergrad*
no credit	*grad*
	postdoc

"Here are some things that I would like to know about you," I explained. "In a minute, I'd like each of you to come up and put a mark under whether you are taking the course for credit or not, and whether you are an undergrad, graduate student, or postdoc. But first, let's work together to put up more questions. Then we can come up and mark off our answers." The idea seemed reasonable enough.

I continued, "I'm curious about one more thing. How many chemists are here?" With a mischievous twinkle in my eye, I added two new categories:

chemist
nonchemist

At this point, a few eyebrows rose. I was well aware that a number of people from fields other than chemistry were present.

"That's right," I said, acknowledging the frown from a physicist. "Not everyone would classify people as chemists or nonchemists. Questions sometimes reveal as much about their authors as about anything else, but we'll get to that in a minute." I pressed them to continue. "I've put up three of my questions. What would you like to know about each other?"

There was plenty that they wanted to know. Some of their questions could be easily framed in terms of categories:

teaching	*parent*
not teaching	*nonparent*

Other questions required that we negotiate which categories to use. For example, somebody wanted to know how many Republicans and Democrats there were. We decided to add the category "other" as well. Another person wanted to know who in the group was Christian. Which categories for religion should we list? Did it matter and, if so, to whom? We ended up listing the categories of Christian, agnostic, atheist, and other.

We also negotiated the rules for answering the questions. Optimist. Pessimist. Cynic. Is it all right to check more than one category? Could we leave a question blank? We decided that both of these were fine and later found that our group included nine optimists, no pessimists, and three cynics, one of whom was also an optimist.

"I'd like to know," stated one of the participants, "who believes all this stuff about cultural inclusiveness in chemistry." This was a tough question to pin down in the format I had given. After considerable discussion, we framed his question in terms of whether we believed that the course content would "probably be useful" or "probably not be useful," or if we were "undecided."

I cut short the discussion that was brewing and urged, "Let's move to answering our questions." We left our seats and converged on the chalkboard, each of us checking off the categories that suited us. Who were we? Who weren't we? What would our responses tell us, and what wouldn't they? How were our questions limiting what we would be able to find out?

Our discussion highlighted several aspects of the data. In some ways, we were quite a diverse group. The class contained undergraduates, graduate students, postdocs, faculty, and academic staff members. We represented the fields of chemistry, physics, science education, and veterinary science, with all but the last having at least two members. We had members from different cultural and ethnic groups as well.

In other ways, we appeared to be a relatively homogeneous group. We held many interests and affiliations in common. Each category, however, had a minority of at least one person. The visibility of those in the minority varied. In some cases, people readily claimed membership in the minority group and tried to locate their colleagues ("Who are the other two cynics out there?"). In other cases, those in the minority didn't choose to reveal their identities and nobody asked them to do so. Certain tallies on the board (such as for religion and political party) stood silently and unquestioned.

We also discussed the process itself. Most of us were familiar with other ways of introducing ourselves, such as speaking to the group one at a time. The experience of having the answers to several questions simultaneously (and anonymously) gave us different information.

FOCUSING THE ISSUES

As an entry point into "culturally inclusive science," this exercise did a better job of laying the groundwork for the course than I had anticipated. Together we had an experience of seeing the limitations of our questions and our answers. It helped us focus on a number of ideas, ones that I suspected would emerge time and again throughout the semester:

1. The consequences of our categories
2. The role of our questions
3. The missing pieces of information
4. The freedom to experiment

Our class discussions are summarized in the sections that follow.

The Consequences of Our Categories

The tendency to put things in categories runs deep on college campuses, if not in our society. Many lines are drawn. Our classes contain majors and nonmajors. Our students are from minority or majority groups. Our faculty are tenured or untenured. We have separate departments of English, biology, and music. We also may have colleges of engineering, medicine, or agriculture.

Scientists contribute their own lines of division. The world is made up of animals and plants; elements and compounds. The world of science includes biology, chemistry, and physics. Each of these fields has further divisions such as zoology, organic chemistry, or astrophysics. There are "hard" sciences and "soft" sciences. There are scientific and nonscientific approaches to solving problems.

Our categories reveal more about our *conceptions* of the world than they do about the actual nature of the world. Furthermore, the divisions that we create take on meaning and value depending on the structures that support them. For example, it may be more prestigious to teach the majors than the nonmajors. Some areas of medicine may be more likely to receive funding than others. Faculty salaries may be higher in the physical sciences than in the social sciences.

Finally, our categories rarely serve to connect that which they divide. Faculty and students may be more aware of their differences than what they share in common. It is a rare event that brings people together as learners regardless of their field. A variety of connections will be needed, however, for those of us working to create culturally inclusive classrooms.

The Role of Our Questions

Chemistry courses, as well as other science courses, require that students answer questions and solve problems. A quick survey of our texts and exams would reveal the importance we place on answering questions correctly. What often is lost is the significance of *asking* questions, and the expertise required to do so.

The right to ask questions is connected to power. Some people may have the right to ask questions; others may not. Some people's questions are attended to; the concerns of others may be left unanswered. How do these dynamics play out in the classroom? Predictably, the issue of power will arise throughout the semester.

Many of us could use coaching in how to ask better questions. One question that we might learn to add to our repertoire is, What are two other explanations that fit the same facts? Similarly, the question What is it good for? may be worth exploring. For the research chemist, this latter question is useful when there is something that cannot be gotten rid of, such as a side product in a chemical reaction. This question is equally useful for the teacher who is confronted with an "undesirable" classroom behavior that is unlikely to go away but perhaps could be constructively channeled elsewhere.

Questions of how best to promote change and educational reform are bound to arise in a seminar course like ours. Students repeatedly ask, How can we change this? Along with this question, I believe that they also need to learn to ask, What enables the current situation to persist? Persistence and change need to be explored together (Watzlawick, Weakland, & Fisch, 1974).

Finally, in an "objective" field such as chemistry, the subjective nature of questions needs to be explored. For example, my earlier question that involved classifying people as chemists or nonchemists revealed something about my worldview (and is reminiscent of census forms that asked if you were white or nonwhite). What does it mean to categorize something by what it is *not*? Who has the right to set the categories? Because it is people who raise questions, all questions, including scientific ones, have a subjective nature.

The Missing Pieces of Information

A colleague once expressed to me his surprise that scientists collected such little information on their students. For example, did we know how many students were reenrolling after previously dropping or failing the course? Did we know who our "satisfied customers" were? What might both these groups teach us? What he viewed as a lack of data stood in sharp contrast to the wealth of information he saw being collected in the laboratory. I think he's right. The trouble is, we don't always know what we need to know about our students. Fortunately, if given the opportunity, our students can usually teach us both what to ask and where to look for possible answers. Furthermore, we need not only to understand our students better but also to know more about ourselves and our discipline.

The data we collect need to be ongoing and timely rather than a snapshot from a single questionnaire. During the semester, we speak with a variety of students who are currently taking chemistry. We also gather demographic data to reveal trends in the years to come.

Finally, we need to take responsibility for the outcomes revealed by the data. For example, continuing students may outperform transfer students. Asian students may experience difficulties rather than being the "model minority" (Suzuki, 1989). Documentation of such outcomes can make possible a level of accountability that is missing from some of our classrooms. A director at the National Science Foundation commented: "The only way I know to ensure we make progress is to emphasize accountability. We have to go into a goals-oriented, no-nonsense mode" (Sims, 1992, p. 1185).

The Freedom to Experiment

Chemists know how to set up and run experiments in the laboratory. We need experiments in the classroom as well. In either locale, a single experiment is unlikely to suffice. Just as it is necessary to persist with an idea in the lab, we need to persist in finding different and improved ways to teach. In the process, we need to allow ourselves (and our colleagues) the opportunity to make mistakes.

I began this course by running an "experiment," that is, I attempted to have us introduce ourselves by checking off boxes on the chalkboard. This idea was actually one in a series of experiments. I tried the idea of taking a class survey by putting a line up on the board and labeling its ends as *Strongly Agree* and *Strongly Disagree*. I then asked each student to put an X on the line representing his or her view on a particular issue, and we discussed the resulting picture. Another time, I asked one group of students to think up soluble salts and list them on the board, and another to do the same for insoluble salts. Again, the composite picture gave us plenty to discuss. It was only on the third round that I asked students to design and answer their own questions.

Looking ahead, I'm wondering how to put this idea to use with larger numbers of students. Over the course of the semester, we may come up with some ideas. In any case, we need to work together to build our repertoire of different ways of asking and answering questions.

These four ideas are by no means a complete set of those relevant to the course. They are, however, a useful subset with which to begin. All relate to each other as well as to the topic of cultural inclusivity in our teaching. These ideas will also be relevant when more controversial topics such as sexism and racism arise later in our discussions.

CULTURAL INCLUSIVENESS

The next time we met, I asked the members of the class what they wanted to accomplish over the course of the semester. I suggested that we divide into small groups to work out some ideas.

Many of the group discussions centered around the term *cultural inclusiveness*. People wanted to clarify what it meant both to them and to their students. Each group kept a written record that I collated and distributed. The comments included:

> "I would like to understand how science is culturally determined, and what needs to be done to make it more *culturally inclusive*—is it just a change in teaching approach or is it a more fundamental problem with science as a paradigm?"
>
> "Am I culturally inclusive right now? Why or why not?"
>
> "Which culture are we including: a race culture or a nonscience culture?"
>
> "First, I would like to discuss how race and ethnicity issues relate to science teaching and to the science research climate. Second, I would like to use this knowledge to analyze ways to appropriately change teaching methods and the science climate."

As we looked through these and other responses, we saw the different ways in which we had expressed the same sentiments: the hope that we would better reach *all* our students, and the fear that we would somehow turn away those who were different from us.

At this point in the course, I offered three questions as possible yardsticks to measure the skills that we might want to develop:

1. How much do you know about the cultural backgrounds of your students?
2. How much do you know about the culture of your own discipline, especially its norms for teaching and learning?
3. How well are you able to teach and learn in ways that are different from those commonly used in your discipline?

Over the next few weeks, we explored each of these questions in turn. In the sections that follow, I summarize our classroom discussions and activities.

How Much Do You Know About the Cultural Backgrounds of Your Students?

Teachers need both an appreciation of and a comfort level with the cultures represented by their students. How do we become knowledgeable about their different cultural norms and values? Most of us already know how. In fact, we have been doing this all our lives as we have come to know a variety of people and places. However, for each one of us there are groups of people who are not in our cultural repertoire, so to speak. When the students in our classrooms match those missing from our repertoire, both we and our students may experience difficulties.

There is no single way to learn "culture." As a class, we explored a number of different avenues. For example, we discussed material taken from the books and journals listed in the Appendix. Conferences and workshops also provided us with resources, and a group of us attended a national conference on Asian Americans.[2] We returned with many stories, including one from a Hmong refugee who was now attending the university:

> Let us imagine for a moment what life would be like for you after having lived for generations in a city in America, and all of a sudden being forced to migrate to the mountains of northern Laos, where there are no televisions or radios, no stoves or refrigerators, no hot water or electricity. Again let us imagine that in leaving your city, you can only bring half of your family with you. . . . Well, for my family, what you are now imagining is a reality, but with the scenario in reverse. (Roop & Roop, 1991, p. 57)

We recognized the strengths of the Hmong people, such as fluency in several languages and an ability to recall the spoken word. We also talked about what it would be like to be from an oral culture where literacy was a relatively new concept. From a colleague who worked in the Hmong community, we learned how using media such as video and film played to the strengths of her students. Later in the semester, at a class "film fest," we watched an educational video produced by Hmong university students.[3]

To get at issues related to cultural stereotypes, we adapted an exercise from another national conference (Kean & Tate, 1991). The goal of our exercise (at least as stated) was to design interview questions that could help us learn about a particular type of student, such as a 45-year-old nurse returning to earn a degree in pharmacy, or a new student coming to the university after 18 years on the reservation. We broke into small groups, each one with a different type of student. As we wrote interview questions, we noted any differences between what we were curious to know and what we thought it appropriate to ask. After sharing our questions with the larger group, we discussed what such an exercise might teach us. We discussed how interviews could set a person up as being able to speak for an entire group rather than as an individual. We discussed the implications of asking students to come in for an interview rather than going to them. Later in the semester, after a lengthy discussion about these and other issues, we invited a group of undergraduates to join us for class. Figure 3.1 lists the discussion questions that we offered them beforehand. We also gave them the opportunity to create their own questions and agenda.

Finally, we acknowledged the time commitment required to extend our cultural knowledge. Small investments, however, can have large payoffs. As a case in point, I told the story of my investing a few hours in locating a map of Puerto Rico, framing it, and putting it up in my office. The reward has been substantial. Students have been pleased to point out their hometowns for me. Through their stories, I have become knowledgeable about different urban and rural areas in Puerto Rico and more aware of the cultural differences on the island.

How Much Do You Know About the Culture of Your Own Discipline, Especially Its Norms for Teaching and Learning?

Chemistry has its own culture, or perhaps what might better be termed its own set of minicultures. Chemists share a number of things, including a core of scientific knowledge ("truth"), a system of symbolic representations, a technical language, professional behaviors and values, preferences about how the discipline should be organized, and strategies for adapting and

FIGURE 3.1. Questions for student panel invited to Chemistry 901.

1. What would you like to know about those of us here in Chemistry 901?
2. What would you like us to know about your experiences in chemistry? You might include: why you are taking chemistry, what you like about chemistry, what you thought your chemistry course would be like, or what it actually was like.
3. How do you choose where to sit in a classroom or lecture hall? When you are already seated, do you notice anything about how people seat themselves around you?
4. When you need to find a lab partner, what is this like for you? Is there anything you might want to comment about?
5. What advice would you like to give to those of us who teach chemistry?
6. If somebody (instructor, student) does or says something that offends you, in what ways might you respond?
7. Do you go to your professor for help?

surviving (Bullivant, 1993). Chemists may even share a dress code, as they have been hailed as the "loose cannons on the frigate of fashion" (Ganem, 1993, p. 10).

It is difficult to perceive the "givens" in one's own culture. Academic disciplines are no exception: "Too often, academics cannot see the profound intellectual or 'cultural' values inherent in their particular disciplines. If we could recognize how culture-bound our disciplines have made us, . . . perhaps integrating multicultural content into our curricula might make more sense to us" (Rodrigues, 1992, p. B1). One of the "givens" to which scientists seem particularly blind is the fact that science is influenced by culture: "We tend to forget that many of the core propositions upon which the sciences rest, such as objectivity, positivism, and empiricism, are cultural products and thus may be culture-bound" (Gordon, Miller, & Rollock, 1990, p. 14). All scientific inquiry requires a perspective, for research is not only investigation but also interpretation. Scientists' perspectives condition what they perceive as important for the advancement of science as well as the design of research and the weight given to conclusions (Frankel, 1993, p. B1).

Well aware that we would have our blind spots, we began an investigation of the culture of chemistry. Our methodology was simple: We would "study" the chemistry building and its occupants. I suggested that people choose their own methods of study and that they feel free to be creative. For example, they might want to read the graffiti on the desktops or eavesdrop at the vending machines. To comply with safety regulations, I provided eye protection to those not already wearing it.

Armed with our ideas of what we would "study," we left the classroom and headed off in different directions. Some checked out the seven floors of research labs. Others went to the library and classrooms. Some interviewed people, some tallied behaviors; others observed the scientific apparatus and the cartoons posted on office doors. Once our tasks were complete, we returned to discuss our experiences:

"I saw a lot of *stuff*, but not very many people."
"The culture of science has certain smells."
"The older looking people were men, but in the classrooms there seemed to be an even male-female split."
"Chemists speak in a lot of jargon."
"There are an awful lot of locked doors."

We examined the results of our demographic surveys. There were more young faces than older ones. The younger people were more ethnically diverse and included more women. Although there were some older women, presumably secretaries by their context, most of the older people were white and male. A seminar room displayed 18 photographs of white, mostly elderly gentlemen. Nothing that we observed contradicted the generalization: "The culture of science evolved in a period when it was being practiced exclusively by men, and that has greatly influenced the outcome. It is a men's game and it continues to be played by men's rules" (Tilghman, 1993, p. A23).

We recalled snatches of conversations that we had heard in the hallways:

"What are you majoring in?"
"Chemistry."
"Oh [dead silence]. You must be *smart*."

We wondered who had decided that scientists were any smarter than other people. We also discussed who might benefit from the idea that chemistry is hard. Chemistry has its mythologies (Bowen, 1992), as does any discipline.

We discussed the classroom practices that some of us had observed. Professors talked fast. Students who put their hands up first were called on. Quizzes and tests were given under the pressure of time. Speed was apparently the norm, if not a virtue. There seemed to be little time to contemplate anything.

We noted that the chemistry building had few connections to the natural world. The building hummed with technical sounds. The windows did not open to the world outside; only a few potted plants dotted the interior landscape. There were, however, plenty of liquids and solids stored carefully in bottles and jars, all presumably once of natural origin. We saw complex apparatus that could manipulate and measure these chemicals, often at arm's length.

We talked ecology. Chemical facts and concepts were presented sequentially in the lecture hall. It seemed easy to miss how the bits of information were interrelated and how they fit into a broader context. The laboratories seemed equally remote from the real world. Given the isolation, it was easy to understand how scientists might come to believe that their work was objective and value-free. Anything that connected the research to social, industrial, or military applications was simply not visible.

At times, we sounded like philosophers. What was scientific "truth"? We cataloged some of the truths that chemists were likely to teach: The universe is logical and ordered. Chemicals are made up of atoms. They react in predictable, reproducible ways. In essence, a "truth" exists, and chemists believe that they have figured out a good part of it. As far as the students are concerned: "Science is taught—or at least it is heard by students in most introductory courses—as a series of sibylline statements. The professor is not indulging in conjecture; he is telling the truth" (Belenky, Clinchy, Goldberger, & Tarule, 1986, p. 215).

Thus, our explorations of the miniculture of the chemistry department brought forth a number of useful ideas. These were useful as we explored the last of my three questions.

How Well Are You Able to Teach and Learn in Ways That Are Different From Those Commonly Used in Your Discipline?

This was a hard one. Those of us who came together for Chemistry 901 were reasonably expert in the usual ways of teaching and learning chemistry. We all had succeeded (more or less) in the current teaching system. And yet, almost to a person, we believed that there were other ways in which to proceed. We were willing to entertain, even push, the questions of how to change the customary ways of doing things.

To reveal how we might frame chemical knowledge in other ways, I asked the group to return to the question of "researching" the culture of chemistry (see the previous section). Perhaps those from other cultures or learning traditions would approach and carry out this same task very differently. As models, I presented the writings of a Native American woman who contrasted Western with Native science (Spencer, 1990) and of a Japanese man who contrasted Western and Eastern science (Motokawa, 1989).

In her writing, the Native American woman explained first her tribal descent and how she had become responsible for passing along an ancient tradition. She had learned the tradition from her father and explained how, in order to keep things in balance, a man should receive the teachings from a woman, and a woman from a man. She then engaged us with a tale of Hawk and Eagle: "When hunting, Hawk sees Mouse . . . and dives directly for it. When hunting, Eagle sees the whole pattern . . . sees movement in the general pattern and dives for the movement, learning only later that it is Mouse" (Spencer, 1990, p. 17). Hawk represented the tendency to look at the specific (Western science), and Eagle represented the tendency to look at the whole (indigenous science). Each complemented the other. She presented to us a personal practice called "go-and-be-Eagle." When doing this, she *became* Eagle in her heart and mind and looked at the world from Eagle's perspective. As Eagle, she was able to learn about the world and conceptualize it in new ways.

The Japanese man offered his reflections after having completed a research appointment in the United States. He commented about how he had come to this country believing science to be universal but had left realizing that people from different cultures think in different ways. He engaged us by recounting a tale of "hamburger science" and "sushi science." Hamburger is cooked and seasoned, and the skills of the chef are evident. Sushi is raw fish and seems to require no cooking skill at all. However, real skills are employed on the part of the sushi chef: "Sushi is also great: we taste the materials themselves. Chefs' skills are hidden: they are devoted to keeping the fresh and natural flavor of the materials. These are two different attitudes toward cooking" (Motokawa, 1989, p. 490). Similar to the differences in cooking philosophies, he saw that there were different types of sciences in the world. Western and Eastern science differed in some fundamental premises. He contrasted scientists who advertised "I" and "my something" to those who preferred to keep silent and let nature speak for itself. He contrasted a science of giants and heroes to one that was more modest in scale:

> In the East, mind and body should walk hand in hand. The size of rules and ideas, and thus the size of mind, should match that of body. . . . The strength of the West and also the problem of the West lie in a habit that people let mind walk far ahead of body. The oversized rules, which are created by oversized minds, are deepening the gap between mind and body. (Motokawa, 1989, p. 499)

From these different perspectives on Western science, Native science, and Eastern science, we approached the "culture of chemistry" for a second time. We began by proposing *how* we might investigate the culture of the chemistry building and its occupants using a different cultural approach. Not unexpectedly, this time our ideas were quite different:

"I would remove myself from my usual work surroundings in order to more honestly listen to my thoughts and feelings about the culture of science."

"The observations would be nonintrusive."

"[I would] observe all night and day to see how the lateness of the day changed things."

"[I would] sit in on a lecture and 'become' that teacher and those students, . . . 'become' that researcher or technician. . . . I don't feel Westerners have the skills to 'become one' with people, things, or abstractions very effectively. Our intuitive skills have not been honed."

In the process of trying out our ideas, we came to new and sometimes unexpected insights:

"It's impossible to tell in advance what you will learn, since that depends on what you observe at each stage. . . . What's different is the placing of the specific phenomena back into the whole rather than saying, 'OK, we understand that now. Let's move on to something else.'"

"I sensed the need to reclaim space for people in the building. It has little color, texture, light, fresh air. There is a need for space that doesn't belong to something or to someone. I think that we could all teach, learn, and do research better in such an environment."

"It turned out that I noticed things that I wouldn't have thought of beforehand."

Again, the exercise provided us with a starting point. After engaging ourselves in it, we were better able to see the norms practiced by science as we knew it and to contrast these with the norms more common to indigenous and Eastern science.

Changes in our norms for teaching and learning are not necessarily large or dramatic. As a case in point, I offered a story about a friend of mine who had spent time in Indonesia. She had presented a lecture, after which her host asked the audience if there were any questions. To her surprise, a lengthy silence followed—upwards of 15 minutes—during which time tea was served. Those gathered *knew* that it took time (and a cup of tea) for people to assimilate the material and come up with good questions.

The period of time allowed for students to come up with questions reflects both how we conceive the questioning process and our social norms for using time. Our teaching repertoire could be increased simply by making changes in how we structure time for generating questions or for a number of other activities. As we make these changes, we might find that our classroom habits change as well, such as any tendencies to favor those who are the quickest to raise their hands or to call on one group of people more than another.

CHEMISTRY, RACE, ETHNICITY, AND GENDER

Our class discussions thus far had sought to raise issues and provide us with new information. Together we had examined some of our current practices in teaching and learning, with an eye for how we might change our goals or accomplish them in different ways.

Some of the tasks in being culturally inclusive seemed overwhelming. For example, we noted that we could spend the rest of the semester (if not the rest of our lives) in increasing our cultural knowledge of the students we teach. However, among those gathered for Chemistry 901, I sensed an urgency to move on. *What* were we going to do in the classroom, and *how* were we going to do it?

I shared in their desire to do something. I don't think they realized, however, that I didn't know just what to do. There was no book that I could pull off the shelf to provide step-by-step directions. There was no consensus in the scientific community regarding cultural inclusiveness. It would require all our resources to move ahead.

Although our path was new, there were many who had gone before us. The pioneers had come from a number of disciplines, including women's studies, ethnic studies, mathematics, history of science, curriculum and instruction, sociology, and counseling psychology. The Appendix contains a partial reading list. A number of people in the class commented that some of our texts were "hard to get through" because of their style or language. In addition, we read several dozen articles and essays.

At this point in the semester, we paused to map out the topics that we wanted to discuss in the coming months. Our list was ambitious: the curriculum, textbooks, laboratory, evaluation, grading, and teaching and learning styles. Three of our discussions are summarized in the sections that follow.

Curriculum

We began with the concept of metaphor, that is, the idea that something is like something else. We noted the metaphors in our language. For example, a person might come through the academic "pipeline" and "climb a career ladder," only to hit a "glass ceiling." Metaphor is more than just a part of our language; it is part of our very thoughts and lives. Metaphor affects "how we perceive, how we think and what we do" (Lakoff & Johnson, 1980, p. 4). Thus, in a real sense, the metaphor becomes the reality.

The metaphors that we hold as educators affect the curriculum, its outcomes, and our role as teachers. We worked in groups to expose some of our underlying metaphors. For example, were schools like factories? Was teaching like a mother robin feeding her young? Was learning like being the captain of the starship *Enterprise,* exploring new worlds and going where no person had gone before?

For the sake of discussion, we picked two metaphors: chemistry as "a terrain to be covered," and the chemistry curriculum as a "bus tour"—specifically, a six-day, 30-country bus tour of Europe. We asked what we might like to change about these metaphors. In the case of "chemistry as a terrain," our answers included filling in some of the potholes, removing some of the land mines, teaching the skill of map reading, setting up a first-aid station, and bringing along a geologist. For the curriculum as a "bus tour," we suggested passing through only one time zone in a day, having breaks for recreation, taking turns driving, traveling on some unplanned routes, and even getting off the bus.

Our metaphors also helped us raise questions. For example, what if we journeyed only as fast as the slowest person? What were the responsibilities of the passengers? Were there other ways to travel? Who was the driver? Which metaphors involved groups and which were individual? Depending on our metaphors, we could see that we would teach differently and would expect different outcomes.

Textbooks

We began by posing a number of questions: Could we teach without a textbook? What kind of textbook (and process of using a textbook) would be ideal for culturally inclusive chemistry? What if the students chose the textbook? How much does the textbook matter? What do the students really do with their textbooks anyway?

We discussed how novels and biographies can add "the human element" to topics in the course. Each of us brought to class a title for possible inclusion in a general chemistry course. Included in our list were *Hiroshima* by John Hersey (human chronicle of the days before and after the bomb dropped), *What Do You Care What Other People Think?* by Richard Feynman (includes a description of the *Challenger* investigation), *Clan of the Cave Bear* by Jean Auel (primitive technologies and natural products chemistry), and *The Mysterious Affair at Styles* by Agatha Christie (a strychnine whodunit) (Southward, Hollis, & Thompson, 1992).

We looked at a preprint of an undergraduate textbook that will use case studies of current issues (in their social, economic, and political context) to introduce topics in general chemistry (Schwartz et al., 1993), and some of us attended a seminar by a member of its editorial board. We wondered whether the textbooks available were driving the courses we would teach, or vice versa. Just after our discussion, a science editor from the publishing industry stopped by my office. She will participate in our discussion next year.

Evaluation

Predictably, questions came up about tests and grading. One of the avenues we explored for evaluation was take-home test questions. We raised issues such as who would write the questions and what types of questions would be useful. We also wanted to know how to easily generate take-home questions, since after the first year, the answers would be at large on campus.

As mentioned earlier, we thought it important that students generate (and answer) their own questions. This would serve many purposes: It would provide practice in posing questions, involve students in their own learning, generate ideas for course content, and, for us instructors, provide a window into the world of our students.

I shared with the class a recent experience. I had come across the statistic that the rainfall on some mountain slopes in Hawaii may exceed 50 feet annually. *Fifty feet of rain a year*? This was inconceivable to me. How many inches was this in a month? In a day? As I was making meaning for myself out of the numbers, I realized that I was doing "conversion factor problems," as we call them in chemistry. More important, these were *my* problems. I was conceiving and answering them on the spot. I came up with other questions that were harder to answer. Where did all the rain go? What was it like to live there? Was agriculture possible? I found myself wondering what questions our students would ask, given the opportunities.

In Chemistry 901, we tried to find materials that would spark questions from a wide variety of students. Intriguing facts and figures (such as the 50 feet of rain a year) could be taken from different kinds of almanacs. As a class, we worked for a while on a geographer's map that showed the countries from which we imported strategic materials. Using this map, we were able to frame some generic questions: What if we could no longer import element X from country Y? How do we use element Z, and how might we recycle it? What if we ran out of element Q on our planet? Questions such as these could be used year after year, each time substituting a different geographic region or chemical element. Such choices could be made by individual students, the class as a whole, or the instructor.

CONCLUSION

Sixteen weeks later, summer was upon us. The semester was ending far before we were ready to: We had no definitive answers, and we had no finished product in our hands. The final word had not been written. Nor should it have been.

What we had learned and experienced in our weeks together was a *process*. We had drawn upon the resources of each individual. We had utilized the strengths of large and small groups. We had raised questions and then refined them. We had noticed some things that were missing. We had argued and discussed and changed our minds and sometimes changed them again. We had allowed for differences and sought commonalities. We had both invited others to come to us and gone to them. We had crossed disciplinary and cultural lines. In short, we had been willing to experiment in a number of different ways.

Rather than finding answers, I believe that we ended up with a better set of questions. I also believe that we shared among ourselves and with others a common hope: "By listening more diligently to what non-traditional voices can tell them, scientists may discover new ways of thinking about, looking at, or solving old problems" (Frankel, 1993, p. B1).

NOTES

1. This graduate course was first offered in 1992 as Race and Ethnicity in the Teaching of Chemistry (1 credit) and was jointly taught with John Moore and Brenda Pfaehler. This chapter presents a composite version of the first two years of the course.
2. Asian Americans: Probing the Past, Living the Present, Shaping the Future, University of Wisconsin–LaCrosse, March 25–27, 1993.
3. *After the war: A family album* [Videotape]. Newist, CESA #7 Telecommunications, IS 1110, University of Wisconsin–Green Bay, Green Bay, WI 54301.

APPENDIX: SELECTED READINGS FROM CHEMISTRY 901

Adams, M. (Ed.). *Promoting diversity in college classrooms*. (1992). New Directions for Teaching and Learning, No. 52. San Francisco: Jossey-Bass.

Banks, J. A., & Banks, C. A. (1993). *Multicultural education: Issues and perspectives*. Boston: Allyn and Bacon.

Border, L. L., & Van Notechism, N. (Eds.). *Teaching for diversity*. (1992). New Directions for Teaching and Learning, No. 49. San Francisco: Jossey-Bass.

Bowers, C. A. (1988). *The cultural dimensions of educational computing*. New York: Teachers College Press.

D'Souza, D. (1991). *Illiberal education: The politics of race and sex on campus*. New York: Vintage Books.

Harding, S. (1991). *Whose science? whose knowledge?* Ithaca, NY: Cornell University Press.

Koshland, D. E., Jr. Minorities in science, science: The pipeline problem. (1992). *Science, 258*, 1057–1276.

Lemke, J. L. (1990). *Talking science: Language, learning and values*. Norwood, NJ: Ablex.

Rosser, S. V. (1990). *Female-friendly science*. Elmsford, NY: Pergamon Press.

Scarcella, R. (1990). *Teaching language minority students in the multicultural classroom*. Englewood Cliffs, NJ: Prentice-Hall.

Tobias, S. (1990). *They're not dumb, they're different*. Tucson, AZ: Research Corporation.

Watzlawick, P., Weakland, J., & Fisch, R. (1974). *Change: Principles of problem formation and problem resolution*. New York: W. W. Norton.

Women in science '93: Gender & culture. (1993). *Science, 260*, 265–460.

REFERENCES

Belenky, Mary, Clinchy, Blythe, Goldberger, Nancy, & Tarule, Jill. (1986). *Women's ways of knowing*. New York: Basic Books.

Bowen, Craig W. (1992). Myths and metaphors: Their influence on chemistry instruction. *Journal of Chemical Education, 69*(6), 479–482.

Bullivant, Brian M. (1993). Culture: Its nature and meaning for educators. In James A. Banks & Cherry A. Banks (Eds.), *Multicultural education* (pp. 29–47). Boston: Allyn & Bacon.

Frankel, Mark. (1993, November 10). Multicultural science. *Chronicle of Higher Education, 40*(12), B1–2.

Ganem, Bruce. (1993, February). Yipes, stripes, scientists got 'em. *Cornell Alumni News*, 10.

Gordon, Edmund, Miller, Fayneese, & Rollock, David. (1990). Coping with communicentric bias in knowledge production in the social sciences. *Educational Researcher, 19*(3), 14–16.

Kean, Elizabeth, & Tate, Maurice. (1991). Enhancing teachers' abilities to teach multiculturally. Fourth National Conference on Race & Ethnicity in American Higher Education, San Antonio, TX, May 31–June 4.

Lakoff, George, & Johnson, Mark. (1980). *Metaphors we live by*. Chicago: University of Chicago Press.

Middlecamp, Catherine H., & Moore, John. (1994). Race and ethnicity in the teaching of chemistry: A new graduate seminar. *Journal of Chemical Education, 71*, 288–291.

Motokawa, Tatsuo. (1989). Sushi science and hamburger science. *Perspectives in Biology and Medicine, 12*(4), 489–504.

Rodrigues, Richard. (1992, April 29). Rethinking the cultures of disciplines. *Chronicle of Higher Education, 38*(33), B1.

Roop, Peter, & Roop, Connie. (1991). *The Hmong in America: We sought refuge here.* Appleton, WI: Appleton Area School District.

Schwartz, A. Truman, Bunce, Diane, Silberman, Robert, Stanitski, Conrad, Stratton, Wilmer, & Zipp, Arden. (1993). *Chemistry in context.* Dubuque, IA: Wm. C. Brown.

Sims, C. (1992). What went wrong: Why programs failed. *Science, 258,* 1185–1187.

Southward, Robin, Hollis, W. Gary, & Thompson, David. (1992). Precipitation of a murder. *Journal of Chemical Education, 69,* 536–537.

Spencer, Paula. (1990). A Native American worldview. *Noetic Sciences Review, 15,* 14–20.

Suzuki, B. H. (1989). Asian Americans as the "model minority." *Change, 21,* 13–15.

Tilghman, Shirley. (1993, January 26). Science vs. women—a radical solution. *New York Times,* A23.

Watzlawick, Paul, Weakland, John H., & Fisch, Richard. (1974). *Change: Principles of problem formation and problem resolution.* New York: W. W. Norton

CHAPTER 4

The Clare Boothe Luce Program for Women in Science at Creighton University

Holly Harris

Creighton University is a midsized, Catholic (Jesuit) comprehensive university located in downtown Omaha, Nebraska. The College of Arts and Sciences, the undergraduate liberal arts school within the university, accounts for approximately one third of the total student body of 6,100. The university was founded in 1878 as an all male school. Women were allowed to attend selected classes in the College of Arts and Sciences beginning in 1923, and in 1931, a separate liberal arts division for women, University College, was established. In 1951, University College merged with the College of Arts and Sciences to form one coeducational undergraduate liberal arts college within the university.

During the Spring 1993 semester the College of Arts and Sciences had an enrollment that was 57% female and 13.9% minority (0.6% American Indian, 3.4% African American, 7.1% Asian or Pacific Islander, and 2.8% Hispanic). A vast majority of the students (more than 95%) were of traditional college age. Women made up 35% of the declared physics majors and co-majors and 46.6% of the declared chemistry majors (chemistry does not offer a co-major) as of the Spring 1993 semester. In the introductory science courses, women constitute 48% of the general chemistry students and 39% of the general physics students. It is significant that the gender balance of the introductory courses is maintained (and in some years exceeded) by the gender balance of the majors.

INTRODUCTORY PHYSICS AND CHEMISTRY COURSES

The Creighton College of Arts and Sciences is committed to undergraduate education. As such, the college works hard to recruit and retain dedicated teaching faculty who are willing to spend a great deal of time and effort becoming excellent teachers. All the changes that have occurred inside the classroom are a result of individual faculty members addressing the call to become excellent teachers. Many of the changes instituted by individual faculty have become department policy and have altered how students' work in a particular course is assessed, but none of the changes has altered course content at the introductory level and therefore cannot be called curriculum innovation.

The introductory courses in both chemistry and physics have historically been taught in small (50- to 60-student) sections, even though the total enrollments in the courses vary from 350 to 500 for chemistry and 125 to 200 for physics. Previously, all the students enrolled in either course came together for multiple-choice, machine-graded exams. A student's grade was based primarily on her or his performance on these exams. The scores of all the students enrolled in the course (all 350+) were compared, and a master curve was constructed. The student's final letter grade was determined by the entire class curve of multiple-choice exam results, with little or no input from her or his individual instructor. Students were given a numerical ranking based on their performance on these exams, and they knew that they had to be in the top 15% of the class to receive an A. Under the old format, the introductory chemistry course had a reputation among students for being highly competitive and cutthroat—a "weed-out" course.

In the fall of 1991, the chemistry department abandoned the common multiple-choice exams and adopted a format in which individual instructors write their own exams and exercise almost full autonomy over their own sections. The overall class ranking was dropped, as was the curve. The exams in the course now range from short-answer, descriptive questions to more involved problem-solving questions. One faculty member has even been known to ask students to pose their own questions on exams. A student's final grade is now based on a variety of activities, including written laboratory reports, homework assignments, and exams. The content of the course has not changed. The faculty who teach organic chemistry have not seen any substantial decrease in the "quality" or preparedness of the students coming out of this revised general chemistry course, only a large increase in the number of students who choose another year of chemistry; fewer students are being "weeded out" unnecessarily.

The physics department adopted a similar change in the fall of 1992, spurred in part by an increasing emphasis on writing across the college curriculum. The general physics course now includes short-answer and essay-type exam questions as well as written and oral laboratory reports. The change in examination and grading policy in both the chemistry and physics departments has been enormously popular with the students. As one student put it, they "are now given the opportunity to explain how much [they] understand of the concepts of science."

All faculty in the physics and chemistry departments have been made aware of the work of Sheila Tobias (1990, 1992). Many of the faculty have individually incorporated her suggestions for making the science classroom less competitive by encouraging students to work together on laboratory and problem sets. Some faculty have formalized cooperative learning via assigned group projects with group grades. A number of faculty are actively trying to change their teaching style by relying less on lecture presentations and encouraging more active participation by all the students in class discussions.

The changes discussed above have a direct benefit for all students enrolled in the introductory courses by making these courses more cooperative and responsive. The majority of the faculty are also aware of and sensitive to issues directly affecting women students. The faculty are becoming increasingly mindful of gender-neutral language and the need to be aware of which students receive attention during classroom and laboratory discussions. All students, male and female, are required to participate fully in the laboratory, using the equipment and instrumentation as necessary. Recently revised manuals written in-house for the general and organic chemistry laboratories (Mattson, 1992; Hulce, Klein, & Jagusch, 1993) make extensive use of the feminine pronoun and feminine names when referring to students in examples and problems.

There is an ongoing discussion within the American Chemical Society on the need to change the content of general chemistry courses. The Division of Chemical Education of the American Chemical Society has created a Task Force on the General Chemistry Curriculum to do just that. The first report of the task force was published in the March 1992 issue of the *Journal of Chemical Education*. The final article in the report (Bodner, 1992) emphasizes the need to address not only the content but also the methods used to deliver the curriculum. By making several changes in how we teach introductory chemistry and physics at Creighton (without changing the content of either course), we have substantially improved the environment for learning science. This improvement has been measured anecdotally by increased student satisfaction with the introductory courses; it has been measured formally by the large increase in students taking the next sequence of science courses and, in chemistry, by the large increase in students declaring a chemistry major.

THE CLARE BOOTHE LUCE PROGRAM FOR WOMEN IN SCIENCE

Creighton College of Arts and Sciences has a reputation for being a good preprofessional school. The departments of biology, chemistry, and physics have always been strong and well respected, attracting a substantial number of majors. Historically, however, the majority of science majors have gone on to medical school or into other health-science–related fields. Many students who come to Creighton with a strong interest in science—both male and female—assume that they will be pre-med only because they are unaware of other career options available to them in science. The assumption that all science majors must be pre-med is even held by some of the nonscience faculty at Creighton. This assumption came under scrutiny when Creighton University received a bequest from Clare Boothe Luce that set up an endowment to promote, support, and encourage the efforts of women who wish to pursue careers in research science (not medicine). The task now for Creighton is to actively promote scientific research, specifically as a career option for women.

Clare Boothe Luce was a playwright, war correspondent, magazine editor, socialite, mother, widow, artist, congressperson, presidential advisor, and diplomat (Sheed, 1982). In all her roles, in every aspect of her life, she was a tireless advocate of women's rights. Though she professed a personal disinterest in science, she recognized that other women were (or should be) interested in careers in science, engineering, and mathematics. As a consequence, she willed approximately $70 million, the bulk of her estate, to establish a program to promote the interests of women in science. She named in her will 14 institutions (including Creighton University), each of which receives the income from $3 million. Other institutions can apply for grants from the income generated by the remaining $28 million held in a general fund. The entire bequest is administered by the Henry Luce Foundation.

The program, as designed by Mrs. Luce, specifically targets women at what she believed are the most vulnerable periods in women's careers: the college, graduate school, and assistant professor years. The Clare Boothe Luce Fund provides money for undergraduate scholarships, graduate fellowships, and assistant professorships. Each institution receiving money from the program must have an explicit proposal for the use of its funds in one or more of the three targeted areas. Creighton University is using its portion of the bequest to fund one assistant professorship, two graduate fellowships in biochemistry, and ten undergraduate scholarships for junior and senior women majoring in any of the sciences.

The Clare Boothe Luce (CBL) Program for Undergraduate Women in Science at Creighton University began in 1989 as a scholarship program. The program had a very low profile on campus initially, affecting only those 10 students who received the Clare Boothe Luce scholarships. This was the case even though those scholarships, given to junior and senior women who show exceptional promise as future researchers, are the only *academic* full-ride scholarships the university offers. Since its inception, however, the program has grown to encompass many aspects of intellectual life in the science departments, and it affects many more women than the 10 who benefit from the scholarship funds. Through the three main components of undergraduate research, external speakers, and an in-house seminar for women students, Creighton University's goal is for the CBL Program for Women in Science to provide a positive experience for all women who major in one of the science disciplines.

Undergraduate Research

Over the past decade, much has been written about the best methods for attracting students, especially women and minorities, to majors and careers in science (Tobias, 1992; *What Works*, 1991). A common thread throughout all these studies is the importance of a strong, positive undergraduate research experience in influencing a student's decision to pursue a career in scientific research.

When a student majoring in one of the humanities graduates from college after four years, he or she will have done what academics in their field actually do: critical analysis of texts or creation of a body of work, be it sculpture, painting, music, or literature. In some of the social science disciplines—history and economics, for example—students are generally required to produce some type of independent work in the more advanced stages of their undergraduate education. The sciences are unique in that a student can obtain an undergraduate degree only by reading about what other people have done in the discipline and perhaps repeating someone else's experiments in the sterile laboratory setting. This situation would be similar to obtaining an economics degree after having copied Adam Smith's *The Wealth of Nations*; the student may obtain a greater understanding of the material and an appreciation of the process of creating such a work, or the student may just get a sore hand.

An undergraduate research experience is the one aspect of a science student's career that allows her or him to experience the day-to-day activities of being a scientist. The frustration, the drudgery, the excitement, and the intensity must be experienced first-hand; there is simply no substitute. The undergraduate research experience is valuable for all students, but, in light of what is known about females' responses to different instructional situations (Rosser, 1990; Belenky, Clinchy, Goldberger, & Tarule, 1986; Gilligan, 1982), it provides added benefits for women. A primary benefit is simply that the undergraduate research experience introduces women to the possibility of a career in research science. Very few people know what a "career in research science" means. Scientists in fiction, on television, and in the movies are generally portrayed as white men, and most often these men are doing things that are a little crazy or, in the most negative portrayals, potentially evil (Brush, 1991). Women are generally not attracted by these images and therefore do not see themselves as scientists, nor do they consider scientific research as a possible career. An undergraduate research experience helps remove those negative impressions for women and allows them to see themselves as scientists: They are doing research; therefore they can do research.

Science and scientists are shrouded in many myths. One myth that presents a particularly negative picture for many women is the impression that a scientist is a loner, working in his lab day and night, never coming into contact with other human beings. Females, in general, are socialized to be "people persons" and are not attracted by the lonely laboratory. The lonely laboratory is a myth, however. By participating in research, students can see that science does not get done by individuals but rather by groups of people working together. Contact between people is imperative for science to proceed.

Participation in undergraduate research allows a student to have a one-on-one interaction with a research advisor. It is through this personal interaction that a student's talent can best be developed and encouraged. Mentoring begins when students and faculty can spend time together in the research laboratory, getting to know each other as people and as scientists. The student can ask questions about such things as the graduate record exams, the importance (or unimportance) of grades, what to look for in a graduate school, and so forth. The mentor can provide direction in these and other matters and can also give immediate praise, encouragement, and direction during the course of a project.

Undergraduate research can aid in the development of participants' self-esteem. Research indicates that the self-esteem of female children declines with the onset of puberty (American Association of University Women, 1991). Female high school and college students continually underestimate their own abilities and attribute good grades and academic success to external factors such as hard work or good teachers rather than to their own talent. During a research experience, women students have the opportunity to work closely with their mentors, obtaining direct encouragement and feedback. In the research laboratory, the mentor and student are on a more equal level than are the teacher and student in a classroom situation. Knowing that the mentor respects and values the student researcher's opinions and ideas provides the student direct, external validation of her abilities as a scientist. This can help maintain or boost the student's self-esteem.

A particular example of the importance of positive mentoring was recently related to me by the student involved and by her research mentor. The student, a junior at the time, was having serious doubts about her abilities as a scientist. She was a B–B+ student and believed that those grades were not good enough; she believed that she should be earning all As in science courses and that the material should be easy if she was going to be successful. During the course of the year, the student began a research project with a faculty member from her major department. Through that interaction, the student received the encouragement she needed to persevere with her studies and the guidance to find and build on her own strengths. The student was encouraged (strongly) by her research advisor to present a paper, based on the results of their research, at a national meeting of a professional organization. The paper was very well received, and the student was approached by faculty members from other institutions encouraging her to apply to their schools for graduate work. The student went on to participate in a prestigious summer research program and spent the fall semester of her senior year pursuing research at a national laboratory. Her initial research experience provided her with the confidence necessary to participate in these other prestigious programs, but the day-to-day interaction with her research mentor provided the critical boost she needed at a crucial time in her career.

A guided independent research project should be just that: guided by the wisdom and background of the research advisor but independent in that the student is allowed (and encouraged) to find her own way to approach the problem, using whatever creativity and insight she possesses. The student is also allowed (and encouraged) to make her own mistakes and to learn from them. During an undergraduate research experience, a student proves to herself that she can master new material on her own; she develops the capacity to read an article from a scientific journal and apply its contents to the problem at hand, to design a new synthetic route, or to interpret data from an instrument with which she has had no previous experience. All these challenges and experiences build a student's self-esteem far better than an A on an exam ever could. A research experience allows the student to participate fully in all aspects of the scientific endeavor, from the formation of the question through the development of the problem to the presentation of the results.

Undergraduate research experiences reward students for creative and independent thinking. Students who participate in undergraduate research develop confidence in their ability to tackle difficult questions, questions that have no immediate or apparent answers. It is precisely these ingredients—encouragement from a mentor, reward for independent thinking, and development of self-confidence—that are crucial for a student's success in graduate school and beyond.

External Speakers

The CBL Program at Creighton attempts to bring in external speakers to present research seminars. Before the CBL Program was instituted, each science department had a research colloquium where Creighton students had the opportunity to learn about current research. Generally the speakers came from within the university or from nearby campuses, as the College of Arts and Sciences' budget didn't provide for importing speakers from far away. With CBL funds, however, we are now able to bring in two to four women speakers annually from across the country to give research seminars.

Attendance at departmental colloquia is strongly encouraged for all students and is required for the students formally participating in the CBL Program. Attendance at these seminars provides a number of benefits for the students. They are introduced to "real science," topics that are currently of prime interest in the research community. Students see that science is not "all done" but that there are still many interesting questions to ask and problems to solve. Creighton students tend to have a strong interest in the biological sciences, so every attempt is made to invite speakers who are working on problems with biological applications. For example, a recent chemistry department seminar was presented by Dr. Debbie C. Crans of Colorado State University on the biological activity of vanadium. These types of seminars provide relevance, the connection between what the students are learning in the classroom and its application to real-world issues that are of interest to them.

The exposure to new topics and techniques presented in a research talk challenges students' abilities to follow an oral presentation. When a student understands even a part of the presentation, her or his self-confidence gets quite a boost. There are two caveats, however. It is imperative that the speaker understand the level of the audience to whom he or she is talking. A seminar meant for the graduate faculty at Cal Tech will be a waste of everyone's time when it is delivered to an undergraduate audience at most colleges. This is not a problem if it is emphasized in the invitation to the speaker that the audience is primarily undergraduate. Recently we found that many graduate schools are delighted to send speakers to undergraduate colleges; it is considered recruiting for potential graduate students, and the schools try to send their best speakers for that purpose.

Faculty should follow up on the seminar, either formally in class or informally in hallway or office conversations. Classroom follow-up emphasizes the relationship between what the students are learning in class and the real-world applications of the formal concepts. It is also important for faculty to share their impressions of a presentation with students, particularly if the faculty member did not understand or follow every aspect of the talk. Students then realize that not everyone understands everything all the time and that is acceptable not to understand certain things immediately. This is usually best accomplished on an informal basis, although there are some instances when it may be appropriate during a class.

When external speakers visit, students are introduced to the social aspects of science. The students observe the interactions between faculty and the invited guest, the informal discussions and sharing of scientific information, the professional gossip, and so forth. During the seminar itself, students observe the variety of presentation styles and see that the question-and-answer portion of the talk is a time for sharing with the speaker the audience's interest in the topic, not a time to tear the speaker to shreds. Our students are strongly encouraged to participate in these visits. The speakers often want (or are at least willing) to meet informally with students to discuss graduate school or other career options. If the speaker has been brought in with CBL funds, she has lunch or dinner with a group of women students and spends an extended period talking with them. This provides a wonderful opportunity for women students to see and talk with other women scientists.

Finally, because of the CBL funding, more than half of our invited speakers are women. The number and quality of the women speakers who visit Creighton emphasize that women can do, should do, and are doing good scientific research. This is an important observation not only for our female students but for our male students and faculty as well.

Seminar for Women in Science

Creighton University offers a seminar for women in science. This 1-credit academic course with pass or no-pass grading is not formally restricted to women, but in the three years that it has been offered, no men have requested to enroll. The discussion-based class meets once a week for 60 to 90 minutes and is very loosely structured; the only formal requirements are that the students attend class and keep a journal. The course has been different each of the 3 years it has been offered.

The seminar is centered around the students' concerns, with reading assignments that vary from the history of women in science to modern critiques of science and practical analyses of the problems and joys of being a woman in science. (A sample reading list is given in the Appendix.) The readings serve mainly to provide background for the discussions. At the beginning of the semester, each student is asked to submit a list of topics that she would like to discuss or questions that she would like answered.

The course syllabus is then constructed from the students' lists of topics. Generally, the students have focused on the more practical aspects of having a career in science; however, because I believe that history is very important, I have included a few historical readings even when they were not requested.

The seminar provides an opportunity for the students to ask questions of the seminar director and other women faculty who sometimes drop in. The women are encouraged to *talk to each other* primarily, not to view the seminar leader as the source of all information or the last word on how to organize their lives. It is not an "encounter group," but it is a place for students to voice their concerns and fears and to hear that other people may have those same thoughts and feelings. The discussion topics have ranged from what the Graduate Record Examinations (GREs) are like and how to apply to graduate schools to debates over the appropriateness of day care for children and how to combine a family and a career.

A topic of particular concern to students in the past 2 years has been sexual harassment. The students have discussed and debated a range of issues surrounding the topic. The evolution of the discussions has been quite interesting. They usually begin by denying that sexual harassment or gender harassment occurs today. One student then timidly relates a story about how a certain male teacher made a comment about her dress, then another student tells about an obnoxious (male) teaching assistant who is constantly propositioning her, then another student adds an anecdote, and so on. In the individual student's mind, the incident is seen as isolated and does not really constitute harassment because she believes that the event was probably her own fault: Sally's dress was too short, Linda should wear bulky sweats to lab (maybe she is leading him on), and so forth. For most of these women, this is the first time that they have told anyone else about these incidents. When the individuals hear that similar incidents happen to almost everyone, it becomes easy to shift the blame and the (often repressed) anger from themselves to the instigator of the behavior. It does not matter (at this stage) whether the behavior is labeled as harassment or not; what is important is the shift in responsibility for the behavior from the woman to the other person involved.

I cannot emphasize enough how important this shift is. It is imperative that women *not* internalize harassment, whether it is called harassment or not. This is particularly true for gender-based harassment. Sexual harassment is much easier to identify, but gender-based harassment is far more common and more dangerous to the self-esteem and success of women.

Examples of gender-based harassment include females being ignored in class (not called on) or, when they are called on, a female student's answer being deemed not as correct as a male student's identical response.

In the laboratory, gender-based harassment occurs when women are assigned the "more feminine" duties such as recording data or observations instead of being asked to set up or manipulate the equipment. Women in science classes are often offered extra help or extra time because it is presumed that they need it. These incidents, which are not overtly harassing (some even mask as being helpful), can be very damaging to the self-esteem of female students. Over the course of 16 years of schooling, women internalize many of these messages, and even the strongest women may begin to believe that they do need the extra help, that they really should not be touching the expensive laboratory equipment, and that their answers probably are wrong. Eventually even the brightest students may leave science because they have come to believe that they just can't do it.

By encouraging the students to discuss these incidents, by identifying them as experiences that are common to many women, the students can begin to see that maybe it is not their fault but rather the fault of the person making the unwarranted presumptions. The students then encourage one another to be more assertive and self-assured. In effect, they challenge one another to stand up to society and disprove the negative assumptions about women.

The discussions during the seminar, regardless of topic, help identify areas of concern common to all the students. Each participant can see that she is not the only woman concerned about child rearing or worried about the GREs or whether she can actually survive graduate school. One of the biggest dangers for a woman in science is to become isolated from other women and therefore from the commonality of women's experiences. When this happens, there is an increased tendency for negative events to become too personalized, and a woman's sense of inadequacy can grow to the point where she believes that there is no other option but to quit. Talking about concerns that women have in common helps put the issues in perspective and gives the students more of a global outlook. Sharing concerns and experiences allows a group to emphasize the positive aspects of a given situation and to provide possible strategies for dealing with the negative aspects.

CONCLUSION

Creighton University has a history of being a supportive environment for women students in chemistry, biology, and physics. These departments have consistently produced a percentage of women majors that is higher than the national average. They have done so with excellent teaching by caring and dedicated faculty in spite of a standard, conservative science curriculum. In the past, however, the science departments have not placed a great emphasis on career direction or long-range follow-up for any one particular group of students.

The Clare Boothe Luce Program has been in effect for only 4 years. In those 4 years, we have seen the percentage of women majors increase substantially in each of the three departments. During the period 1978–1990, the percentage of biology and chemistry majors who were women was relatively steady at 30±2% and 29±3%, respectively. Since 1989, there has been a steady increase in the percentage, to a high of 46% of biology majors and 58% of chemistry majors being women. The total number of physics majors is so small that meaningful statistics cannot be gathered over this short a time. It is too soon to tell, however, if the program is really successful in helping these women *stay* in science after they leave Creighton University.

The only portion of the program that costs a large amount of money is the scholarships themselves. The bulk of the program could be implemented for less than several thousand dollars a year, with the money used primarily to bring in external speakers. The majority of the program takes just time, effort, and commitment. Obviously, the scholarships are for the students, but their overwhelmingly positive response to the seminars and the research experiences leads me to believe that these are the important aspects of the program, and these aspects could be easily replicated elsewhere.

APPENDIX: A SAMPLE READING LIST FOR THE WOMEN IN SCIENCE SEMINAR

Alic, Margaret. (1986). *Hypatia's heritage*. Boston: Beacon Press.

Brush, Stephan G. (1991). Women in science and engineering. *American Scientist, 79*, 404–419.

Gornick, Vivian. (1990). *Women in science*. New York: Simon & Schuster.

Hubbard, Ruth. (1989). Science, facts, and feminism. In Nancy Tuana (Ed.), *Feminism and science* (pp. 119–132). Bloomington, IN: Indiana University Press. [Original work published 1988 in *Hypatia, 3*(1)]

Jordan, David S. (1985). The higher education of women. In Louise M. Newman (Ed.), *Men's ideas/women's realities: Popular science, 1870–1915* (pp. 96–104). New York: Pergamon Press. (Original work published 1902)

Kass-Simon, G., & Farnes, Patricia (Eds.). (1990). *Women of science: Righting the record*. Bloomington, IN: Indiana University Press.

Keller, Evelyn Fox. (1977). The anomaly of a woman in physics. In Sara Ruddick & Pamela Daniels (Eds.), *Working it out* (pp. 77–91). New York: Pantheon Books.

Keller, Evelyn Fox. (1987). Women scientists and feminist critiques of science. *Daedalus, 116*(4), 77–91.

Smith, A. Lapthorn. (1985). The higher education of women and race suicide. In Louise M. Newman (Ed.), *Men's ideas/women's realities: Popular science, 1870–1915* (pp. 147–152). Elmsford, NY: Pergamon Press. (Original work published 1905)

Tobias, Sheila. (1990). *They're not dumb, they're different: Stalking the second tier.* Tucson, AZ: Research Corporation.

Yentsch, Clarice, M., & Sindermann, Carl J. (1992). *The woman scientist.* New York: Plenum.

Zuckerman, Harriet, Cole, Jonathan R., & Bruer, John T. (Eds.). (1992). *The outer circle: Women in the scientific community.* New Haven: Yale University Press.

REFERENCES

American Association of University Women. (1991). *Shortchanging girls, shortchanging America.* Washington, DC: Author.

Belenky, Mary F., Clinchy, Blythe M., Golberger, Nancy R., & Tarule, Jill M. (1986). *Women's ways of knowing.* New York: Basic Books.

Bodner, George M. (1992). Why changing the curriculum may not be enough. *Journal of Chemical Education, 69*, 186–190.

Brush, Stephen G. (1991). Women in science and engineering. *American Scientist, 79*, 404–419.

Gilligan, Carol. (1982). *In a different voice.* Cambridge, MA: Harvard University Press.

Hulce, Martin, Klein, Francis M., & Jagusch, Christian R. (1993). *Organic chemistry laboratory manual.* Omaha, NE: Creighton University.

Mattson, Bruce M. (1992). *Laboratory for general chemistry, an environmentally responsible manual.* New York: McGraw-Hill.

Rosser, Sue V. (1990). *Female friendly science: Applying women's studies methods and theories to attract students.* Elmsford, NY: Pergamon Press.

Sheed, Wilfrid. (1982). *Clare Boothe Luce.* New York: E. P. Dutton.

Tobias, Sheila. (1992). *Revitalizing undergraduate science: Why some things work and others don't.* Tucson, AZ: Research Corporation.

What works: Building natural science communities. (1991). Washington DC: Project Kaleidoscope.

Part III
MATHEMATICS

CHAPTER 5
The Four-Component System
A Nontechnological Interactive Learning Environment Where Women Count

Bonnie Kelly

Returning to college after 16 years, I entered graduate school as an older student intent on obtaining an education degree in secondary-school mathematics. Short of student teaching, I finished that degree and then went on to obtain my master of science degree in mathematics. As a graduate assistant with a diverse viewpoint—different from that of most graduate students and most of the instructors in mathematics—I saw the need for an integrated and consistent approach to instruction in undergraduate mathematics.

During the summer of 1989, due to the poor math preparation, horrific math phobia, and general math ennui of my college algebra students, I experimented with a combination of teaching strategies such as group learning, peer teaching, and active student participation. These particular strategies had already worked for my high school students, but because I had done my own learning primarily through the lecture method, the tendency to doubt the efficacy of these strategies for teaching college-level mathematics was high. But out of necessity, and because I didn't want students to fail or to dislike a subject as beautiful as math, I proceeded to incorporate alternative methods in the summer course as well as in the following academic year.

I found them to be very successful. There was an increase in student attendance, student involvement, and student accomplishment with respect to grade improvement and course retention. I saw in myself an increased awareness of and confidence in the ability of my students to do mathematics, and I saw in my students a new self-confidence in their own ability to perform competently in mathematics.

I noticed that my female students showed the most improvement. They gave the most positive feedback on the evaluation form. In the newly formed Four-Component System, their grades outstripped the males', and their confidence in their math ability grew.

With the support of the Mathematics Department at the University of South Carolina, insightful advice and comments from mathematics professors, and an innovative instructional grant awarded to me by the provost's office, two test projects involving the Four-Component System were initiated in the spring and fall semesters of 1991.

These projects proved to be successful quantitatively and qualitatively both for the students in the classes and for the graduate students who taught the courses. An immediate result was the increased confidence indicated by the female graduate assistants in their ability to control their classes and by the international graduate students in their competence to communicate with students from different backgrounds. A further result was that the graduate assistants received higher teaching evaluation scores from their students.

DESCRIPTION OF THE FOUR-COMPONENT SYSTEM

The Four-Component System (FCS) is a replicable instructional system that upgrades the instructional climate presented to undergraduate students and improves their mathematical aptitudes and attitudes. Because each component stands on its own, instructors can choose any or all of the components to provide support and reinforcement for instructional goals. As a whole, the four components work synergistically to produce active and successful teaching and learning.

The specific instructional objectives of the FCS are to help the beginning instructor learn how to teach effectively and efficiently, to standardize teaching methods and streamline instructional delivery, and to produce coherence and consistency in the instruction itself. The specific performance objectives are to help students learn to comprehend mathematics on their own; to increase their ability to read, write, speak, and listen mathematically; to help them build self-confidence in their own mathematical abilities; and to develop personal motivation and enthusiasm for studying mathematics.

The FCS combines four reliable strategies to provide students with a rich array of instructional activities. The Focus Sheet gives students a daily agenda, and the Recap Quiz provides students and instructors with feedback communication. Forward Homework promotes study and preparation, and the Group Test initiates and supports cooperative learning. Figure 5.1 provides a schematic diagram of the FCS, with each component described in greater detail in the following paragraphs.

FIGURE 5.1. The Four-Component System: An interactive learning environment.

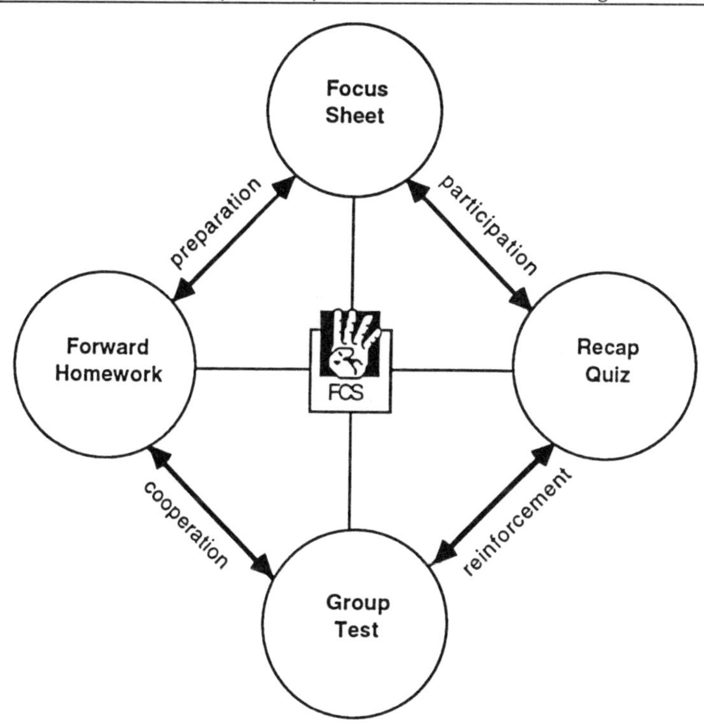

The Focus Sheet, which provides the daily agenda, is essentially a lesson plan that is used by the instructor and the students. The purpose of this one-page synopsis of the upcoming lecture is to focus the attention of both the instructor and the students on the material to be taught. It eliminates excessive boardwork and note taking and provides students with a study guide of important concepts as well as a variety of questions that may appear on a test. The Focus Sheet is divided into the following sections: Focus, Objectives, Terms, Key Facts / Procedures, Review Problems, and Homework (Forward and Backward).

Figure 5.2 provides an example of a Focus Sheet. Notice that the terms are only listed, not defined. This practice streamlines the lecture so that the concepts can be covered efficiently. Because the terms are always defined in the textbook, students are expected to know them. As in other disciplines, students in Four-Component mathematics are expected to read ahead to prepare for the next lecture. To help them accomplish this responsibility, Forward Homework is assigned.

FIGURE 5.2. A sample Focus Sheet.

FOCUS: Real Zeros of Polynomial Functions
OBJECTIVE(S): To determine and find the real zeros of a polynomial
TERMS: roots/zeros, **Descartes' Rule of Signs,** variation in sign, **Rational Zero Test,** lead coefficient, constant, possible rational zeros

KEY FACTS:

1) **TEST to DETERMINE ZEROS:**

DESCARTES' RULE of SIGNS ⇒ determines the **number** of **zeros** of **f(x)**

⇓ ⇓

number of **positive** real **zeros** ≤ **number** of **variation** in **sign** of **f(x)**

number of **negative** real **zeros** ≤ **number** of **variation** in **sign** of **f(-x)**

number **less than by an **even** integer**

RATIONAL ZERO TEST ⇒ determines the **possible zeros** of **f(x)**

⇓

$f(x) = a_n x^n + a_{n-1} x^{n-1} + \ldots + a_1 x + a_0$

⇓

$a_i (i = 1, \ldots, n)$ must be integer coefficient

⇓

$$\text{possible rational zeros} = \frac{\pm\text{factors of constant}}{\pm\text{factors of lead coefficient}}$$

REVIEW PROBLEMS:
1. Find all real solutions of: $y^4 + 6y^3 - 13y^2 + 10y - 4 = 0$
2. Find all rational zeros of: $f(x) = 2x^3 - 3x^2 - 23x + 12$

ASK ANALYSIS: Can I...find the real zeros of a polynomial?

HOMEWORK:

Adapted from Larson & Hostetler (1989). *College Algebra, Second Edition.*

Forward Homework is used in combination with Backward Homework, the traditional homework model for providing after-class practice. Forward Homework combines text reading with exercises that will be covered in the next lecture. Students learn explicitly that "This is what we are doing in the next lecture, so come prepared." The Forward Homework problems are elementary and imitative of solved examples in the text. Forward Homework lets students know that the instructor has clear expectations for student involvement and success and says to students, "You can do this. You can read mathematics and solve problems on your own. And we're counting on you to do this."

The Recap Quiz also has the expectation of success built into it. This quiz is given at the end of each lecture and is designed to give immediate feedback on whether the students have at least nominally assimilated the concepts. It usually takes about 5 to 10 minutes and consists of two problems with two important emphases. The first problem is an elementary problem based on a concept from the current lecture. To connect the lecture content with the previous lecture, the second problem is more complicated and requires students to use knowledge learned in the previous lecture.

The Recap Quiz continually provides assessment by requiring students to process small bits of information that they can easily accommodate. This recap of previously taught concepts teaches students that active listening and learning are required from them at all times. They learn that true understanding cannot be accomplished without actively participating in the classroom and doing homework as well. In addition, the instructor learns what students have assimilated by monitoring their active and frequent input. The Recap Quiz expects successful involvement on everyone's part. Figure 5.3 provides examples of typical Recap Quiz questions.

FIGURE 5.3. Sample quiz questions.

Based on the Focus Sheet just presented, this sample quiz reflects one concept of the day's lecture, that is, Rational Zero Test which gives:

$$\text{possible rational zeros} = \frac{\pm \text{ factors of constant}}{\pm \text{ factors of lead coefficient}}$$

The second question is based on the previous lecture which was on synthetic division.

Quiz

Question 1: Using the Rational Zero Test set up all possible zeros of

$$f(x) = 2x^3 - 3x^2 - 23x + 12$$

Question 2: Using synthetic division divide

$$2x^3 - 3x^2 - 23x + 12 \text{ by } (x - 1)$$

The fourth component is the Group Test. In addition to two traditional exams—midterm and final—a group test is given every 2 weeks. This test is a group problem-solving session (GPSS), which is counted in the students' grades. The instructor selects two to four students who represent a wide range of abilities and social compatibilities to work in groups. If group dynamics decompose, the groups are rearranged. At all times during the group sessions, the instructor is present to observe and to give aid if necessary. The problems encountered in a Group Test are usually harder and more thought-provoking than the text exercises. In general, the problems range from technical derivations to detailed applications.

The Group Test, an example of which is displayed in Figure 5.4, involves cooperative learning and reciprocal teaching that requires students to explain concepts to their group cohorts. It forces students to examine and articulate to themselves and others the degree to which they understand the problem. To do this, students mentally construct mathematics in their own minds and then verbalize and defend their mathematical constructs. This process occurs in the absence of the traditional test with its accompanying stress.

In the Group Test, the stress and panic encountered in traditional testing are lessened so that students can demonstrate what they have learned: mathematical knowledge rather than strategic knowledge necessary to manage the stress of testing. The Group Test builds student mathematical self-esteem and confidence and simultaneously fosters student network-

FIGURE 5.4. Sample problems from a Group Test (group problem-solving sessions).

Problem 1: Find all zeros of

$$g(x) = \frac{(1+2x^2)e^{2x} - 3x^2e^{2x}}{(1+2x^2)^3}$$

Problem 2: Your aunt has promised to give you $1000 on your twenty-first birthday, three years from now. Since you are attending college, you ask her for the money now. "Of course," she replies, "but you know we can earn 10% compounded quarterly in a money market account." She then hands you a check for $750. Has she reneged on her promise? Why or why not?

ing and the development of support systems, needed particularly by undergraduate students. In short, the Group Test promotes learning.

BENEFITS OF THE FOUR-COMPONENT SYSTEM

From my personal observations and from the confidence surveys I distributed during the first classroom period, I found that female students sometimes have a very different perspective from male students concerning the difficulty of a course in mathematics. From the perspective of the female students, mathematics is a course to be feared and possibly failed. From the male students' perspective, math is just another subject. For instance, in one class, on the confidence survey all the males believed that they were quite good in the subject and expected to get at least a B for the course grade. Two thirds of the females expected to receive a C or better; the other third expected to fail. All the female students indicated that they were not confident in their ability. When the first Group Test was graded, all the females received a B or better, but half the males scored no higher than a C. No females in this class failed at the end of the course; two males did. There were, of course, other factors to be considered here, yet I observed in subsequent classes this same tendency of females to underestimate their ability in math. In addition, females seem to have a unique perception of participation within the classroom. In general, comments from female students indicate that they believed that the best students in class were male because they asked the most questions and seemed to know what they were talking about. In reality, a lot of the questions from male students indicated that they did not understand and were not really listening. Because female students associate class participation with command of a subject, they refrain from asking questions in class. This reinforces the perception of their inability to achieve in math.

I now work primarily with African American students and have found that the same perspectives and perceptions are at play not only in female students but in black males as well. These aspects of learning in the traditional lecture-oriented classroom can prevent success. Substantial references to support these observations can be found in various journals and books that deal specifically with mathematics (Chipman, Brush, & Wilson, 1985; Hyde, Fennema, & Lamon, 1991a, 1991b; Kenschaft & Keith, 1991), as well as those in developmental psychology (Brown & Gilligan, 1993) and those on gender bias and gender differences in the sciences (American Association of University Women [AAUW], 1992; Matyas & Malcolm, 1991; Rosser, 1986; Rosser & Kelly, 1994), which are directed to science and cognitive studies in general.

Females after a certain age tend to be less sure of themselves and more easily intimidated (AAUW, 1992; Brown & Gilligan, 1993). Although many of the male students subscribe to the theory that there is no such thing as a stupid question and will ask anything that they are unsure of, many of the female students believe that their lack of understanding is their own fault, or at least their own problem (Chipman, Brush, & Wilson, 1985; Kenschaft & Keith, 1991). The irony is that many of these same females have just as strong an understanding of the math concepts as the males; they simply tend to doubt themselves unnecessarily (AAUW, 1992; Hyde, Fennema, & Lamon, 1991a, 1991b). The problem is not the math; it is their self-confidence with the math and their fear of pushing the envelope of their experience (Kenschaft & Keith, 1991; National Research Council & National Academy of Sciences [NRC & NAS], 1989).

The FCS provides a wide variety of benefits for instructors and undergraduate students of mathematics. First, students who are afraid to speak up in a full class or to ask or answer questions have an opportunity to contribute their questions and answers in the smaller setting of the group problem-solving sessions (Kenschaft & Keith, 1991; Skolnick, Langbort, & Day, 1982). Second, students lead group discussions of mathematical concepts, thus building confidence in their capability as problem solvers (Chipman, Brush, & Wilson, 1985; NRC & NAS, 1989). By feeling and receiving support, not intimidation, students are encouraged to attempt and succeed at educated risk taking (Kenschaft & Keith, 1991; Skolnick, Langbort, & Day, 1982). Third, in a small group setting, students become more aware of mathematical concepts as applied to themselves (Case, 1991; NRC & NAS, 1989). They appreciate mathematics for itself and not as an inconvenience that prevents them from getting a degree (Goodman, 1991). Problems that seem to be monumental when confronted by the lone student can now be attempted with the support of the group (Skolnick, Langbort, & Day, 1982). Fourth, small groups acknowledge and foster a student's confidence and ability. This is necessary in other math courses as well as in life itself (NRC & NAS, 1989). Small groups allow networking and friendship building (Kenschaft & Keith, 1991). Fifth, in a Group Test, students have more time to formulate questions and answers. They are listened to by their peers and communicate in the language of their peers (Kenschaft & Keith, 1991). They cooperate with other students, thus enhancing teamwork. Sixth, entry-level undergraduates are very anxious regarding their math abilities. "Math anxiety" and "math avoidance" are predominant infirmities (AAUW, 1992; Brown & Gilligan, 1993; Chipman, Brush, & Wilson, 1985). The FCS reduces these infirmities by using Forward Homework and Recap Quizzes to reinforce the notion, "Don't be scared, just come prepared." Finally, students prefer and perform better in situations in which everyone wins (Kirwan, 1991). They are fully aware that the success of their peers in no way lowers their own. In stark contrast to courses in which grades are controlled by the bell curve and or by a student's class rank, the FCS rewards initiative and involvement. Each student has the opportunity to achieve an A.

It is very important that the students, and the instructor as well, understand that there will be no grading curve. It may be difficult for an instructor to give final grades that are substantially higher and produce a higher class average than usual. Overcome this fear! If the students are learning, it is all right for everyone's grade to be high. There may be some peer pressure for the instructor to have a broader range of grades, but that misses the point. If students are to help one another learn, and to learn from one another, they must be absolutely assured that they are not in competition for a ration of As and Bs. In several of my courses, all the students ended up with As and Bs. Some other faculty members made comments about this, but the standardized midterm and final tests demonstrated that this was not grade inflation but actually a measure of increased student achievement.

There is, at present, a national call for reform in mathematics (David & NRC, 1990; Kirwan, 1991) and a similar one in the sciences (Matyas & Malcolm, 1991). The purpose of this call is to foster stronger recruitment, higher retention, and lower attrition rates of female and minority students in such disciplines. The FCS offers a practical response to help revitalize mathematics at the precalculus and college algebra levels.

TESTING THE FOUR-COMPONENT SYSTEM

The FCS has been tested twice by the University of South Carolina Mathematics Department. The first study was conducted during the spring of 1991 and involved 7 sections of college algebra. Three sections served as experimental sections, taught using the FCS instructional model, and 4 sections served as controls, using the traditional instructional approach. The second study was conducted during the fall 1991 semester and involved 15 sections of precalculus. Eight sections were experimental and 7 were control. In each study, all the students were pretested using a departmental standardized placement test. Additionally, each student was required to take a common, uniform midterm, prefinal, or both of 2 hours' duration. These tests were written by an objective observer who was a faculty member and were purposely designed to be difficult. Minimal partial credit was given.

The courses for both studies were taught by graduate teaching assistants. The sections were distributed as equally as possible with respect to the times at which the sections were taught and the instructors' gender, race, cultural background, expertise, experience, and age. The results for college algebra are summarized in Table 5.1. The close pretest scores, which were out of a possible 25 total, indicate that the groups did not vary in aptitude at the beginning of the semester. The experimental group scored approximately 24% higher in the midterm exam.

Confidence surveys were also given to the students at the beginning and end of the semester. The students rated their mathematical confidence on a scale of 1 to 4. At the end of the semester, the experimental group experienced a larger increase in math confidence than did the control group.

When retention was represented as the proportion of students who did not withdraw from the class, the experimental group had a higher retention rate than the control group. The control group had 141 students out of preliminary 164, and the experimental group had 115 out of 124.

As the data from Table 5.2 reveal, positive results were obtained in the precalculus project as well. Again, the experimental group and the control group had similar pretest scores: 15.9 as compared to 16.0 out of a total of 25. The experimental group had a significantly higher mean midterm score than the control group, approximately 28% higher. The experimental group also had a significantly higher mean prefinal score than the control group, approximately 25% higher.

To measure student confidence levels in specific course objectives, confidence surveys were administered during the first and last days of class. Note that only the experimental group exhibited an increase in mean confidence level. Amazingly, the mean confidence level of the students in the

TABLE 5.1. Statistical analysis summary: College Algebra Project 111.

Measure	*Control*	*Experimental*
Pretest value	10.9	11.4
Mean midterm score	46.2	57.3*
Mean confidence change	.1324	.6719*
Retention	86%	93%*

$p < .05$*

TABLE 5.2. Statistical analysis summary: Precalculus Project 115.

Measure	*Control*	*Experimental*
Pretest values	15.9	16.0
Mean midterm score	41.3	52.9*
Mean prefinal score	38.2	47.7*
Mean confidence change	-.0396	.1667
Retention	92%	97%*

$p < .0001$*

control group decreased over the semester. A secondary analysis of confidence change, according to gender, revealed that female students in the experimental sections had an increase in confidence of .096, and female students under traditional instruction had no increase. Male students in the experimental sections increased in confidence by .26, and the confidence of males in the traditional sections decreased by .078.

To determine retention in the program, a coding scheme was used. Retention was given a value of 1 if the student took the pretest and the prefinal and a value of 0 if the student took the pretest but not the prefinal. This scheme was used under the assumption that if a student was still an active member of the course, he or she would take the prefinal, which counted in the grade received for the course. The retention percentages shown are derived from matching the students' Social Security numbers for both tests. The results broken down by race and gender are summarized in Table 5.3. Observe that the experimental group had not only an overall higher retention rate than the control group but also higher retention among the so-called at-risk groups.

QUALITATIVE DATA FROM STUDENTS

Students in each study were given the opportunity to respond to open-ended questions that tapped their reactions to the FCS course. Three students' comments are included to represent the overall views of students.

One female student stated, "I have always disliked math greatly and have tried to avoid it at all costs. This method takes the fear out of learning

TABLE 5.3. Statistical analysis summary by race and gender: Precalculus Project 115.

Group	*Control (%)*	*Experimental (%)*
Female		
African American	94	98
Caucasian	91	97
Male		
African American	93	98
Caucasian	92	95

math and makes it much easier to comprehend. I am actually not dreading coming to class and enjoy learning the material."

A second female student wrote, "I feel that the Four-Component System is beneficial to most if not all undergraduate students. It allows you to isolate the most important elements in each chapter and learn them well; not just for the test or exam, but for the rest of your life. Many may think that the group problem-solving sessions are an easy way to get good grades on a test, but quite the opposite is true. Many concepts are more readily understood when explained in a number of different ways. Often a teacher explains a concept one way and if another student can explain in different words or using another example it often 'clicks.' This is the second time in Math 115 and I had a terrible time the first go-round. This method of teaching has given me a new outlook on math and I'm quite confident that I will enter calculus next semester with a more than adequate background."

Finally, a male student responded, "The course provides the students a way to more comfortably ask questions because the groups are a way to be more at ease with the people because they become your friends. It makes it easier to arrange help with the people in your class after class if you don't understand."

SUMMARY OF THE FOUR-COMPONENT SYSTEM

To summarize, the FCS for teaching undergraduate mathematics is a replicable system for mathematics as well as other disciplines. Plans are currently being made to expand the system to other courses, to create more teaching-learning guides, and to introduce diskettes as part of the system.

The FCS is unique in that it intertwines proven strategies into a comprehensive, effective structure. It combines traditional lectures with actively attentive students and balances traditional testing with cooperative learning. It coincides with the instructor's style of teaching and provides the instructor with tools to enhance the students' learning and appreciation of the discipline of mathematics.

In short, the FCS approach offers students the genuine opportunity to experience success in an academic discipline that has historically served as a "gatekeeper" to block student access to a degree in higher education.

REFERENCES

American Association of University Women. (1992). *How schools shortchange girls.* Washington, DC: AAUW Educational Foundation.

Brown, Lyn Mikel, & Gilligan, Carol. (1993). *Meeting at the crossroads: Women's psychology and girls' development.* Cambridge, MA: Harvard University Press.

Case, BettyeAnne (Ed.). (1991). *Preparing for college teaching* (preprint). Washington, DC: American Mathematical Society, Mathematical Association of America, and Society for Industrial and Applied Mathematics.

Chipman, Susan, Brush, Lorelei, & Wilson, Donna. (Eds.). (1985). *Women and mathematics: Balancing the equation.* Hillside, NJ: Lawrence Erlbaum.

David, Edward E., & National Research Council. (1990). *Renewing U.S. mathematics: A plan for the 1990's.* Washington, DC: Board on Mathematical Sciences, National Academy Press.

Goodman, Billy. (1991). Toward a pump, not a filter. *MOSAIC, 22*(2), 12–21.

Hyde, Janet Shibley, Fennema, Elizabeth, & Lamon, Susan J. (1991a). Gender differences in mathematics performance: A meta-analysis: Part 1 of 2. *Newsletter of the Association for Women in Mathematics, 21*(3), 20–27.

Hyde, Janet Shibley, Fennema, Elizabeth, & Lamon, Susan J. (1991b). Gender differences in mathematics performance: A meta-analysis: Part 2 of 2. *Newsletter of the Association for Women in Mathematics, 21*(4), 20–23.

Kenschaft, Patricia Clark, & Keith, Sandra Zaroodny (Eds.). (1991). *Winning women into mathematics.* Washington, DC: Mathematical Association of America.

Kirwan, William (Chair) and Members on the Mathematical Sciences in the year 2000. (1991). Moving beyond myths: Revitalizing undergraduate mathematics. *Notices of the American Mathematical Society, 38*(6), 545–559.

Larson, Roland, & Hostetler, Robert P. (1989). *College algebra* (2nd ed.). Lexington, MA: D. C. Heath.

Matyas, Marsha, & Malcolm, Shirley. (1991). *Investing in human potential: Science and engineering at the crossroads.* Washington, DC: American Association for the Advancement of Science.

National Research Council & National Academy of Sciences. (1989). *Everybody counts.* Washington, DC: National Academy Press.

Rosser, Sue V. (1986). *Teaching science and health from a feminist perspective*. Elmsford, NY: Pergamon Press.

Rosser, Sue V., & Kelly, Bonnie. (1994). From hostile exclusion to friendly inclusion. *Journal for Women and Minorities in Science and Engineering, 1*(1), 29–49.

Skolnick, Joan, Langbort, Carol, & Day, Lucille. (1982). *How to encourage girls in math and science: Strategies for parents and educators*. Englewood Cliffs, NJ: Prentice-Hall.

CHAPTER 6

Toward a Feminist Algebra

Mary Anne Campbell
Randall K. Campbell-Wright

Mathematicians on the whole have not been particularly responsive to feminists' work concerning the influence of mathematicians' gender (largely male) on the discipline or the varying impact of mathematics on the sexes. However, a basic sense of justice and decreasing numbers of white men seeking careers in mathematics have driven professional societies such as the Mathematical Association of America and the American Mathematical Society to work at including more women and under-represented minorities ("Special Issue," 1991). Questions of motive aside, there has been a concerted effort from many directions to appeal to women.

We applaud the progress that has been and continues to be made in improving pedagogical techniques to account for student learning styles (Cooney & Hirsch, 1990; McLeod & Adams, 1989), to counteract math anxiety (Kogelman & Warren, 1978; Tobias, 1978), and to address the issue of why women tend to have better high school and college grades but worse Scholastic Aptitude Test (SAT) scores than men (Kelly-Benjamin, 1990; Kimball, 1989). We are also keenly aware of feminist critiques of bias in the foundations of science and mathematics (Keller, 1985; Harding, 1986; Rosser, 1990), and we join them in challenging the notion that there is such a thing as "pure" mathematics (free from the social upbringing and values of its practitioners). Our chapter treats pedagogical techniques and feminist critiques together by focusing on the content of mathematical "word problems," the context in which students most directly experience the tone of what they see as mathematics.

Feminists have long understood the negative impact of sexist language and stereotyping on women studying mathematics. However, old habits fade slowly, and textbooks evolve more out of a need to avoid offending adoption committees than out of a desire to effect social change. The superficial solutions of many textbook authors—simply removing pronouns and replacing some male names with female names—are not sufficient. Women have been gratuitously inserted into the world of mathematics, but the content of textbook problems hasn't changed much.

We seek to empower women by building a collection of affirmative word problems for use in standard college algebra courses. Moreover, the principles that are described and illustrated in this chapter can be used at any level of mathematics to create examples that are not merely nonnegative. These principles include:

- Presenting female heroes and breaking gender stereotypes
- Analyzing sex similarities and differences intentionally (and not using sex as an arbitrary category)
- Confronting mathematical metaphors that are religious or violent (and ultimately misogynous)
- Imagining examples that unveil the mathematics that already exists in the world of women, thus affirming women's experiences and providing encouragement to continue studying mathematics

A feminist teacher who is empathetic and imaginative can not only avoid bad textbook problems but can also construct good classroom (and textbook) examples that empower women and other marginalized people. It is hoped that the examples and principles detailed here will facilitate that process.

FEMALE HEROES AND BREAKING GENDER STEREOTYPES

The idea of presenting female heroes and breaking gender stereotypes in mathematics textbooks is our most basic principle. It has much the same effect that altering one's sexist speech habits does: In addition to placing inclusive paradigms in public view, it changes one's own perception of reality. It is a good—and absolutely necessary—way to begin changing attitudes (ours and our students').

Admittedly, the presentation of female heroes can be difficult, for women's accomplishments have been either devalued or erased altogether as well as constrained. To use a sports example, the larger average body size of men is an advantage in many of the sports of force and contact that our society values. It remains to be seen whether different socialized patterns of eating and exercising might produce closer average male and female body sizes and how much this convergence could affect maximal performance. Rather than sex, perhaps body size could be the exclusive determiner of competition categories. For the time being, we can present to our students applications based on the accomplishments of Olympic gold medalist Bonnie Blair:

> At the 1994 Winter Olympics, Bonnie Blair skated the 500-meter race in 39.25 seconds to win the gold medal. What was her average speed in miles per hour?

We must, however, heed the lessons of male African American athletes, namely, that the economic success of a few individuals is not representative of the economic status of (male) African Americans as a whole. By presenting exemplary achievements by sportswomen as though such a high standard were ordinary, we ignore their economic—and usually racial—advantages. Women are invariably a hegemonic underclass within a particular economic, racial, and sexual preference or orientation community (although it must be admitted that women certainly help perpetuate oppression over less powerful groups, such as children). Although female heroes should be given equal representation in mathematics education, these and other positive portrayals of women should not be subject to facile interpretation as being somehow representative of "the status of women." The status of women is something too complex, too interwoven with other social valuators such as sexual preference or orientation, race, and class, to be contained neatly within any particular schema, in this case, sports. Inasmuch as the status of women is falsely perceived as an easily measurable given, the presentation of female heroes should be balanced with applications concerning ordinary women who must, for instance, meticulously balance the expenditures of households and small businesses:

> Ruth figures that she can afford $40 a month to make payments on aluminum siding, which she can have installed for $950. If she puts it on her department store credit card (with an annual interest rate of 19%), how long will it take her to pay off the aluminum siding?

Breaking gender stereotypes in general goes hand in hand with the presentation of female heroes. Women are athletes, career professionals, and blue-collar workers, and men are nurses, secretaries, flight attendants, and other support personnel. The danger in setting out to break stereotypes is not in providing fuel for academic derision and classroom jokes (which might even be taken as a small sign of success); rather, the danger we face is that if we do not consistently overturn all stereotypes, students will glibly accept any stereotypes that we allow into our curricula as "normal." At this point in the game, the purpose is still to jar people out of complacency.

(Sexist language is, of course, an issue too. "Male nurse" is just as insidious as "housewife," both terms implying appropriate occupations and behaviors for women.) Nonstereotypical roles, then, should be the standard for feminist writers and teachers of mathematics:

> Malhab wants 50 shrimp on a party platter. If the store has large shrimp that range from 30 to 40 per pound, how many pounds should he buy?

Finally, watch that men who are taking on roles traditionally assigned to women do not in the process co-opt women. A classic case would be a woman who cooks (for her family)—she is called a mother or a cook. A man who cooks (as a paid occupation) is called a chef.

Sexuality serves an odd function in mathematical applications. It is rare for there to be both women and men in an exercise without romance—and, by heterosexist extension, gender—being an underlying issue if not the focus:

> Peter is meeting his girl friend Melissa at the airport. They haven't seen each other in 6 months. He is precisely 120 feet away from Melissa when he sees her walking toward him. They start running at the same moment, he at 15 feet/second, she at 12 feet/second (she is carrying luggage). How many feet does Peter run until they meet? How long does it take him? (Grossman, 1992, p. 92)

We cannot hope to rectify stereotypical representations of women and men (those of women thus being devalued) in our teaching of mathematics if we ultimately fall back on heterosexual romance as normal ideology. We must present women and men whose relationships are other than romantic. Even more importantly, we must present women and women and men and men whose relationships are romantic:

> Susan and Debbie are a couple financing their $70,000 home over a period of 15 years. Their annual interest rate is 8.75%. How much will Susan and Debbie's monthly house payments be?

To accomplish these goals—that is, to portray female heroes and to break gender stereotypes—is absolutely necessary as an initial step toward the inclusion and valuing of women in mathematics. But to work only at these goals is superficial and demeaning toward women, for the rents in our social fabric—and in our mathematics—are much more severe. From these basic beginnings, we move toward the mending of more subtle areas.

SEX SIMILARITIES AND DIFFERENCES

A primary rationale for word problems is that they ground mathematical study in human experience. The experiences presented, then, should reflect reality.

Mathematics textbook authors have traditionally been careless about their presentation of sex as a category of analysis in examples. Counting and comparing the boys (or men) and girls (or women) in a group is a common exercise, often with no meaningful purpose whatsoever. A current college algebra text contains the following problem:

> The Senior Birdwatchers' Club, consisting of 4 women and 2 men . . . plan to elect a president, a vice-president, and a secretary. . . .
>
> 3. In how many ways can they elect their three officers if the president is required to be female and the vice-president, male?
> 4. In how many ways can they elect their three officers if the president is to be of one sex and the vice-president and secretary of the other? (Fleming, Varberg, & Kasube, 1992, p. 375)

Of course, no club that we know of—and certainly not a birdwatchers' club—requires the president to be female and the vice president to be male. This problem illustrates the flippancy of using sex as an arbitrary category for counting problems; more seriously, it encourages dangerous misconceptions about how affirmative action works in practice. We would rather see a problem that reflects and addresses reality:

> A department has 12 women and 10 men who are equally qualified. If they choose 3 men to promote, what is the probability that they acted fairly (without regard to gender)?

When there is a reason to consider women and men as categories, the political content of the problem grabs the attention of students, who are then more likely to care what the answer is.

Textbook authors are increasingly aware that they should consider the sexual politics of the situations in which they place people. They are also aware that the politics are volatile. One way that authors try to avoid trouble is by making sex invisible:

> A landscape contractor has two employees plant the shrubbery around a new office building. The older employee could do the job alone in two days, whereas the newer employee would take three days working alone. How many days will it take them working together? (Hall, 1992, p. 125)

However innocent the intentions of some authors, supposedly sex-neutral examples compound the problem of sexual politics even as they attempt to avoid it. Studies show that people (especially men) habitually replace sex-neutral images with male images (Bailey & Bailey, 1987, p. 17). Sex-neutral language is impossible; we feminist mathematicians must be responsible for the sexual politics of our language usage.

When it seems reasonable to consider women as a group, textbooks often do not; rather, math textbooks have customarily used sex categories in such a way that the male is the presumed norm and the female is made invisible. Older college algebra texts often contained exercises on life insurance, using mortality probability tables (Rees & Sparks, 1969, p. 466 ff.). Although it was well known that women have different (usually longer) life expectancies than men, only the male mortality table was presented even when an occasional woman appeared in the exercises (Rees & Sparks, 1969, p. 475). Women were either invisible or were forced into a male model.

Disappointingly, these problems have tended to disappear from standard college algebra texts rather than to undergo the obvious transformation. We would like to see the return of life (and other) insurance problems as a major application of probability principles, with data included for both sexes and various socioeconomic classes, sexual preferences or orientations, races, and ethnic groups. The political impacts of such comparisons are startling, and the importance of mathematical analysis becomes clear to students.

A favorite exercise of ours is to collect the height, weight, and sex of each student in a class (anonymously, of course) in order to construct a linear model for each sex and to provide a rough comparison of average body characteristics (Figure 6.1). We can then show the class what American national averages look like (Figure 6.2). The slopes of these lines show that women's bodies are generally less dense than men's (although there is certainly overlap). This phenomenon is due to general body composition as well as body shape. Since this simple comparison reveals such clear and immediate consequences, it is unconscionable that the medical community continues to apply a male model to women's health.

But just as there is overlap in the data for women and men, students can find a startling convergence in women and men who train and push their bodies athletically. A comparison of women's and men's times in competitive running shows both sexes regularly breaking records, but with women gaining on men. Linear models suggest that women could overtake men in the 2032 Olympics (Figure 6.3).

It can be appropriate and compelling to analyze the status of women and men using mathematics, but there should be a reason for sex categories and comparisons. One of the worst sexisms in algebra texts is to pre-

FIGURE 6.1. Height and weight of University of Tampa college algebra students.

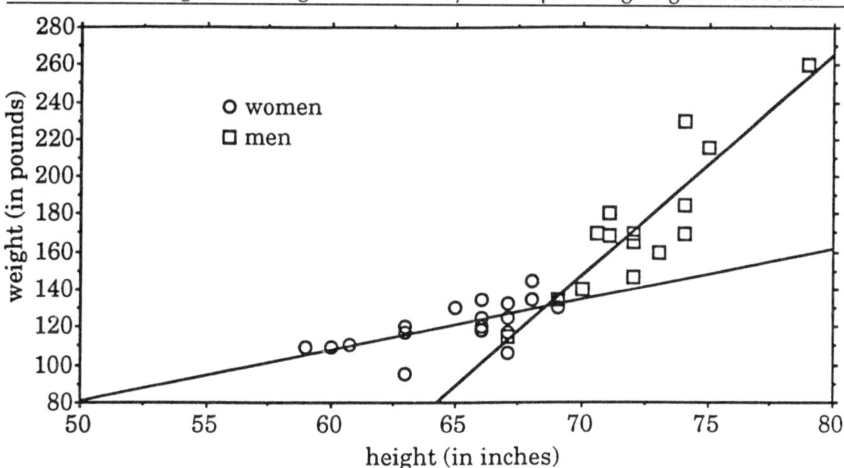

tend that sex categories matter in a context where they clearly do not or to pretend that sex categories are not important in a situation where they obviously are. As long as society uses sex similarities and differences to describe itself, mathematicians will act in response. We feminist mathematicians, however, must recognize that our responses themselves participate in the makeup of society. Consequently, in our classrooms we must expose the fallacy of the male norm.

FIGURE 6.2. Average height and weight of American 20- to 24-year-olds.

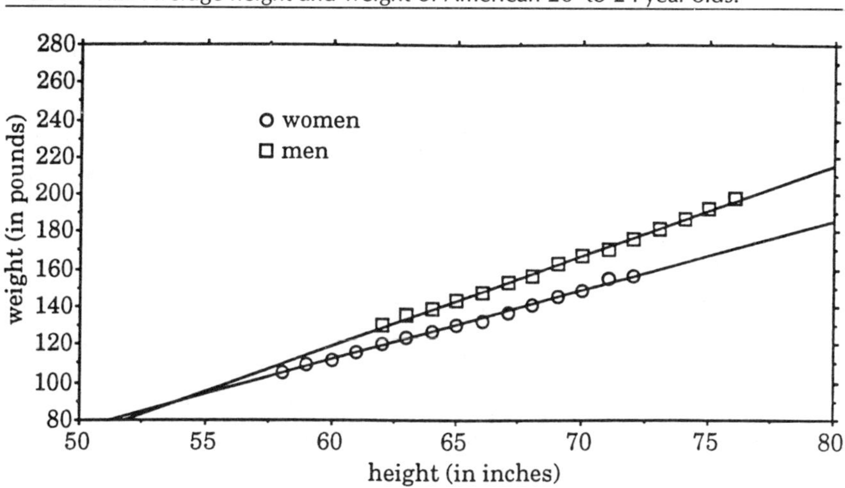

FIGURE 6.3. Olympic 200 meter gold medal times.

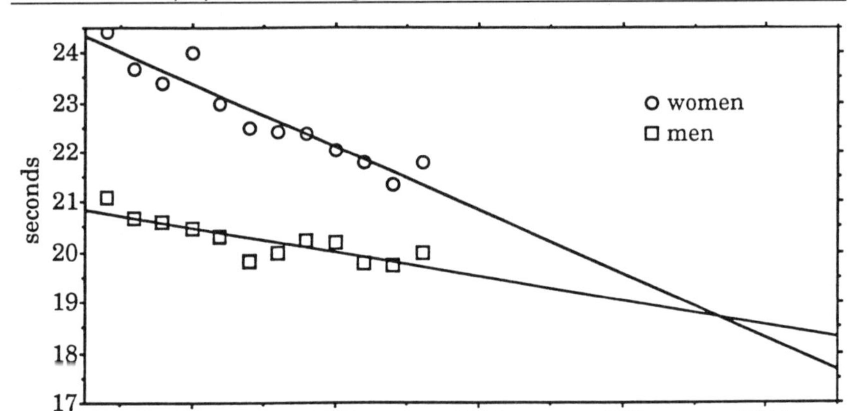

METAPHOR

Metaphor plays a central role in the construction of mathematics as well as the teaching of mathematics. A good metaphor can provide a means for a student to connect a mathematical concept to her or his life. A questionable metaphor can mislead or alienate a student. It is no surprise to feminists that the male-centered metaphors on which mathematics is based disproportionately alienate female students. We mathematicians are responsible for the metaphors we choose, and we need to consider carefully the implications of each one.

Mathematics is often seen as a divine mystery. Religious metaphors can perpetuate this distance by granting the instructor a divine authority. Students are often told to "take this rule on faith." Are we asking for faith in the instructor? The book? Mathematics is often portrayed as an eternal system of rules that one learns to obey rather than as a set of principles constructed and agreed upon by humans as useful. Thus we see a current college algebra book stating matter-of-factly that Euclid's *Elements* is, "next to the Bible, the most influential book ever written" (Fleming, Varberg, & Kasube, 1992, p. 83). A more humble approach would be to show the student not only that she or he can use mathematics each day but also that she or he can construct new mathematical concepts personally.

Images of violence are also endemic in mathematical writing. On the surface level, there are the popular sports metaphors and the less common but still prevalent war metaphors. On deeper levels, metaphors of violence pervade our very approach to mathematics. It is not coincidental, then, that this violence in math is sexually politicized; mathematics is portrayed as a woman whose nature desires to be the conquered Other.

Although metaphors of war are unquestionably violent, sports metaphors are only potentially so. That is, it is not merely the individual sport under discussion that warrants the label of "violent" but also the degree of violence with which it is presented. For example, we have the violence of Project PASS, a multimedia program recently developed by GTE and the National Football League to teach geometry and statistics to seventh graders through football applications (Leggett, 1992, p. 12). But a Bonnie Blair application contains a sports metaphor that we can call up confidently in terms of its nonviolence and its positive valuation of women.

The more systemic violence in mathematics—or at least in our approach to mathematics—runs rampant. One often hears terms like "manipulate," "choose a method to attack the problem," "use brute force," "grind out the answer," "exploit the previous theorem," "the numerator dominates the denominator," and "if you torture the data it will confess" at all levels of mathematics. There is even a recent general interest book called *Conquering Mathematics* (Motz & Weaver, 1991).

It is disappointing and alienating for a college algebra book to introduce chapter 1 with Albert Einstein's quote of his uncle's definition of algebra: "'Algebra is a merry science,' Uncle Jakob would say. 'We go hunting for a little animal whose name we don't know, so we call it *x*. When we bag our game we pounce on it and give it its right name'" (Fleming, Varberg, & Kasube, 1992, p. 2).

To discount the violence in mathematics is to deny the interdependence of science and society, to ignore the responsibility of science—even the "pure science" of mathematics—toward society. Mathematical research has real consequences in society, and its presumed indirectness is no excuse for irresponsible attitudes. One step toward recognizing the implications of mathematics on society is admitting to the social violence that lies in mathematics.

A feminist mathematician realizes that the direction of violence is toward women both socially and in mathematics. This violence toward women plays on the notion of sexual difference (heterosexism) and on its seemingly indigenous devaluation of the Other (women). At the level of college algebra, the battle of the sexes is played out in this modern *Taming of the Shrew*:

> John plans to take his wife Helen out to dinner. Concerned about their financial situation, Helen asks him point-blank, "How much money do you have?" Never one to give a simple answer when a complicated one will do,

> John replies, "If I had $12 more than I have and then doubled that amount, I'd be $60 richer than I am." Helen's response is best left unrecorded. (Fleming, Varberg, & Kasube, 1992, p. 90)

At a deeper level, Bertrand Russell's famous description of mathematics as a "beauty cold and austere" (1917/1957, p. 57) begs the question of the tacit misogyny of the accepted mathematical paradigm. (That it is so famous is strong evidence.) This same violent-romantic juxtaposition comes through eerily in a current text's reassurance about student attitudes toward "word problems": "We want to destroy those mental blocks and give you one of the most satisfying experiences in mathematics" (Fleming, Varberg, & Kasube, 1992, p. 95).

It is the task of feminist mathematicians to examine our own complicity in these attitudes and to look toward an as yet unenvisioned future that is not (hetero)sexist and violent. The established mathematical metaphors can be transformed. A theorem can be useful or "friendly"; there are families and networks of related mathematical concepts. The hope is to replace subtly misogynous attitudes with women-identified attitudes and thereby to engender a socially responsible mathematics.

Male fascination with nuclear war technology brought radioactivity into college algebra as the classic example of exponential decay. All college algebra books include exercises on the half-lives of radioactive elements:

> If a radioactive material decays continuously at the rate of 0.5% per year, determine the half-life of this material; that is, find the time for each gram to decay to one-half of a gram. (Hall, 1992, p. 376)

If radioactivity is included as an example in order to raise scientific literacy, then it makes sense to at least follow through with calculations concerning the safety of nuclear wastes in addition to the usual exercises on archaeological dating (with carbon 14). Better yet, the distance between students and the concept of exponential decay could be reduced dramatically by transforming the war metaphor of radioactivity into the healing metaphor of medicine:

> The half-life of an antibiotic in the bloodstream is about 8 hours. This means that when 64 milligrams of the drug are absorbed in your bloodstream, the number of milligrams D remaining after t hours is given by the function $D = (64)2^{-t/8}$. Graph this function for $t \geq 0$ and find the number of milligrams of the antibiotic remaining in the bloodstream after (a) 0 hours, (b) 8 hours, (c) 16 hours, and (d) 24 hours. (Steffensen & Johnson, 1992, p. 362)

Drug half-lives illustrate the same point about exponential decay that radioactive decay does—but in a more familiar and personal context. Surely drug half-lives deserve equal time with radioactive decay exercises.[1] The question is, should a mathematics text focus on impressing the student with applications to high technology or on connecting the student to the subject matter?

Mathematicians alternate between denying and glorifying the role of metaphor in research and teaching. That metaphor is so important to the construction of mathematics is evidenced by the tedious debate over whether mathematics is "created" or "discovered." In any event, devising new metaphors can serve as a valuable source of connection to people who have not felt welcome in the mathematical world our male-identified system has brought about. An inclusive mathematics for our changing world will incorporate newly imagined metaphors with the increased participation of women and peoples of color at all levels of mathematics.

EMPOWERING WOMEN WITH ALGEBRA

One way to empower women is to allow access to traditionally male-performed tasks. Another way is to depict men in traditionally female-performed roles. Yet another way is to demonstrate the value of women's experiences as lived by women.

One of the reasons that mathematics texts seem so foreign to female students is that the books tend to build on stereotypically male activities such as throwing balls and driving trains rather than on the sort of realistic, day-to-day mathematics that many women and some men are likely to find more interesting and familiar (although they may not necessarily think of those experiences as mathematical). Thus, one major goal of this chapter is to demonstrate that women's experiences—even as lived within our sexist society—contain mathematical sophistication ignored by male-identified mathematicians.

To truly include women, an algebra course must reach the experiences of those women with real applications that students care to answer. Food is a good source of nontrivial(izing) examples. Women are the cultural guardians of food, and word problems about cooking and nutrition can draw on what women already know, thus reinforcing women's capability to perform mathematics well.

A college algebra course often begins with a review of fractions. Fraction properties are wonderfully illustrated by the following problem:

The cake recipe below makes two cocoa layers and one orange layer. Rewrite the recipe to make one cocoa layer and one orange layer.

ORANGE COCOA CAKE

½ cup HERSHEY'S Cocoa
½ cup boiling water
¼ cup (½ stick) butter or margarine, softened
¼ cup shortening
2 cups sugar
⅛ teaspoon salt
1 teaspoon vanilla extract
2 eggs
1½ teaspoons plus ⅛ teaspoon baking soda, divided
1 cup plus 3 tablespoons buttermilk or sour milk, divided*
1¾ cups all-purpose flour
¾ teaspoon grated orange peel
¼ teaspoon orange extract
Orange Buttercream Frosting (recipe follows)

Heat oven to 350° F. Grease three 8- or 9-inch round baking pans; line with wax paper. In small bowl, stir together cocoa and water until smooth; set aside. In large mixer bowl, beat butter, shortening, sugar, salt and vanilla until creamy. Add eggs; beat well. Stir 1½ teaspoons baking soda into 1 cup buttermilk; add to butter mixture alternately with flour. In small bowl, measure 1⅔ cups batter. Stir in remaining ⅛ teaspoon baking soda and 3 tablespoons buttermilk, orange peel and orange extract; pour into one prepared pan. Stir cocoa mixture into remaining batter; divide evenly between remaining two prepared pans. Bake 25 to 30 minutes or until wooden pick inserted in center comes out clean. Cool 10 minutes; remove from pans to wire racks. Cool completely. Place one chocolate layer on serving plate; spread with Orange Buttercream Frosting. Top with orange layer; spread with frosting. Top with remaining chocolate layer; frost entire cake.
10 to 12 servings

*To sour milk: Use 1 tablespoon white vinegar plus milk to equal 1 cup; use ½ teaspoon white vinegar plus milk to equal 3 tablespoons.

ORANGE BUTTERCREAM FROSTING

⅔ cup butter or margarine, softened
6 cups powdered sugar
2 teaspoons grated orange peel
1½ teaspoons vanilla extract
4 to 6 tablespoons milk

In large mixer bowl, beat butter, 1 cup powdered sugar, orange peel and vanilla until creamy. Add remaining powdered sugar alternately with milk, beating to spreading consistency. (*Hershey's Chocolate Classics*, 1988, p. 31.

> [Hershey's is a registered trademark. Recipe courtesy of the Hershey Kitchens and reprinted with permission of Hershey Foods Corporation.])

This is a great critical-thinking exercise because some measurements are halved, some are cut to two thirds, and some are left alone. One University of Tampa student responded to this problem by saying that she appreciated it because it got her started in college algebra with a familiar situation. Another student reported that when her sorority needed to combine two recipes for a bake sale, she knew that she could do it because that was what she had been doing in math class. This example also leads into a discussion of a commercial revision of the recipe, which would require converting and adjusting some of the measurements to make them practical.

Motion problems (and their analogues) and mixture problems are mainstays of college algebra. Consider how the classic principles are illustrated by these household examples:

> A crock pot recipe for baked beans says that they should be cooked on low for 11 hours or on high for 4½ hours. If you have 8 hours in which to cook the beans, how long should they cook on low and how long on high to get the proper amount of heat? (After calculating the exact, algebraic answer, consider how you might go about estimating to arrive at a reasonable approximation.)

> How much full-strength coffee and how much 50%–caffeine coffee would you mix in order to have a pound of coffee with two thirds the usual amount of caffeine?

All students (but especially women) find it enlightening to learn some of the basic formulas of nutrition. Nutritionists tell us that we should watch the percentage of calories from fat in our food. However, labels usually give fat content by weight. Because all fat contains 9 calories per gram (carbohydrates and protein each contain 4 calories per gram), one can set up formulas (Figure 6.4) that can be applied to any food label containing standard nutrition information:

> A 1-cup (226-gram) serving of Campbell's Homestyle Beef Noodle Soup contains 80 calories, 5 grams of protein, 8 grams of carbohydrates, and 3 grams of fat. Compute the percentage of weight that is fat. Also compute the percentage of calories that come from fat.

The same information can be used to illustrate the mathematical definition of matrix multiplication (Figure 6.5).

FIGURE 6.4. Nutrition formulas.

$$(\text{fat cal }\%) = \frac{9\ (\text{fat weight})}{(\text{total cal})} \times 100$$

$$(\text{carb cal }\%) = \frac{4\ (\text{carb weight})}{(\text{total cal})} \times 100$$

$$(\text{prot cal }\%) = \frac{4\ (\text{prot weight})}{(\text{total cal})} \times 100$$

As these nutrition examples show, many food applications can be approached through an understanding of the units of measurement involved. In fact, all students would profit from a greater emphasis on units analysis in algebra, as a means of both setting up equations to solve problems and solving problems outright. However, few algebra books have sections on units.[2]

Cooking situations provide teachers with an accessible means not only of calculating units but also of expressing them accurately and realistically. Only the most inexperienced of cooks would persist in measuring out 6 teaspoons of spice instead of 2 tablespoons. Furthermore, there is a huge difference between 3 cups and 3 ounces; the purpose of precise notation should become unmistakably clear to students.

Consider the following units examples as evidence of the meaningful mathematics that can arise from a woman's experience:

> Maria wants to buy a microwave oven as a housewarming gift for a family member. She wants to get one about the size of the one she has at home, but microwaves are sold by cubic feet, and she no longer knows how big hers is. Maria finds that her microwave measures 11 inches by 15.5 inches by 7.5 inches inside. How many cubic feet is that?

> I often bring a container of yogurt to school for lunch, but recently I started thinking about bringing pudding instead. A 1-cup portion of Breyer's yogurt costs 65¢. On the other hand, I can buy enough Royal pudding mix to make 4 cups for 85¢. Of course, I have to mix

FIGURE 6.5. Nutrition matrices.

$$\begin{array}{r} \\ \\ \text{peanut butter} \\ \text{bread} \\ \text{jelly} \end{array}
\begin{array}{c} \text{fat} \\ (\text{gm}) \\ \\ \\ \\ \end{array}
\left[\begin{array}{ccc} 32 & 12 & 18 \\ 2 & 20 & 8 \\ 0 & 28 & 0 \end{array}\right]
\left[\begin{array}{c} 9 \\ 4 \\ 4 \end{array}\right]
\begin{array}{l} \text{fat} \\ \text{carb} \\ \text{prot} \end{array}
=
\left[\begin{array}{c} 408 \\ 130 \\ 112 \end{array}\right]
\begin{array}{l} \text{peanut butter} \\ \text{bread} \\ \text{jelly} \end{array}$$

Column headings: fat (gm), carb (gm), prot (gm); cal per gm; cal.

> the pudding with 4 cups of my own milk. A gallon (1 gallon = 16 cups) of skim milk costs $2.33. Find the price per cup for pudding. Is it cheaper than yogurt?

Price comparisons are often the first experience people have with units. Using that experience, then, is an effective way to relate mathematical topics:

> A pizza restaurant charges $6.50 for an 8-inch square pizza. The owner is thinking of introducing a 10-inch round pizza. What price should she charge for the round pizza to keep the same price per square inch?

A revealing incident occurred recently when the topic of units came up in college algebra. I (Randall Campbell-Wright) brought a tape measure to class and asked a woman to measure the dimensions of the room so that the class could convert that volume to gallons. She asked me to get someone else to do it, saying that she didn't know how to use the tape measure. In a flash the woman next to her said, "Let me do it with you. You hold one end," and they proceeded to measure the room. (A spontaneous guessing contest ensued in one class to see who could guess the volume of the classroom in gallons. The winners? Two men who own or work with swimming pools.) Our experience has shown that units analysis can be a viable source of connection and empowerment to students.

Another neglected topic in algebra is that of proportions. The usual approaches generally look either dull:

> Find an explicit formula for the dependent variable [if] . . . y varies directly as x, and $y = 12$ when $x = 3$. . . . (Fleming, Varberg, & Kasube, 1992, p. 179)

or disturbing:

> The maximum range of a projectile varies as the square of the initial velocity. If the range is 16,000 feet when the initial velocity is 600 feet per second,
> a) write an explicit formula for R in terms of v, where R is the range in feet and v is the initial velocity in feet per second;
> b) use this formula to find the range when the initial velocity is 800 feet per second. (Fleming, Varberg, & Kasube, 1992, p. 179)

How disappointing! We suggest a question that inevitably perks up students' ears:

> A 7-ounce chocolate bar consists of 16 squares. How many squares should one use in a recipe that calls for 4 ounces of chocolate?

The algebra answer of $x = 9.14$ squares of chocolate leads to the legitimate discussion of whether estimation is as good as algebra in this case. Situations involving proportions call for flexibility from instructors. Students who know how to cook know that although a cake needs a precise amount of leavening to rise effectively, the cook has freedom regarding flavoring ingredients (although still within limits) to suit her or his own taste and ingredient supply. A chili recipe is perhaps the height of flexibility. Of course, there are many compelling examples in any number of household situations:

> Juan's neighbor gives him 62 limes, which Juan squeezes to get 11½ cups of juice. How many limes should Juan ask for to get 25 cups of juice?

The content as well as the presentation of college algebra can be adjusted to make women feel more welcome and to motivate the use of implicit personal experience with mathematical situations. The result can be exactly the sort of empowerment that enables people to approach novel situations confidently.

CONCLUSION

We have attempted in this collection of algebra exercises to fuel the imaginations of feminist teachers who realize that new and affirmative paradigms are needed to replace the limiting stereotypes that are only slowly fading. In this pursuit we join socially conscious scholars such as Frankenstein (1989), whose mathematics review book for adult students addresses a variety of social situations through mathematical analysis. However, this process of paradigm shift is an ongoing project. We have recorded some positive reactions from University of Tampa algebra students (mostly white, mostly middle to upper-middle class) but realize that our own imaginations are limited by our personal experience.

Genuine interaction among an increasingly diverse pool of students and faculty will bring about a reevaluation of ways to build context and metaphor that incorporate factors such as race, religion, sexual preference or orientation, and differing ability in more than just a passing way. It is our fervent hope that our ideas may quickly become outdated by deeper analysis.

Certainly the time has come to look at how the content of mathematics needs to change in order to reflect and to nourish the sensibilities of an increasingly diverse pool of participants. The increasing participation of women and minorities will change the agenda—that is, the questions as well as the answers—of mathematics.

NOTES

1. Our survey of nine college algebra books with a 1992 copyright found 8 medical exercises and 100 radioactivity exercises. Six of those 8 medical exercises were in one book (Steffensen & Johnson, 1992).

2. Our survey of nine college algebra books with a 1992 copyright found no books with a section on units, although Larson, Hostetler, and Munn (1992) do use units better than most authors. Sad to say, none of these books states that the units on both sides of an algebraic equation must be the same.

REFERENCES

Bailey, Gerald D., & Bailey, Gwen L. (1987). Teaching parents how to identify and use sex-equitable instructional materials. *Feminist Teacher, 2*(3), 14–19.

Cooney, Thomas J., & Hirsch, Christian R. (Eds.). (1990). *Teaching and learning mathematics in the 1990s: 1990 yearbook.* Reston, VA: National Council of Teachers of Mathematics.

Fleming, Walter, Varberg, Dale, & Kasube, Herbert. (1992). *College algebra: A problem solving approach* (4th ed.). Englewood Cliffs, NJ: Prentice-Hall.

Frankenstein, Marilyn. (1989). *Relearning mathematics: A different third r—radical math(s).* London: Free Association Books.

Grossman, Stanley I. (1992). *College algebra* (2nd ed.). Fort Worth, TX: Saunders College-Harcourt.

Hall, James W. (1992). *College algebra with applications* (3rd ed.). Boston: PWS-Kent.

Harding, Sandra G. (1986). *The science question in feminism.* Ithaca, NY: Cornell University Press.

Hershey's chocolate classics. (1988). Lincolnwood, IL: Publications International.

Keller, Evelyn Fox. (1985). *Reflections on gender and science.* New Haven, CT: Yale University Press.

Kelly-Benjamin, Kathleen. (1990). *The young women's guide to better SAT scores: Fighting the gender gap.* Toronto: Bantam Books.

Kimball, Meredith M. (1989). A new perspective on women's math achievement. *Psychological Bulletin, 105,* 198–214.

Kogelman, Stanley, & Warren, Joseph. (1978). *Mind over math.* New York: Dial Press.

Larson, Roland E., Hostetler, Robert P., & Munn, Anne V. (1992). *College algebra: Concepts and models.* Lexington, MA: Heath.

Leggett, Anne. (1992). Barbie. *Newsletter of the Association for Women in Mathematics, 22*(6), 12.

McLeod, Douglas B., & Adams, Verna M. (Eds.). (1989). *Affect and mathematical problem solving: A new perspective*. New York: Springer-Verlag.

Motz, Lloyd, & Weaver, Jefferson Hane. (1991). *Conquering mathematics: From arithmetic to calculus*. New York: Plenum.

Rees, Paul K., & Sparks, Fred W. (1969). *Algebra and trigonometry* (2nd ed.). New York: McGraw-Hill.

Rosser, Sue V. (1990). *Female-friendly science: Applying women's studies methods and theories to attract students*. Elmsford, NY: Pergamon Press.

Russell, Bertrand. (1957). *Mysticism and logic*. Garden City, NY: Doubleday Anchor. (Original work published 1917)

Special issue on women in mathematics. (1991). *Notices of the American Mathematical Society, 38*, 701–777.

Steffensen, Arnold R., & Johnson, L. Murphy. (1992). *College algebra: A problem-solving approach* (2nd ed.). New York: HarperCollins.

Tobias, Sheila. (1978). *Overcoming math anxiety*. New York: Norton.

World almanac and book of facts 1993. (1992). New York: Pharos.

Part IV

COMPUTER SCIENCE

CHAPTER 7
Girls and Technology
Villain Wanted

Jo Sanders

Just as with science and mathematics, many girls decline opportunities available to them in K–12 computing. Beginning usually in the middle school grades but sometimes earlier, girls are significantly underrepresented in after-school computer clubs, as computer contest participants, at free-access times using the computers, and in advanced computer electives. They are also underrepresented in relation to other technologies, such as in-school video studios.

Girls who avoid technology in grade school are, to put it mildly, at a disadvantage in college. I have heard stories—no studies yet—that more women than men are uncomfortable with computerized libraries. Is this causing them to do more poorly in research assignments? Women who avoid technology do without the powerful tools of word processing, data bases, graphics, desktop publishing, and others. And of course, women who avoid technology are not very likely to major in science or engineering.

We know that there are considerable gender imbalances in the technical workforce. Here's a quick review of what we know for the computer field.

- Women constitute about one third of all employed computer specialists. The higher the occupational category, the fewer the women.
- In 1991, women earned 16% of the PhDs awarded in computer science (U.S. Department of Education, 1993). In the last decade, they have advanced their share of the PhDs by one third of a percent per year. At this rate, women will achieve parity with men in 110 years, or in our great-great-great-great-great-granddaughters' generation.

In lower-level education, researchers in many small studies have found significant and repeated gender differences in advanced computer course enrollments, free-time use of school computers, computer club membership, and computer contest participation, although there have been no large-scale national studies (Sutton, 1991). Girls are greatly underrepresented in high school advanced placement (AP) computer science courses (Girls Clubs, 1988). The National Assessment of Educational Progress, in the most recent national survey of computer competence and use in schools (Martinez & Mead, 1988), reported that boys demonstrate a higher level of computer competence than girls and that both boys and girls agree that boys like computers more than girls.

Whose fault is this? Why are girls underrepresented in technology programs and courses in school? Well, here are some *non*-reasons.

- Teachers, administrators, and counselors aren't the problem. They don't forbid girls to use the computers or take advanced courses.
- Male teachers aren't the problem, because girls' computer avoidance is seen just as often with female teachers.
- Lack of access isn't the problem—after all, the computers aren't kept in the boys' bathrooms.
- The machine isn't the problem. It works just as well with female fingers and brains as with male.
- And no computer gene has been found.

In my experience, educators often misperceive the nature of the influences that result in lopsided enrollment figures. Although some of them surely ascribe the cause to innate sex differences, most probably assume that girls avoid advanced computing because computer teachers continually say grossly sexist things to them in class, or because counselors urge them to take home economics instead, or because parents aggressively discourage their daughters from taking more than the minimum required. In other words, they assume that a villain exists (Sanders, 1993). Since few teachers personally observe these situations or commit these acts themselves, they are often genuinely puzzled at the overwhelmingly male nature of so many computer clubs, contests, and courses.

I agree that egregious situations of this sort, although they sometimes occur, are rare. Much more common are the subtle influences, the ones most educators miss unless they bring an active feminist orientation with them into school or unless they have been taught to recognize them.

I find the subtleties and trivialities—the "picky things"—fascinating. Individually they have no effect, but cumulatively they cause girls to decline opportunities that are available to them in technology (Sandler & Hall, 1982). The subtle influences do not arise out of an evil male conspiracy to keep girls and women out of computing, math, or science. The notion that the gender imbalance is men's fault has a certain elegant simplicity that is tempting to many, but it is simply not valid.

The truth is far more interesting and complex than that. The overwhelming male presence in computing is a chicken-and-egg issue. Because mostly boys and men use computers, girls conclude that computing is not appropriately feminine, which leads them to decline computing opportunities available to them, which leaves computing environments male, which leads girls to conclude. . . .

Because the subtle influences are cumulatively so powerful and at the same time so often unrecognized, I would like to spend the rest of this chapter tracing them.

THE COMPUTER CULTURE

Computers started as extremely large, complex number-crunching machines, each aspect of which tends to be male-identified. Many of us remember the popular image of the computer 2 or 3 decades ago: a roomful of whirring tapes in tall machines with many incomprehensible dials and knobs, staffed by white men in white lab coats. Both the "machine" aspect and the "esoteric technical" aspect are, of course, male-identified. A decade or so ago, video games became prevalent. At the time, they were called "computer games," which of course they are. Video games started and continue to exist largely as games of conflict, war, and destruction in fantasy environments. Combat as a theme rarely appeals to girls, which is perhaps why Ms. Pacman—married, with children, and distinctly unwarlike—was a notable exception. Indeed, video arcades are typically occupied by young men in their teens and twenties; to the extent that girls are present, they are watching the boys play.

Many essential elements of the computer culture are primarily male. Picture for a moment a computer enthusiast or, in other words a jock, hacker, or computer nerd. I'm sure you aren't visualizing a girl. Instead you are probably thinking of a teenage boy who is thin, wears large glasses, has few friends, and has bad skin.

Computer language, apart from the ferociously in-group nature of the technical jargon, has some features that probably originated with male hackers. To start a computer you "boot" it, with connotations of kicking. A system failure results in a "bomb," that is, it "crashes." You use a "hard" drive with lots of "RAM." And so forth.

Public computer environments, visible to the average person, are largely male. Besides the video arcades, computer stores are also staffed and frequented for the most part by men. I have noticed that computer exhibits in shopping malls show the same pattern. Certainly computer trade shows are put on primarily by men for men, but nonaficionados rarely attend.

User groups—"clubs" of people who use certain kinds of computers and meet to share software and trade information—tend to be mostly male.

T-shirts, the human equivalent of the bumper sticker, tell a great deal about our preoccupations and concerns as a society. At a recent computer education conference, I saw several T-shirts for sale:

- An illustration of a floppy disk, with the words "I may be over 40, but I'm not floppy."
- An illustration of a tousled woman, with the words "Compute, compute, compute! That's all you ever want from me!"

BIT BIT
BYTE BYTE
MEGABYTE MEGABYTE

- The word *bit* was printed at the neckline of the shirt and "megabyte" was printed at the nipple level. Obviously, these shirts appeal to men.

Electronic bulletin boards are excellent places to find misogynist and pornographic material, such as the blonde "jokes" making the rounds on a variety of boards. Some samples:

Dumb
- What do you call a blonde with half a brain?
  Gifted.
- How can you tell when a blonde has used your computer?
  There's whiteout all over the screen.

Cruel
- How do blondes commit suicide?
  They put spikes on their shoulder pads.
- How do you drown a blonde?
  Put a mirror at the bottom of the pool.

Obscene
- What is the best protection against rape?
  Dye your hair blond: no one "rapes" a blonde.
- What does a blonde put behind her ears to attract men?
  Her ankles.

Computer magazines for sale on newsstands cater to and reflect a largely male audience. Photographs and illustrations in articles and especially ads are mostly of men, except for the glamorous women in secretary roles. Nearly all the articles are written by men. Increasingly, computer magazines contain numerous ads for pornographic software.

And speaking of pornographic software: Leisure Suit Larry, who "scores" by seducing as many women as possible in a bar, is now tame stuff. One program illustrates its graphics capabilities by showing a gyrating woman with rotating breasts. Another permits the user to choose among a French maid, a bar girl, and a nun; undress them; and manipulate a throbbing penis in contact with various parts of her body. There are programs called "Sex Vixens From Space" and "Leather Goddesses of Phoebus." Now we have the interactive CD-ROM "Virtual Valerie," which *Newmedia Magazine*, in the April 1993 issue featuring articles on "digital sex," called "an unusual product with tremendous sales" (p. 8). Its editor wrote that the small ads for "adult-oriented CD-ROM titles . . . pull in as much or more response than many of the full-page and double-page ads in our magazine" (p. 8).

This chapter is not the place for a full discussion of "compusex," but clearly it is a growing issue in the computer culture and one that caters to a male audience in a way that, whatever we might think of pornography, is hardly attractive to most women.

PARENTAL FACTORS

Studies have shown that parents buy computers more often for their sons than for their daughters. The National Assessment of Educational Progress survey on computer competence mentioned earlier found that boys' families were more likely to own computers at all three grade levels surveyed (3rd, 7th, and 11th). "In the eleventh grade, boys were 40 percent more likely to have access to a computer at home" (Martinez & Mead, 1988, p. 47). In a survey I carried out, I found that 11% of the girls didn't even use their home computers, as opposed to only 3% of the boys (Sanders, 1985). Moreover, I have often heard that families with children of both sexes place the computer in the son's bedroom.

In addition to buying home computers for their children, parents also buy enrollments to summer computer camps. In a survey of 23 computer camp directors (Miura & Hess, 1983), it was found that female enrollment declined with age, "curriculum" level, and cost. Girls were a third of the computer campers when the tuition cost under $100 but only a sixth when it cost over $1,000.

CURRICULUM FACTORS

The educational software industry has improved greatly since the early days of educational computing. Fewer arcade games adapted to educational purposes are being published. But most school districts have less than princely software acquisition budgets, and they continue to use the old violent, antagonistic software in which correct answers are rewarded by something exploding or in which the central character is a clever, resourceful male person sometimes interacting with an exceedingly stupid female person in need of rescuing. For example, an old but still popular math program shows a male detective searching for clues near a voluptuous "dumb blonde" who is holding a cocktail glass while reclining on a chaise lounge.

There is still a lot of software that pictures males when it needs to picture a person in a neutral context. The telecommunications program I use, for example, signals the telephone-connect stages by showing a man with glasses. A hand holding a telephone has a white shirt cuff and cufflinks below the jacket sleeve. Although this male standard is not actively alienating, it cumulatively reflects the assumption that those who telecommunicate are male.

Then there are classroom programming projects designed purely to exploit the power of the technology. This is not bad per se, of course, but we do know that many girls are drawn to technology and science as solutions for real-world problems such as pollution and disease. When computing is taught as an abstract exercise devoid of meaning and importance to people's lives, it tends to appeal more to boys.

Many schools participate in computing contests, and the magazine *The Computing Teacher* often publishes the results. In one recent article, for example, the winners in the elementary, junior, and senior Pascal divisions and the senior BASIC division were identified (Piele, 1990–1991). All were boys. (Interestingly, all the faculty advisors named were women.) This common pattern communicates to girls that boys do computing, not girls.

Cooperative learning is taking place in computing classrooms across the country, and it will become more prevalent as computers are used as learning tools in other school subjects. Many software titles in mathematics, science, and other areas are now designed to be carried out by small groups of students rather than by a student working alone. Although research has shown that girls prefer and benefit from cooperative learning (Lockheed & Klein, 1985; AAUW, 1992), this approach can boomerang at the computer. In mixed-sex groupings, boys often wind up being the researchers, thinkers, and decision makers, and girls wind up being the note takers and keyboarders (Grossman & Grossman, 1994). This does not promote self-confidence in one's computing skills.

BIASED TEACHER BEHAVIORS

I can't imagine any teacher deliberately setting out to lower girls' achievement, aspirations, and persistence in a subject, yet girls do exhibit lower achievement, aspirations, and persistence in computing as well as in mathematics and science. This reminds me of one of my favorite cartoons, in which a teacher is giving a lesson on human rights and explaining her belief that boys and girls are equal. She is proud of the fact that there is no sex bias in her class. But she reminds Bill that boys don't fiddle with their hair, tells Cynthia that scratching is not ladylike, and insists that Anne shouldn't lift a stool. As she concludes the lesson she sighs with satisfaction: "Oh, it feels so good to have the chance to liberate young people!"

The American Association of University Women (AAUW) report *How Schools Shortchange Girls* identified biased teacher behaviors as a significant factor in the gender gap in science and mathematics:

> Two recent studies find teacher-student interactions in science classes particularly biased in favor of boys. Some mathematics classes have less biased patterns of interaction overall when compared to science classes, but there is evidence that despite the more equitable overall pattern, a few male students in each mathematics class receive particular attention to the exclusion of all other students, male and female. (AAUW, 1992, p. 70)

Although there have been no comparable studies of computer classrooms, I strongly suspect that the same dynamics are at work: Computers are as male-identified as math and science, and girls are as underrepresented in computer courses as they are in math and science. The teacher behaviors that have been documented are (Sadker & Sadker, 1982; AAUW, 1992; Klein, 1985):

- Calling on boys more than girls
- Accepting boys' called-out answers more than girls'
- Waiting longer for boys' answers
- Asking boys more interpretive questions and girls more fact or yes-or-no questions
- Giving girls more neutral responses ("okay," "uh-huh"), and boys more complex responses
- Giving boys more attention, both positive and negative
- Positioning their bodies more toward boys
- Circulating more to boys' desks
- When students have difficulty completing tasks, giving boys suggestions for how to solve problems but solving girls' problems for them ("learned helplessness")

Biased teacher behavior can be as inadvertent as the following true story, which occurred to the daughter of a friend. With much trepidation, she decided to take advanced physics despite the fact that she would be the only girl in the class. Shortly after the beginning of the term, she was walking down the hallway with some of her advanced physics classmates when her physics teacher from the preceding year came upon them. "Ah, here they are," he called out cheerfully, "the advanced physics group . . . and the advanced physics groupette!" Already uncomfortable at being the only girl, she felt singled out and embarrassed and dropped the course shortly thereafter. Although the incident cannot be said to have caused her to drop out, it nevertheless helped tip the scale in that direction. Nor can the teacher be said to have intended this to happen; indeed, he was probably completely unaware that his words had any effect at all and probably even intended to congratulate her. Nevertheless, against the background of her lack of self-confidence concerning her role in the class, she took his words as negative.

PEERS' ATTITUDES

A few years ago, I did a study on girls' attitudes about computer use at the middle school–junior high level (Sanders, 1985). I found that it wasn't the predominantly male cast of the computer room that kept girls away, as I had thought, but rather the absence of their girlfriends. This is a subtle but significant difference, since the presence of a few important girlfriends would make the environment far more attractive. Their need for same-sex peers at this age is apparently extremely strong. By the same token, girls also reported that their girlfriends' lack of interest in computing was far more powerful in discouraging their computer use than any other factor.

We must also remember the visual impact on a girl looking at a computer room full of boys. Particularly in the earlier grades, I have heard many reports from teachers of boys expressing their enthusiasm for computers by pushing girls out of the way and even off the chairs. And when boys make disparaging remarks about girls' computer ability or sexist "jokes," which teachers fail to challenge and prohibit, the computer environment can be extremely unpleasant for girls.

Individually, each incident of the sort I've described above is nothing. Several are nothing. It is when the incidents form patterns, day after day, week after week, year after year, that girls get the—entirely unintended—message: You do not belong in computing (or math or science). The message becomes a self-fulfilling prophecy.

I have a personal interest in the subtle, cumulative influences that make girls drop out of computing, math, and science. I dropped out of math and science as a girl and have regretted it ever since. Having done very well in math in high school, I signed up for calculus in college. Those were the early days of "programmed learning," which at that time meant a book with questions on the left side of the page, answers on the right, and a plastic flap that slid up and down to uncover the answers as you progressed. I ground to a halt at the place where the concept of a limit was introduced. I retraced a few steps but still could not understand how the answer was obtained. Now I realize that the problem was a fault in the writing, but at the time, I thought that there was something wrong with my math ability. I went to see the professor, who for all intents and purposes said, "There, there. Many students have trouble getting the idea of a limit." I do not recall his saying "many girls," but I doubt that he would have let a male student off as easily. I learned the rest of the material as best as I could by rote memory, got a humiliating C as my final grade, and never took another math course.

From my adult perspective, the end of my science career is even sadder. I had taken 5 years of science in high school and loved it. In college I signed up for genetics and did well. In the final exam, the professor—a colorless, rather boring sort—asked a colorless, boring, but complex question, the answer to which required knowledge of much of the course material. I knew it thoroughly and decided to answer the question in a more interesting way, so I wove the answer into an elaborate story I made up about butterflies. I was proud of my ingenuity: Now here was a blue book the professor would enjoy reading! I couldn't wait to see his reaction. When I got the exam back and saw an "A" written on it with no further comment, I was crushed. The butterfly story had been my attempt to individualize and personalize the science. By ignoring it, the professor effectively insisted on the anonymity of science as well as my own—something that I was uncomfortable with and could not accept. I never took another science course.

It is clear to me now that I must have been looking for reasons to drop math and science. These were awfully slim reasons, but obviously any reason would do. This was especially so in science: The professor did nothing at all to discourage me, just failed to encourage me. When the deck is stacked, however, doing nothing can be enough to achieve the predictable result.

Although I've tried, I can't remember any precursors to my readiness to drop those courses. I was good at math and science, enjoyed them, and earned excellent grades, but something subtle must have made me doubt my ability or my desire to continue. I certainly remember feeling relieved when I dropped them, as if an unstable or inappropriate situation had been corrected, as if I'd gotten too far out on a limb and was retreating to a safer place. Another thing that strikes me is the pain of failure and loss I recall to this day in each experience—pain that I have discovered is shared by other women, sometimes to the point of tears, with stories of their own about computing, math, or science.

WE CAN STEM THIS TIDE

The subtle male-associated or male-dominated influences I've described—the computer culture, parental factors, curriculum factors, biased teacher behaviors, and peers' attitudes—are real, but they don't have to be determinative.

From 1990 to 1993, I directed the Computer Equity Expert Project[1] in which 200 K–12 educators, representing every state, learned about girls' avoidance of computing, math, and science and provided training to their faculty members to change it (Sanders & McGinnis, 1991a, 1991b). Here are some of the results in computer courses and extracurricular activities at participating schools that occurred over a year and a half or less:

- In New York, the ratio of girls to boys in the computer lab after school was 2:25 before the project. Now it's 1:1.
- In Oregon, programming went from 23% female before the project to 35% after. Advanced programming went from 0% to 65% female.
- In Pennsylvania, the before-and-after female enrollment figures are: computer applications, 45% to 55%; BASIC, 40% to 52%; Pascal, 30% to 41%.
- In South Carolina, female enrollment in programming went from 30% to 57%.
- In Kansas, female enrollment in advanced computer courses rose 134%.
- In Virginia, the AP Pascal class went from 0% to 50% girls, and female membership in the computer club is up 30%.

I could cite dozens of such examples. Similar results occurred for math and science. The 200 trainers achieved these remarkable outcomes by learning and then conveying to their colleagues an understanding of the subtle forces described above. This is an approach that works extremely well in educational groups because it removes the blame that is often attached to educators whose female students accomplish less than boys in technology, math, and science. And as we have seen, much of the blame is misplaced, since few of the discouraging influences are deliberate or even conscious. Another advantage is that men (as well as women) begin to care about helping to solve the computer gender gap, which they can't realistically be expected to do when they are being blamed for keeping innocent, defenseless little girls out of computing on purpose!

Of course, it's not enough to know—you have to do. To accomplish the successes they had, the trainers and their colleagues carried out a stunning array of hundreds of strategies designed to reverse the message girls receive from so many quarters that they don't belong in computing, math, or science. Here is a small selection of what they did in computing:

- Identified summer programs in computing and urged girls to participate.
- Held a Saturday "Computer Brunch" for girls and an adult female of their choice, with food donated by local businesses.
- Started a computer club for girls in a middle school.
- Had girls staff the computer booths at Open School Night for parents and showed gender-equity videos near the food table.
- Invited women engineers to speak to students.
- Issued personal invitations to girls to join the rocketry club.
- Accompanied girls to an engineering fair at a local university, where the tour guides through the facilities were female engineering students.
- Recruited girls for a middle school computer video crew.
- Started an equity team composed of girls who teach younger children keyboarding and word processing.
- Helped girls do the annual student yearbook in multimedia format.

Beyond these strategies, all of which worked just fine, I'd like to add a few principles for educators to keep in mind. After all, educators are the ones in the best position to counteract the "computing is male" message sent to girls.

1. Teach technology as a tool to solve real-life problems rather than as a glitzy toy.
2. Do not permit sexist materials, "jokes," or behavior in your classroom, ever.
3. Notice the girls who hang back and pull them in, and make sure that girls take their turns at more than keyboarding and note taking.
4. Encourage girls to participate in friendship groups at the computer.
5. Eliminate biased teaching behaviors you may have by becoming conscious of them.[2]
6. Make a point of praising girls for real achievements and urging them to develop their skills further. Urge the especially talented ones to consider careers in technology.
7. Be aware of the little, picky, trivial things and keep them from adding up. Teach your colleagues how to recognize them too.

The end of my story is that not all educational progress in gender equity needs to be dramatic. It doesn't always have to be evaluated to death, or be in the form of an official directive from the school board, or require specialists with multiple degrees, or even be expensive. It is possible to make a profound difference in girls' lives just by paying attention to the little things in school. I think that's pretty nice to know.

NOTES

1. The Computer Equity Expert Project was funded for $1.1 million by the National Science Foundation, IBM, Hewlett Packard, Intel, Xerox, American Express, Westinghouse, and Chevron and was conducted at Women's Action Alliance, New York.

2. The GESA program—Gender/Ethnic Expectations, Student Achievement—developed by Dolores Grayson from Canyon Lake, California, has had much success in teaching teachers how to become aware of and eliminate biased behaviors in the classroom.

REFERENCES

American Association of University Women. (1992). *How schools shortchange girls.* Washington, DC: AAUW Educational Foundation.

Girls Clubs. (1988, April). Press release.

Grossman, Herbert, & Grossman, Suzanne. (1994). *Gender issues in education.* Boston: Allyn & Bacon, pp. 132–137.

Lockheed, Marlaine E., & Klein, Susan S. (1985). Sex equity in classroom organization and climate. In Susan S. Klein (Ed.), *Handbook for achieving sex equity through education* (pp. 189–217). Baltimore: Johns Hopkins University Press.

Martinez, Michael E., & Mead, Nancy A. (1988). *Computer competence: The first national assessment.* Princeton, NJ: Educational Testing Service.

Miura, Irene, & Hess, Robert D. (1983). Sex differences in computer access, interest and usage. Paper presented at the American Psychological Association Conference, Anaheim, CA.

Piele, Donald T. (1990–1991, December/January). A decade of digital dexterity: 1990 ICPSC results. *The Computing Teacher,* 33–35.

Sadker, Myra Pollock, & Sadker, David Miller. (1982). *Sex equity handbook for schools* (2nd ed.). New York: Longman.

Sanders, Jo. (1985, April). Making the computer neuter. *The Computing Teacher,* 23–27.

Sanders, Jo. (1993, September). Closing the gender gap. *The Executive Educator,* 32–33.

Sanders, Jo, & McGinnis, Mary. (1991a). *Computer equity in math and science.* New York: Scarecrow Press.

Sanders, Jo, & McGinnis, Mary. (1991b). *What is computer equity?* New York: Scarecrow Press.

Sanders, Jo, & Stone, Antonia. (1986). *The neuter computer: Computers for girls and boys*. New York: Scarecrow Press.

Sandler, Bernice, & Hall, Roberta M. (1982). *The classroom climate: A chilly one for women?* Washington, DC: Project on the Status and Education of Women.

Sutton, Rosemary E. (1991). Equity and computers in the schools: A decade of research. *Review of Educational Research, 61*(4), 475–503.

U.S. Department of Education. (1993). In *Chronicle of Higher Education*, June 2, p. A25.

CHAPTER 8

Accommodating Diversity in Computer Science Education

Caroline M. Eastman

As instructors we deal with large numbers of students. They come from many backgrounds and groups. The institutions we work for must attend to the needs of different groups and monitor differences in performance. But as instructors we face individuals, not groups. The diversity among individuals transcends their group memberships. Women differ among themselves; so do men. Instructors must be aware of actions that can have differential effects on different groups of students. But differences in group means do not allow us to draw firm conclusions about specific individuals.

The problems inherent in accommodating and encouraging women in computer science can thus be viewed as a special case of accommodating diversity in all our students. Some of the approaches and techniques recommended here are specific to the discipline of computer science, but almost all apply equally to other computing disciplines, including computer engineering, computer and information science, and management information systems, and most are applicable to any scientific discipline. Although the focus of this chapter is undergraduate education in computer science, many of the comments and suggestions are applicable at the graduate level as well.

STUDENT DIVERSITY

There are many dimensions to student diversity, including not only gender, race, and ethnic background but also differences in personal and career goals, language abilities, physical abilities, and sexual orientation. All these differences can influence the approaches and skills students bring to the study of computer science.

Gender

Males and females differ in their use of computers and their approaches to course work. There is some evidence that females prefer different examples and kinds of software and do better if given the opportunity for collaborative rather than competitive work (Turkle, 1984). Turkle (1984) discusses styles of computer use by children, distinguishing between children who approach the computer as an object to control and children who approach the computer as an entity to collaborate with. She found that girls often adopt the collaborative approach and boys often adopt the controlling approach.

Perspectives focusing on college-level education are given by Frenkel (1990) and Pearl et al. (1990). They present a variety of reasons for relatively low numbers of women in computer science; these include the use of gender-biased software, problems with self-esteem, limited computer resources in schools, educational environments that tend to favor males, and gender discrimination in both education and employment. Frenkel (1990) and Moses (1993) discuss the recent decline in the percentage of females enrolled in computer science programs. It appears that we are losing ground in attracting and retaining female computer science students.

Race

Students of different races may also differ in their computer backgrounds and their approaches to course work. However, racial differences in this area have not been as extensively studied as gender differences. In many regions, race has an impact on precollege educational opportunities to use computers and thus influences the background that students bring to college work. Gruman (1990) addresses the problems of both women and minorities in computer science. Frenkel (1990) briefly discusses minority students.

Olognunju (1991) describes a longitudinal study of black computer science students at a historically black institution; many of the results might be relevant to other kinds of institutions as well. Positive factors supportive of student success included a variety of role models (including guest lecturers), the opportunity for professional activities and honors in student organizations, and the opportunity for collaborative work in courses and cooperative education. Negative factors included inadequate computer resources, limited computer access, and limited course availability. Some of these areas can be addressed even when funding is limited.

Ethnic Background and National Origin

Students from different ethnic groups and cultures may have different approaches to and attitudes about learning. Many computer science students, especially at the graduate level, are foreign students. Language background and attitude toward education may vary from group to group. Yahya (1992) provides an overview of some of the issues involved. The emphasis is on differences in language backgrounds, the use of different alphabets, expectations about computer interfaces and interactions, and differences in social and legal environments with respect to computers.

Personal and Career Goals

College students have a variety of personal and career goals. They may place different emphases on family and career. Some may be interested in research careers, others in more applied areas. Course work should accommodate a variety of career goals, and students should be encouraged to formulate their own goals.

Language Ability

Many computer science students initially perceive technical majors as requiring low levels of communication skills. However, they eventually discover that extensive written and oral communication is required of most computer professionals. Computer systems require extensive documentation and user manuals; the process of software development requires both written documentation and oral presentations. Diversity in language abilities should be recognized, and students should be helped to improve their communication skills.

Physical Ability

Some students have disabilities of various kinds and may need specific accommodations, including special equipment. Even students who are not officially classified as handicapped have different levels of physical abilities. For example, some computer equipment is designed for right-handed people and is more difficult for left-handed people to use.

Sexual Orientation

I am not aware of any studies indicating potentially significant differences in attitudes or approaches to the study of computer science that are related to sexual orientation. However, instructors should be aware of differences in student sexual orientation when selecting examples and assignments. An example involving a database for a heterosexual dating service may cause some students to feel excluded.

ACCOMMODATING DIVERSITY

There are a number of approaches that can be used to accommodate student diversity in computer science classes. Some are specific to the discipline of computer science; others are of more general applicability.

Platform Flexibility

In some computer science courses involving computer work, it is essential that all students use the same hardware and software for assignments. This is more likely to be the case in introductory courses or in courses introducing specific languages or systems. However, in other courses, more flexibility may be possible. Allowing students a greater choice of computer systems and possibly even programming languages gives them a wider selection of times and locations for work; some may even be able to work at home.

One semester I taught a compiler course offered to both graduate and undergraduate students. I allowed students a choice of languages (C or Pascal) and a choice of hardware platforms (PC's or departmental minicomputers). This flexibility resulted in a much higher rate of successful completion, especially for undergraduates, than is usually the case when fewer options are allowed. I am currently teaching an introductory course in which several students are using their PC's for much of the course work. They have a variety of motives, including the facilitation of child care.

Collaborative Work

In a typical computer science curriculum, there is usually at least one course (software engineering) that requires an extensive group project. A small group of students designs and implements a software system. They must work both with one another and with potential users. This may be the only group assignment in the curriculum.

Increased use of group and collaborative work in the computer science curriculum is currently being recommended for pedagogical reasons. For example, Wilson, Hoskin, and Nosek (1993) present evidence of improved performance when group work was used in a database course.

Many of the problems involved in software design and development are essentially communication problems; these are best encountered in group activities. However, this curricular change also has the potential of improving our ability to accommodate student diversity. Some students may learn better from the structured interaction required to work in pairs and teams. Students also have the opportunity to improve interpersonal skills.

However, some students learn best from individual work, so a mixture of individual and collaborative assignments should be used. I once gave an assignment in an advanced course that could be done either individually or in pairs, at the students' option; neither choice resulted in a grade advantage. In a class of 40 students, 16 chose to work individually and 24 chose to work in pairs. Four of the female students worked individually; two worked with male partners, and two worked with each other.

Students may fall into stereotypical roles in group work. It is important to structure assignments to ensure that students play a variety of roles. Instructors may either assign students to groups or allow them to choose their own. Often a middle ground allows students to work with others with compatible schedules and ensures that all students have partners or groups.

Examples and Assignments

Computer science is a technical discipline. Most of the material presented in courses involves systems, languages, algorithms, and proofs, which are gender neutral. However, presentation of this technical material often involves the use of examples. The examples may involve data, such as an employee database, or algorithms selected from a particular domain. It is important to use examples that represent a diversity of human interests and experiences in order to capture student interest and make all students feel comfortable (Rosser, 1990). This applies both to examples used in texts and to examples developed by the instructor.

Text and reference materials containing sexist language and examples should be avoided. I have rejected potential textbooks because they used blatantly sexist examples; it is important to provide feedback to publishers about such problems. Fortunately, books that are explicitly sexist are less common than they used to be. However, many books now contain more subtle sexism (Rosser, 1990). For example, it may be difficult to avoid computer science texts that use generic masculine pronouns.

Closely related to the choice of examples is the selection of problems for programming assignments. Some assignments involve fairly abstract problems, and others involve specific application domains. In many cases, an assignment can be structured either way. For example, sorting is studied in intermediate courses. An assignment to implement a sorting algorithm could use as data a list of integers, a list of words, or a list of employee surnames. The first case would be relatively neutral; the second and third might not be.

Scheduling Constraints

Adequate time should be given for all assignments. Giving programs and other assignments to students without sufficient time to complete them may well disadvantage students with extensive outside commitments. Although the time allowed should be somewhat more than the minimum required, excessive time may simply encourage students to put the work off until shortly before the due date. It would be interesting to collect data on actual assignment completion times and relate these to student characteristics. I am not aware of any studies investigating this issue specifically, but it would be easier to conduct such studies in computer science than in other fields because computer-based assignments are easy to track (by computer!).

In many cases, computer assignments must be completed in specific laboratory areas. It is important to ensure that adequate facilities are available to avoid excessive contention in which less assertive students may lose out. All students should feel safe and comfortable working in the labs. If the labs are located in an area where night access is problematic, adequate day hours should be provided. Also, sufficient lab hours should be available so that students with various outside commitments can find enough convenient hours.

Advising and Other Student Interactions

Studies indicate that females are more likely than males to become discouraged by academic problems and to attribute their problems to their own personal shortcomings (Pearl et al., 1990; Rosser, 1990). All students should receive appropriate feedback about their work, including positive comments about work well done and negative comments about work that is incorrect or needs improvement. If there are problems, constructive comments should be made for improvement. Encouragement and support are important both outside and inside the classroom.

Communication Skills

Most computer science students readily acknowledge the importance of learning to communicate with computers. However, the design, development, and use of computer systems also involves communication with other people. Computer science students must have the opportunity to develop both oral and written communication skills. In most undergraduate programs, there is a required software engineering project course that involves both extensive written documentation and presentations. Other courses, however, usually provide little or no opportunity to work on communication skills. Such opportunities should be provided throughout the curriculum. Short written assignments or presentations can be incorporated into most computer science courses. Pesante (1991) discusses some of the issues involved.

Mentors and Role Models

The importance of role models for students is well documented. However, most computer science departments in the United States and elsewhere have relatively few female faculty and even fewer minority faculty. The levels are generally below those needed to ensure full gender and racial integration (Kanter, 1977), and they provide an insufficient diversity of examples to students.

One woman faculty member is only one woman; she has specific strengths and interests that differ from those of other women. It is useful for students to be exposed to a variety of role models who represent different professional and personal options. For example, I am currently the only female faculty member in a small computer science department. I am married, white, and do not have children; my research area is information systems. I am not in a position to offer a personal example of how to balance the often competing demands of children and career.

One way to compensate for low numbers of female and minority faculty is to use female and minority teaching assistants and adjuncts. In addition, many women and minorities work in the computer field in various capacities; they can be invited to give guest lectures and colloquia. Some female students might benefit from participation in Systers, an electronic network group for women only.

Of course, faculty can and should mentor and support students unlike themselves. None of us are dealing with clones of ourselves. Women need to support all students, not just females. Myers (1992) presents suggestions and advice for male faculty who want to be more supportive of female students.

Social and Ethical Issues

Social and ethical issues associated with computers and computing are usually covered in computer science curricula. Many of the technological changes in this area have differential impacts on different groups. For example, women have been more likely than men to suffer medical problems resulting from extended use of computer terminals. Computer equipment and facilities are not equally available to all segments of society, and it is not clear whether these differences exacerbate already existing differences. Computers are often anthropomorphized, frequently with male personas. Females and males may well have different perceptions of ethical issues presented by computers, reflecting more general differences in ethical attitudes. Considerations such as these should be incorporated in course discussions of social and ethical issues.

CONCLUSIONS

Many of the recommendations made here with the goal of accommodating diversity are consistent with current trends in computer science curricula (Denning et al., 1988, 1989; Tucker et al., 1990). For example, there is increased emphasis on laboratory exercises, including closed labs. Closed labs are structured laboratory assignments (usually involving programming or program use) designed to be completed during a scheduled laboratory period. They provide an alternative to the commonly used open lab assignments, typically involving a program to be completed at the student's convenience and handed in later. Closed labs may provide increased opportunities for collaborative activities, although open labs may also be done collaboratively. In addition, many females (and males) might appreciate the structured time frame for a closed lab, which contrasts with a traditional programming assignment.

Making the effort to accommodate student diversity can benefit all students. For example, I used a large type size in handouts in a course to accommodate a visually impaired student. The resulting materials were easier for everyone to read (including me), and I have continued to use large type sizes. Providing more diversity in educational activities should help all students without disadvantaging any of them.

REFERENCES

Denning, Peter J., Comer, Douglas E., Gries, David, Mulder, Michael C., Tucker, Allen, Turner, A. Joe, & Young, Paul R. (1988). *Report of the ACM task force on the core of computer science*. New York: ACM Press, Association for Computing Machinery.

Denning, Peter J., Comer, Douglas E., Gries, David, Mulder, Michael C., Tucker,

Allen, Turner, A. Joe, & Young, Paul R. (1989). Computing as a discipline. *Communications of the ACM, 32*(1), 9–23.

Frenkel, Karen A. (1990). Women and computing. *Communications of the ACM, 33*(11), 34–46.

Gruman, Galen. (1990, July). Getting women and minorities into computer science. *IEEE Software*, 87–89, 92.

Kanter, Rosabeth Moss. (1977). *Men and women of the corporation*. New York: Basic Books.

Moses, Louise E. (1993). Our computer science classrooms: Are they "friendly" to female students? *SIGCSE Bulletin, 25*(3), 3–12.

Myers, J. Paul, Jr. (1992). Men supporting women computer science students. *Proceedings of the Twenty-Third SIGCSE Technical Symposium on Computer Science Education. SIGCSE Bulletin, 24*(1), 63–66.

Ologhunju, Amos O. (1991). The plight of a minority in computer science: An educational manifesto. *SIGCSE Bulletin, 23*(1), 219–225.

Pearl, Amy, Polloack, Martha E., Riskin, Eve, Thomas, Becky, Wolf, Elizabeth, & Wu, Alice. (1990). Becoming a computer scientist. *Communications of the ACM, 33*(11), 47–57.

Pesante, Linda Hutz. (1991). Integrating writing into computer science curricula. *SIGCSE Bulletin, 23*(1), 205–209.

Rosser, Sue V. (1990). *Female-friendly science: Applying women's studies methods and theories to attract students*. Elmsford, NY: Pergamon Press.

Tucker, Allen B., Barnes, Bruce H., Aiken, Robert M., Barker, Keith, Bruce, Kim B., Cain, J. Thomas, Conry, Susan E., Engel, Gerald L., Epstein, Richard G., Lidtke, Doris K., Mulder, Michael C., Rogers, Jean B., Spafford, Eugene H., & Turner, A. Joe. (1990). *Computing curricula 1991: Report of the ACM/IEEE-CS joint curriculum task force*. New York: ACM Press, *IEEE* Computer Society Press.

Turkle, Sherry. (1984). *The second self: Computers and the human spirit*. New York: Simon & Schuster.

Wilson, Judith D., Hoskin, Nathan, & Nosek, John T. (1993). The benefits of collaboration for student programmers. *Proceedings of the Twenty-Fourth SIGCSE Technical Symposium on Computer Science Education. SIGCSE Bulletin, 25*(1), 160–164.

Yahya, Adnan H. (1992). Local considerations in computer science curricula development. *SIGCSE Bulletin, 24*(1), 123–128.

CHAPTER 9
Attracting and Retaining Women in Graduate Programs in Computer Science

Noni McCullough Bohonak

Increasing the number of women and minorities in graduate computer science programs is important for the health of American technology and for social justice. With technology moving faster than ever before, the United States must meet the demand for science researchers and educators. To meet this demand, it is important that all talented students be encouraged and allowed to excel.

WHY SHOULD WE INCREASE THE NUMBER OF WOMEN?

The number of women and minorities completing graduate computer science programs does not seem to be increasing (National Science Foundation [NSF], 1990c). The pipeline that supplies American women and minorities to graduate programs in computer science begins at the moment of birth for every female and minority child and ends at the beginning of graduate school. The number of women who complete a graduate degree in computer science at the PhD level is only a trickle compared to the number that should have entered the pipeline (Alper, 1993).

Data have been collected about the status of scientists in the United States by the NSF (1990a, 1990b, 1990c, 1992) and Gries and Marsh (1992). These studies looked at the number of women, minorities, and men entering undergraduate through graduate programs in science, mathematics, and engineering. Of the many studies on women in computer science, the annual Taulbee survey (Gries & Marsh, 1992) seems to be the most well known because it appears in several important publications. It is recognized by computer professionals to reflect the status of computer science education for the year in which the study was conducted. In the statistics collected for the 1989–1990 Taulbee survey (Gries & Marsh, 1992), the percentage of women who earned PhDs remained constant in the 10–14% range. African Americans remained at 1% and Hispanics at 2%.

Data collected by the NSF (1992) around the same time found that the number of women who earned PhDs in the years 1980 through 1990 increased, but those who held citizenship in the United States actually dropped from 86% to 74%. The Taulbee study and the other NSF reports cited earlier confirm that there was a large increase in the number of foreign students earning PhDs. Apparently, American women continue to avoid graduate computer science programs, at least at the PhD level.

WHAT IS GOING ON ALONG THE PIPELINE?

According to the American Association of University Women (AAUW) study (Horwitz, 1992) and the work of the Sadkers (cited in Manning, 1994), most girls have already lost interest in mathematics and science before entering high school. When they enter college, they are poorly prepared in the background needed to handle a difficult program in science, mathematics, or engineering. This should change as more programs are introduced to encourage girls and minority students to study those subjects once avoided by them. Although we occasionally hear or see expressions of optimism for the future, it may be too early to detect any change for girls. *USA Today* (Kelly, 1993) reports that minorities are showing some gains at the K–12 level.

Working to increase the number of female students entering undergraduate computer science programs is important. But what happens once they have enrolled in a program? Undergraduate computer science programs have not been receiving the same attention as some engineering programs. There have been several successful programs that involve the attraction and retention of female and minority engineering students. Programs similar to the California Minority Engineering Program (Fields, 1987) have been successful in retaining both female and male minority engineering students by using tutoring and special support. Although such programs look as if they are segregating female and minority students from the traditionally white male engineering population, they are really designed to prepare students to interact with groups in which they have not had much experience as equals.

A report on the problems of women engineers by Saigal (1987) indicates that the more the white male majority is exposed to women and minorities in the sciences, the greater the acceptance of them. Interaction with women and increased numbers of women result in less prejudice toward them. In situations in which there are only one or two women versus larger groups of women, a greater amount of male prejudice has been found. Saigal also notes that, when men attain doctorates, their prejudices toward women are lessened. Although single-sex education may benefit females and produce twice as many women science doctorates as coeducation (Tidball, as cited in Ivey, 1987), it does not teach the students how to interact with the other sex. The technique of segregating students must be balanced carefully with the integration and education of all students as part of a group.

WHAT ABOUT NONTRADITIONAL STUDENTS?

Nontraditional students, including women and minorities, can also be entered into special programs and eventually graduate with a terminal degree in computer science. Nontraditional students are usually classified as students who are older than 25. In 1984, the University of California at Berkeley (UC–Berkeley, 1991) recognized that there was a national shortage of women and minority computer scientists and believed that an increase in diversity among computer scientists would be beneficial. Based on the belief that there were many women and minorities who lacked the technical and mathematics courses required for a graduate program, a unique reentry program was started. Among the types of support given were free tuition, free tutoring, and an equipment loan program. Students were not only advised on undergraduate matters but were also helped by advisors through the graduate school application process.

Unlike many reentry programs of the early 1980s, this program was not designed to place people in jobs, and it was not designed to prepare students for the UC–Berkeley graduate computer science program. The goal of the program was to help students enroll in graduate computer science programs at highly ranked universities throughout the United States. Once in the program, the students were given rigorous classes in the core computer science curriculum. Depending on the student's background and any work and family commitments, the normal course load was two courses each semester for a total of three semesters. This was considered full time because of the intense nature of the courses.

The UC–Berkeley report indicates that 43 students had completed the program by May 1991, with 34 admitted to graduate programs. Many were offered fellowships or teaching assistantships normally reserved for the top graduate students in a program. Students have been accepted at Stanford, MIT, Carnegie-Mellon, UCLA, UC–Davis, UC–Santa Cruz, Oregon Graduate Center, Brown, Dartmouth, Rutgers, and the Universities of Illinois, Washington, Texas, Wisconsin, Arizona, Colorado, and Michigan. No information was given about the success of these students. Some type of follow-up indicating their success or failure and any problems encountered would be of use to evaluate this type of program. The program still exists today with some modifications, and it is a good model for anyone wanting to start such a program to prepare students for graduate school. But it is important that, once these students actually enter a graduate program, they graduate. Unfortunately, the nature of many of our computer science programs makes it difficult for both traditional and nontraditional students to succeed. This is especially true for women.

WHAT ABOUT SPECIAL PROGRAMS?

Matyas and Malcom (1991) looked at several programs to see whether they had any features designed specifically for the recruitment and retention of undergraduate women in sciences. In addition, they looked at what is being done to recruit and retain graduate students and faculty. Of the programs studied, less than 10% had any specific feature for the recruitment and retention of undergraduate women in science. When such a program component did exist, special fees were charged and the workers were faculty volunteers rather than trained professionals. The number of programs for graduate students was even smaller in scale, with efforts aimed mostly at recruitment or some type of financial support. They did find that there was some active recruitment of faculty members. However, the concept of an interactive support system for both graduate students and faculty did not exist. Once women arrive on campus as new graduate students or faculty, they are left to handle a system that may be so unfriendly that they leave.

DOES THE TRADITIONAL PhD PROGRAM NEED CHANGING?

Brownhill (1989) listed some gender-related issues that she believes discourage women from entering PhD programs. Among these issues was the "unfriendly environment" that exists for many women seeking PhDs. Since the 1980s, this "chilly climate" has described what women faced inside and outside the classroom (Hall, 1982; Hall & Sandler, 1984; Sandler & Hall, 1986). Levstik's description of the "PhD experience" of the early 1980s (cited in Brownhill, 1989) describes the same experiences found today. The typical graduate student is expected to have minimal outside commitments and a wife to handle all the "real-life" problems that might come up. Women are expected to arrive without any distractions that might interfere with their university activities, and a woman arriving with children may be totally unacceptable. Levstik reported that there was at least one case in which a woman faculty member refused to accept female advisees with preschool children. The roles of scientists and women should not be mutually exclusive.

Graduate programs must take into account that it is healthy to have a life outside of the academic environment. It is entirely possible that many male students would thrive under a less traditional PhD program that allows them to have outside activities. Some PhD programs still follow the traditional pattern of students attending on a full-time basis under the belief that part-time students will not go on to attain their PhDs. Perhaps it is the rigidity of the traditional program that causes students' inability to complete their PhDs. After all, the concept of undergraduate education has been changing from the traditional 4 years of college right after high school to 4-plus years sometime after high school. We are making it convenient for students to complete their undergraduate degrees by providing locations that are accessible to more people, providing classes on weekends and at night, and allowing students to work part time toward an undergraduate degree. With the start of new distance learning programs, more students could have access to graduate programs without traveling to a university on a daily basis.

The University of North Carolina at Charlotte (UNC–Charlotte) responded to a need for engineering doctoral programs in the Charlotte area by offering a joint program with North Carolina State University (NCSU). The degree was conferred by NCSU, but students used the latest telecommunications facilities to attend classes on the UNC–Charlotte campus rather than traveling hundreds of miles to Raleigh, where the class was being taught. Several degrees were available through the program until recently, when UNC–Charlotte received approval to offer its own doctoral degrees in engineering at the Charlotte campus.

Another alternative PhD program exists at Nova Southeastern University in Fort Lauderdale, Florida. Nova offers a PhD in computer science specifically designed for working computer science professionals. It allows students to attend classes on weekends and use telecommunications facilities to conduct research. Many of the students are actively engaged in high-level research on the job, which is comparable to the research conducted on a campus.

Although experimentation is just beginning with alternative PhD programs in the sciences, it is hoped that existing PhD programs will look closely to see whether new paths toward the PhD can be found. But even if the path toward the degree is changed, the problems in the existing degree path must be addressed, or they may be transferred to the new path. In 1989, a report on women entering the computer science field was done by Leveson (1989) for the NSF Cross-Directorate Activities Advisory Committee. Although much of her material was anecdotal or based on her own opinions about educating women in computer science, the information was collected from a large number of women throughout the United States. She includes some comments on the effect of the large number of noncitizens or foreign-born students and teachers on women.

American graduate programs in science have been inundated with foreign students. There is also a large number of foreign male faculty members in these programs. Many of these foreign students and faculty—both men and women—hold different cultural views on whether and how to accept women as colleagues (McMillon, 1987). Vetter (1988, 1989) has done extensive work with women in engineering and has found a "language barrier" that affects all American students. This refers to the fact that these faculty usually speak accented English and are not completely familiar with the American education system and culture. Although students have used a faculty member's accent as an alibi to explain their lack of performance, Vetter's study indicates that a professor's foreignness has been used to describe a situation in which women feel that they are being sexually harassed or not taken seriously. She believes that the lack of female faculty members in engineering programs makes it difficult to resolve such problems, resulting in the loss of women to business programs, where the climate is less difficult.

Data from the NSF (1990a, 1992) and Vetter's (1988) report show an increasing number of foreign students entering computer science and engineering programs. The proportion of foreign women drops as they go from undergraduate to graduate degrees. This indicates that there is an increase in male graduate students at the PhD level. Both undergraduate and graduate programs are becoming sensitive to the increase in the number of foreign faculty, but they may not be aware of the effect that the influx of male foreign students has on other students, especially women.

From time to time, the "foreign student or teacher" problem has appeared in newspapers and on television. On March 13, 1989, Ronald Rosenberg wrote two articles for the *Boston Globe* that expressed the concerns of Vetter and others about why women are not choosing computer science and engineering careers. According to the articles, the associate dean of engineering at Stanford acknowledged that a problem exists with both students and faculty as they begin to interact with women on an equal basis. Students who come from a culture that discounts women as colleagues do not accept women students as equals. The associate dean further noted that some male foreign students have been known to challenge female faculty members inappropriately. This may also be happening with American-born students and faculty. We must not make foreign-born and -educated faculty the scapegoats. We cannot discount the reports of problems with students and teachers from cultures where women are not accepted as equals, but we should not single out one group as being responsible for the wrong attitudes toward women. If a diversity among scientists is important, the inclusion of foreign-born students and faculty is good. A computer science department made up of American-born men and women can be just as damaging to the future of our students.

Even the most caring faculty members, male or female, can succumb to their own prejudices. A faculty member may end up hurting a student by trying to help the student in the wrong way. For example, a student might be perceived by a faculty member as being less prepared than the other students and be graded more easily because of some generalization based on his or her gender or race. It would be better to recognize that this is a student with potential who needs extra help and to try to help that student reach the level of the other students. A fine line must be drawn between keeping an eye open for students who may need help and generalizing that all students of a particular race or gender need help.

WHAT HAVE WE LEARNED FROM UNDERGRADUATE PROGRAMS?

A practice that affects not only women and minorities but all students is the attempt to use certain courses as part of a filtering process. Unfortunately, many undergraduate departments pick a difficult course and use that as a filter to keep unqualified students from advancing in various science programs. The course is so rigorous that only a select few survive. Freshman calculus courses have been used as filters for years. Even when a concerned mathematics department tried to increase students' rate of success, one member found that other factors may have been affecting the failure or dropout rate. Treisman (1983, 1989) at UC–Berkeley (cited in Watkins, 1989; Wieneke & Certain, 1990) has done and is doing much to change how freshman calculus courses are taught. Treisman's initial work —trying to find a way to help minority students succeed in calculus— brought to light new information that is useful to all students at the undergraduate level and could be used at the graduate level.

Treisman's work with minority students has done much to change the way that these students are supported as they study mathematics. His comparison of a group of successful Asian students with a group of not-so-successful African American students resulted in a change in the way many universities handle minority assistance programs and might help in the retention of women and minorities in graduate computer science programs. One factor that may help explain how groups differ was found: The Asian students made their studies part of their social lives. A particularly difficult homework problem might be the topic of conversation at dinner. Students worked together to find a solution to the problem, making sure that each member of the group understood it. They formed formal study groups and tried to help one another understand the subject matter. They also tried to help one another cope with other university and nonuniversity problems. Students from the African American group separated their academic lives from their social lives. They tried to study alone and handled nonacademic problems on their own. The concept of group learning or collaborative learning can be beneficial and is a technique that many of us are trying. This seems to give students the peer support that educators believe is beneficial. It moves the student toward being the center of the learning model, replacing the old teacher-centered concept.

Computer science departments can work toward graduating qualified women and minorities by making sure that freshman computer science courses are not used for filtering. They should make sure that there is no filter in the graduate programs either. Rather than making the program so difficult that only the best survive, why not choose students who have potential and help these students achieve their fullest potential by incorporating some new learning methods?

DO MINORITY WOMEN HAVE SPECIAL NEEDS?

There is another issue that must be addressed if all women are to succeed. Minority women have special problems. Malcom, Hall, and Brown (1976) concluded that the difficulties encountered by white women aspiring to become scientists were minimal compared with those of minority women. Women's and minority organizations expect minority women to be active participants in both, which results in the women spending too much time with both groups. If a choice between the groups has to be made, a woman is confronted with having to deny either her race or her gender. Many of the minority women in the report indicated that early racism changed to sexism as they entered graduate schools. In fact, it was often difficult to determine whether it was racism or sexism that these students were encountering. Many of the women had experienced problems with gender bias from minority males and race bias from a group they perceived to be middle- and upper-class women.

IS THERE AN IDEAL GRADUATE COMPUTER SCIENCE PROGRAM?

Financial support is important for both traditional and nontraditional students, especially women and minorities. Many universities have access to funding, but it is often tied to a specific area of research in which the student may not be interested. In 1992, I sent a request to the Office of Sponsored Research at the University of South Carolina at Columbia asking for possible funding sources for women seeking PhDs in computer science. In spite of the office's helpfulness and diligent search, only a handful of programs was found. Of the programs, American Telephone and Telegraph (AT&T), the American Association of University Women (AAUW), and International Business Machines (IBM) were the only ones that offered assistance for women in computer science. Letters requesting information resulted in replies by AT&T and the AAUW; IBM did not reply. AT&T seemed to tie the funding to the student's research area. The AAUW was interested in funding work toward a doctorate in computer science, with the stipulation that the recipient be actively working to increase the number of girls and women in the sciences. No federally supported programs were on the list. These data tend to dispel the myth that women are singled out and given financial support. Industry, foundations, and government need to provide funding.

Special programs should be designed to help women and minorities. Although the programs should include faculty, staff, and members of the community, the primary staffing should consist of professionals with backgrounds in education and one of the science, math, or engineering areas. This is where funding is important. Without money, programs may consist of faculty members who are concerned but already overworked, or faculty members who are unable to find jobs in their own disciplines.

We must find new ways to handle the education of our graduate students in computer science if we want to attract all of America's talented students, traditional and nontraditional. Each faculty member must develop his or her own successful teaching style. Even if a program does not seek alternative methods of teaching, we need to look at what is happening within existing programs. Graduate programs must become sensitive to the concept of "minority" within a program. The concept of "ethnic isolation" can apply to any group, whether the group consists of women, African Americans, Native Americans, Hispanic Americans, non-Americans, or even white American males, who may no longer be part of the majority. When a former majority becomes a minority, they experience the same problems that other minority groups have experienced in the past. We all need to examine our teaching methods for unintentional and intentional biases toward our students.

Do doctoral programs have to be limited to an intellectually elite group of people? The life experiences of nontraditional students could be helpful in shaping student research. Since many nontraditional students have special problems, we need to examine how computer science doctoral programs work to see what changes could relieve these problems. Could alternative methods be employed without weakening the program? Perhaps we need to research the problem further. We certainly need to see new studies similar to the "Findings & Recommendations From the Report of the Task Force on the Engineering Student Pipeline" (1988) or Treisman's work (1983, 1985, 1989, 1992) with minority calculus students.

Finally, my participation in a project designed to improve the retention of women in mathematics, science, and engineering must be mentioned, since it is an example of what can be done now to benefit our current and future students. Funded by an NSF grant (HRD-9053892-A) that was awarded to the University of South Carolina, the project brought together a widely diverse group of faculty from several campuses in the system to try to improve teaching methods for women. Participants included male and female students from several races, many age groups, and faculty born in and outside the United States. Each member was exposed to the work of educators addressing the problems of women and minorities in science, mathematics, and engineering. In addition, participants shared ideas about what seems to be working within their own disciplines. Although we were a very diverse group, we came with one goal in mind: We wanted to know what we could do in our classes to attract and retain more women. Each member of the group selected a class and redesigned it using methods thought to work well with women. Although the work was time-consuming, it was not unreasonable. But there was one topic that kept coming up in the final reports. When teaching methods consisted of those thought to be successful with women, positive results were found not only for the women but for minorities and other students in the class as well. And it confirms my opinion that a successful program depends on a concerned faculty willing to take risks in an effort to attract and retain all potential students in graduate computer science programs.

REFERENCES

Alper, Joe. (1993, April 16). The pipeline is leaking women all the way along. *Science, 260*, 409–411.

Brownhill, Carrie. (1989, August). *Factors affecting the decisions of women to enter doctoral programs in computer science* (Report). University of California, Irvine.

Fields, Cheryl M. (1987, September 30). What works: California's minority engineering program. *Chronicle of Higher Education, 34*(5), A33.
Findings & recommendations from the report of the task force on the engineering student pipeline. (1988, May). *Engineering Education, 78*(8), 778–780.
Gries, David, & Marsh, Dorothy. (1992, January). The 1989–90 Taulbee survey. *Communications of the ACM, 35*(1), 133–143.
Hall, Roberta M. (1982). *The classroom climate: A chilly one for women?* Washington, DC: Project on the Status of the Education of Women.
Hall, Roberta M., & Sandler, Bernice R. (1984). *Out of the classroom: A chilly campus climate for women?* Washington, DC: Association of American Colleges.
Horwitz, Elinor L. (1992, Summer). Taking the lead. *AAUW Outlook, 86*(2), 10–15.
Ivey, Elizabeth S. (1987, Fall). Recruiting more women into science and engineering. *Issues in Science and Technology, 4*(1), 83–87.
Kelly, Dennis. (1993, November 3). "Encouraging" gains in minority math, science. *USA Today*, p. 4D.
Leveson, Nancy. (1989, December). *Women in computer science: A report for the NSF CISE cross disciplinary activities advisory committee* (Report). Washington, DC: National Science Foundation.
Malcom, Shirley Mahaley, Hall, Paula Quick, & Brown, Janet Welsh. (1976). *The double bind: The price of being a minority woman in science* (Report No. 76-R-3). Washington, DC: American Association for the Advancement of Science.
Manning, Anita. (1994, February 2). How bias in coed classrooms holds girls back. *USA Today*, p. 5D.
Matyas, Marsha Lakes, & Malcom, Shirley M. (Eds.). (1991). *Investing in human potential: Science and engineering at the crossroads*. Washington, DC: American Association for the Advancement of Science.
McMillen, Liz. (1987, August 12). Step up recruitment of women into science or risk U.S. competitive edge in field, colleges are warned. *Chronicle of Higher Education, 33*(48), 9, 12.
National Science Foundation. (1990a). *Science and engineering personnel: A national overview* (NSF 90-310). Washington, DC: Author.
National Science Foundation. (1990b). *Academic science and engineering: Graduate enrollment and support, fall 1989* (NSF 90-324). Washington, DC: Author.
National Science Foundation. (1990c). *Characteristics of recent science and engineering graduates: 1990* (NSF 90-316). Washington, DC: National Science Foundation.
National Science Foundation. (1992). *Women and minorities in science and engineering: An update* (NSF 92-303). Washington, DC: Author.
Rosenberg, Ronald. (1989a, March 13). Engineering losing its luster among students. *Boston Globe*, p. 1, col. 5.
Rosenberg, Ronald. (1989b, March 13). More women shun engineering as other careers beckon. *Boston Globe*, p. 8, col. 1.
Saigal, Anil. (1987, December). Women engineers: An insight into their problems. *Engineering Education, 78*(3), 194–195.
Sandler, Bernice R., & Hall, Robert M. (1986). *The campus climate revisited: Chilly*

for women faculty, administrators, and graduate students. Washington, DC: Association of American Colleges.

Treisman, Philip Uri. (1983, June 3). Improving the performance of minority students in college-level mathematics. *Innovation Abstracts V* (17). Austin, TX: University of Texas at Austin, National Institute for Staff and Organizational Development. (ERIC Document Reproduction Service No. ED 234 874).

Treisman, Philip Uri. (1985). A model academic support system. In R. B. Landis (Ed.), *Improving the retention and graduation of minorities in engineering handbook* (pp. 55–65). New York: National Association of Minority Engineering Program Administrators.

Treisman, Philip Uri. (1989, November 9). Testimony of Philip Uri Treisman to the Committee on Governmental Affairs United States Senate, 101st Cong., 1st Sess. (S. Hrg. 101-561), pp. 39–42.

Treisman, Philip Uri. (1992, November). Studying students studying calculus: A look at the lives of minority mathematics students in college. *College Mathematics Journal, 23*(5), 362–372.

University of California at Berkeley. (1991). *Questions and answers about the computer science reentry program*. Berkeley, CA: Author.

Vetter, Betty M. (1988, May). Demographics of the engineering student pipeline. *Engineering Education, 78*(8), 735–740.

Vetter, Betty M. (1989, November 9). Statement before the Committee on Governmental Affairs United States Senate, 101st Cong., 1st Sess. (S. Hrg. 101-561), pp. 42–46, 87–95.

Watkins, Beverly T. (1989a, June 14). Berkeley mathematician strives "to help people get moving." *Chronicle of Higher Education*, p. A16.

Watkins, Beverly T. (1989b, June 14). Many campuses now challenging minority students to excel in math and science. *Chronicle of Higher Education*, pp. A13, A16–A17.

Wieneke, William R., & Certain, Phillip. (1990, April 6–7). The freshman year in science and engineering: Old problems, new prospectives for research universities. Report of a Conference Sponsored by The Alliance for Undergraduate Education, Ann Arbor, MI, with support from the National Science Foundation. (ERIC Document Reproduction Service No. ED 352 249)

PART V

ENVIRONMENTAL SCIENCE AND GEOSCIENCES

CHAPTER 10

Female-Friendly Geoscience

Eight Techniques for Reaching the Majority

Darlene S. Richardson
Connie J. Sutton
Karen R. Cercone

Until the 1960s, encyclopedias and histories of science wrote of "men of science" without any conscious recognition that "women of science" were thus excluded. Until the mid-1980s, most textbooks used pictures of white males wearing white lab coats to portray "the scientist" (Matyas, 1985). Women in science had been so marginalized that mention was made of only the few "extraordinary" women scientists (Richardson & Sutton, 1993). Whereas it is true that few male scientists are mentioned in textbooks, some of the males who are routinely incorporated in textbooks have been included for dubious reasons (Richardson & Sutton, 1993). For example, Tycho Brahe is mentioned in every introductory astronomy book, but his contributions to astronomy as a science are not as important as those of Annie Jump Cannon. Brahe's routine observations of the skies proved useful to later astronomers such as Kepler, even though Brahe himself did not contribute significantly to the field. Cannon, however, utilized data to develop the stellar spectral classification system used today to categorize newly discovered stars.

Even though women now represent approximately 30% to 40% of the students in medical schools, business schools, and law schools, women have not made such inroads in the physical sciences (Brush, 1992). Undergraduate women in the earth and space sciences, for example, make up about 20% to 25% of the geoscience majors; women represent 15% to 20% of graduate students, with wide-ranging estimates of 5% to 15% of PhDs in geoscience being awarded to women (Coates, 1986; Crawford, Moody, & Tullis, 1977; Richardson, 1990). Over 50% of the women geoscientists employed are in academic positions (Mara, 1977), although they are disproportionately distributed among the lower faculty levels and in part-time or temporary positions. Women geoscientists occupy about 10% of the full-time, tenure-track positions in the geosciences, but they constitute 40% of the nontenure track, part-time academic positions (Suiter, 1992; White & Lewis, 1992). The percentage of women who choose to major in the earth sciences compares favorably with the percentage of women who choose to study physics (5%), but unfavorably with the percentage of women who major in biology (35%). Women with bachelor's degrees in geoscience earn 60% as much as their male colleagues with the same degrees and training. This salary disparity is the greatest of any of the scientific disciplines (Suiter, 1992).

One of the questions that face us as we look at the distribution of women students in the sciences is why the percentages of women in the life sciences (biology, psychology, nursing) are higher than the percentages of women in the physical sciences. We are pleased that more national associations of geoscientists and employers readily recognize that the underrepresentation of women in geoscience is a problem that should be addressed. National associations began to show an interest in women in geoscience—who they are, what their subfields are, their representation in various employment sectors, their training, and so on—beginning in 1973 in Canada (Allman, 1975). Women geoscientists were the subject of a symposium called Women and Careers in Geoscience, which explored historical perspectives, educational opportunities, and career advancement at the Geological Society of America (GSA) annual meeting in 1976 (Crawford et al., 1977). This early (if 1976 is early) American symposium was sponsored by the American Geological Institute (AGI). Since then, several national geoscience conventions have had workshops on how to make geology more appealing to women—and to men (the GSA national meeting held in November 1993 was an example). The United States Geological Survey has a poster of geologists at work in which each geologist is female. Clearly, on a national level, women are encouraged to study the geosciences.

We asked ourselves why women are choosing not to study the physical sciences. Part of the answer lies in factors over which we have little direct control: Girls turn away from science at an early age, and our societal values have placed girls and women on the margins of science (Hall & Sandler, 1982; Suiter, 1992). Sutton's (1988) work with teenage girls demonstrated that making girls aware of employment opportunities in science and the better salaries associated with jobs in science, mathematics, and technological fields, along with mentorship, does increase the number of girls taking math and science in high school. Another part of the answer lies in the general scientific illiteracy in the United States (Hartwig, 1992). Tobias's (1990) division of the first tier and the second tier and Sigma Xi's (1989) naming of the 15% cohort and the 85% cohort define those who choose to study science and those who do not. Most American college students (approximately 85%) choose *not* to major in science. Most students (indeed, most Americans) do not understand how science affects their lives (American Association for the Advancement of Science [AAAS], 1990). Instead of making science more relevant and more accessible to students' lives outside the classrooms, we science teachers tend to stress what is "bitty, remote, boring and hard" (Claxton, 1992, p. 49). The way science is traditionally taught in the college classroom tends to "disconnect" students from their personal experiences and everyday knowledge.

Various attempts have been made to make college science courses more interesting, relevant, and pertinent to college students and thus increase their lifelong interest in and understanding of science. Some of these efforts have been directed to the nonscience major specifically (see Bennick, Costello, Lavallee, Shahn, & Szalay, 1990) and some to all students (see Johnson, Johnson, & Smith, 1991); others have transferred pedagogical techniques from women's and ethnics studies (see Rosser, 1986, 1990). These efforts to transform both pedagogy and curriculum share common goals: to improve the science classroom climate, to help students appreciate how science affects their everyday lives, and to facilitate students' understanding of science. The aims of these reform movements are similar to those of the AAAS's (1990) call for "radical reform of science curriculum." Students should understand that science, as a human endeavor, develops in a particular societal context. This context determines the kinds of questions scientists ask, which questions are legitimate, and which answers are correct.

We have attempted to integrate many changes in our courses: We have changed our pedagogical styles, rethought course goals and content, revised our lectures to include the development of earth science ideas in terms of scientists' philosophical foundations (Richardson, 1992; Schneiderman, 1992), and made the inclusion of students' personal experiences an explicit goal in our geoscience courses. The nature of our discipline—the earth sciences with the subdisciplines of geology, meteorology, oceanography, and astronomy—impels us to emphasize change. Earth and life on Earth have a history—they have not always been as they are now. Stars have a beginning and an end. Rocks can change from one to another. Continents have "danced" over the surface of the Earth. Students recognize that the physical world changes as they themselves change. We believe, as do others (Merritts & Shane, 1992), that by improving the ways in which we teach geoscience, we can engage student interest, improve the abilities of our students to do science, and promote active learning, which is most likely to translate to lifelong interest in the geosciences.

HOW TO CHANGE HOW WE TEACH GEOSCIENCE

In contrast to recommendations from Crawford et al. (1977) and Suiter (1992), we believe that it is not sufficient or even advisable to change the student to fit the way we teach science. Rather, we should restructure the ways in which we teach geoscience to engage and enlighten our students (Sutton & Richardson, 1993). We have followed the outlines of good teaching practice in general (Chickering & Gamson, 1987) and in geoscience in particular as described by Boardman and Buchwald (1990), Palmer (1991), Buchwald (1992), and Keller (1992). We are continually challenging our assumptions about both what and how we teach. Field trips, telescope observations, laboratory work, and hands-on experience with all types of scientific equipment, including microcomputers, are integral to both our nonmajors and majors courses. We encourage student-to-student exchange and collaboration as well as frequent interactions between faculty and students. Some of the methods we describe below are appropriate for upper-level classes with enrollments under 25; other methods are applicable to even large lecture classes with much higher enrollments.

These techniques for good undergraduate practice demonstrate to science students how science is done; we do not teach students just a bunch of loosely connected facts. The geosciences are normally divided into four major subdisciplines—astronomy, geology, meteorology, and oceanography—which we integrate in our lectures and upper-level laboratory exercises. We use examples from all subdisciplines to illustrate techniques that encourage students to become active learners.

Faculty in some universities and colleges will find that some of these techniques are more applicable to their individual situations than others, but putting any of these recommendations into practice will benefit all students in the class, not just women and nontraditional students. Indiana University of Pennsylvania (IUP) has approximately 13,000 undergraduate students. Although most students are drawn from the tristate region (Pennsylvania, Ohio, and West Virginia), we have students from all states and from 60 other countries. The student body is approximately 10% to 20% minority (in terms of race or ethnicity) and is about 55% female. These techniques have worked well for us in our service courses (where the student enrollments mirror IUP as a whole) and in our courses for majors (about 20% to 40% of our majors and minors are women).

EIGHT TECHNIQUES TO ENGAGE STUDENTS IN THE GEOSCIENCES

The first four techniques apply generally to the good practice of education; the remaining four are more specific to teaching the geosciences.

1. Teachers clearly demonstrate the relevance of science to their own and students' lives.

AAAS (1990) argues that material that can translate into other parts of the student's life is most meaningful to the student. In our lectures, we continually emphasize the relationship of a particular topic to human life or the life and health of the planet. In speaking of glaciers, for example, it is boring to simply list the nomenclature of glacial erosive effects. But if we ask the students to think about what can be preserved in rocks to indicate past glacial episodes, students themselves generate a list of glacial effects that the teacher can then name. Critical thinking in the lecture room is emphasized by asking students to give various interpretations of scientific data (Is global temperature increasing, decreasing, or remaining the same?) or to look at the potential beneficial and adverse effects of global warming. Analysis of the gas wells drilled on campus and their potential for contamination, for example, demonstrates to students that earth science is not a collection of dull facts confined to the classroom and regurgitated on the test. International examples of geoscience processes, as well as teachers' personal experiences, enliven the class and help students realize that we all do not perceive nature in the same way (Merchant, 1980; Montgomery, 1991). As an example, our measurement of time comes to us from the early Arab world rather than from the early Greek and Roman worlds. We make a point of drawing on the personal experiences of foreign students in the class as well as those of American students from other parts of the United States.

2. Assessment methods are diverse and emphasize context and how science is practiced.

Journals, papers, presentations, in-class and out-of-class graded and ungraded writing exercises, graded and ungraded quizzes, and tests are used in combination to encourage students to draw on their strengths. Large classes generally preclude many writing assignments, but even in our classes of 150 students, students prepare at least three written assignments. Test questions emphasize context and the interrelationships and interactions of science and society. We can ask students to insert themselves in the place of those making decisions for their communities and ask the students to make those decisions based on scientific facts. For example, the professor makes a proposal to the class, which pretends that it is the Egyptian parliament, to develop groundwater resources for an expensive irrigation project to make the Sahara bloom. The class questions the professor, who generally gives evasive answers in her role as a developer who wants $2 billion for the project. The students then decide what types of data they need to make informed judgments, plan how to acquire those data, and finally decide whether to fund the proposal. Memorization of facts and formulas is deemphasized in favor of conceptual learning, especially for nonmajors. Collaboration and cooperation among students and between teacher and student are important aspects of each of our courses. Students write about what they have learned and thus learn through writing. Some majors courses have oral presentations as an important component in assessing speaking and organizational skills. Critical analysis and synthesis are other important skills we assess through problem solving, integration of previously learned material with new material, and understanding of the interaction of geoscience processes and society.

3. Nonsexist language is used throughout the courses.

It is important to use nonsexist language in lectures, assignments, and examinations. We do not realize how much language colors our perceptions until we make an effort to use nongendered language (Rosser, 1986). In order to eliminate these subtle messages, we speak of humans rather than man; we use he/she or alternate she and he when speaking of the generic geologist; we do not always refer to extinct organisms as he or it but instead alternate between he and she, since all were sexed. It jolts us out of our complacency when we refer to *Tyrannosaurus rex* as she. We incorporate the contributions of men and women geoscientists as well as those of non-Westerners.

4. Students are encouraged to question assumptions and to be comfortable with uncertainty and ambiguity.

Scientific information changes rapidly as new techniques reveal different aspects of the natural world (Bruffee, 1992). We encourage our students to be open to new ways of studying the world. For example, the application of fractals and chaotic processes to understanding geological, meteorological, oceanographical, and astronomical processes presents new ways of discovering how small changes in one factor might create catastrophic changes in the whole system. Self-organized criticality and the use of microcomputers permit geoscientists, among others, to model dynamic systems such as weather systems, earthquakes, and turbulence in ocean currents. Our previous assumptions that large-scale geoscience systems work toward equilibrium are challenged by chaos theory. One of the underlying assumptions of many evolutionary scientists is a belief that evolution is driven toward increasing complexity. Recent studies (Yoon, 1993), in contrast, hold that there is no overall trend toward complexity in evolution. Some species of ammonites, for example, became more complex with time; other species of ammonites became less complex with time. Thus, students are encouraged to question "what everyone knows" and to become comfortable with uncertainty.

5. Nonmajor students are separated from geoscience majors in introductory labs.

The students who are on a professional track in the geosciences require more detailed development of complex topics, particularly in the laboratory context, and also need to learn the special language of their discipline to prepare them for their upper-level courses. In contrast, nonmajors need to understand the broader picture and look at geological processes, for example, in terms of end result (such as development of landscape), in a context that is readily visible to them. All too often, nonmajors are frustrated and bored by the intense memorization and detailed characterization required in lab work designed for majors.

We have therefore separated majors and nonmajors in labs but kept them together in lectures. In the laboratory exercises, all students are expected to use different types of equipment and to obtain hands-on experience with both simple and sophisticated instruments. We emphasize that collaboration and cooperation in the laboratory do not mean that one student monopolizes the equipment while the other students take notes. The laboratory exercises pique students' interest by presenting problems they solve rather than merely requiring them to memorize the physical properties of minerals or to define an isobath. For example, we discuss why quartz sand is used to make glass. What are the physical properties of quartz—which students discover for themselves—that make it useful to us?

6. Classes incorporate reading materials other than textbooks.

Both nonfiction and fiction are used to convey the excitement and relevance of science to students on levels that they can easily grasp and in formats that they are most likely to encounter once they graduate. Few of us read textbooks for pleasure, but many of us read magazines, technical journals, fiction, and nonfiction. One of our aims is to encourage lifelong learning and appreciation of the geosciences. Nonfiction books such as John McPhee's *The Control of Nature* (1989) and *Basin and Range* (1981) relate geological processes to the personal experiences of ordinary people. John Horner's *Digging Dinosaurs* (1988) recreates the excitement of finding fossil dinosaurs and how paleontologists can construct family relationships among some dinosaurs. Science fiction, such as David Brin's *Earth* (1990) and Michael Crichton's *Jurassic Park* (1990), allows students to imagine how geoscience processes today might lead to a different future. Journal articles on the space program, life in the oceans, development of storms, and interaction of life with physical processes help students apply what they have learned in lectures to another context.

7. Field trips are an integral part of all geoscience courses.

Field trips that emphasize concepts covered in lectures and laboratories are a significant part of the experiences of majors and nonmajors alike. This type of hands-on experience allows students to study rocks in a much larger scale than in the laboratory. They can train their telescopes on sunspots or actually understand the problems—mechanical and human—associated with drilling for water, gas, or oil. Field trips oriented toward understanding environmental problems help the students relate their knowledge gained in lectures to "real-life" problems that they can expect to face in their personal lives or in their lives as citizens.

8. Field trips do not stress competitive physical accomplishments.

Instead of the traditional field emphasis on masculine traits such as physical endurance in hiking and prowess in rock climbing (the competitive urge to be the first one on top of the mountain), field experiences are tailored to the level of physical confidence of and support needed by each student. Often, those students who rush to the outcrop or hurry to be the first swimmer to reach the coral reef have neglected to study the rock structures or the other marine life-forms on the journey. We establish constructive group dynamics among students by assigning field partners and grading students on participation in group-focused activities. Daily camping tasks such as food preparation, vehicle maintenance, and camp cleanup are not divided according to sex but by interest and talents. In addition, two or more people carry heavy equipment, not just one strong male. Field observations are made by all members of the group, and students understand by group discussion among themselves and with the field trip leaders that not all observers agree on the causes of the observed phenomena.

CONCLUSION

We have found that the above techniques help us connect students to the geosciences, particularly by engaging students' interests (and, therefore, their active participation) in lecture, laboratory, and field experiences. Not all apply to every college environment, but putting any of them into practice will have the benefit of making geoscience friendly not only to women but also to all other students. In addition, these techniques help us connect with the students: By valuing their personal experiences and their contributions to our classrooms and laboratories, we interact with them in a less authoritarian manner. Students most often rise to our expectations of them —that is, that they be active participants in their own learning and not just passive note takers.

REFERENCES

Allman, N. J. (1975). Women geoscientists—why not? *Geoscience Canada, 2,* 145–149.

American Association for the Advancement of Science. (1990). *The liberal art of science: Agenda for action.* Washington, DC: Author.

Bennick, Alfred, Costello, Robert, Lavallee, David, Shahn, Ezra, & Szalay, Fred. (1990). *Foundations of science: Instructor's manual for science 101–102.* New York: Hunter College of the City University of New York (photocopy).

Boardman, Shelby, & Buchwald, Caryl. (1990, May). Maintaining geology enrollments during a period of decline. *Journal of Geological Education, 38,* 194–196.

Brin, David. (1990). *Earth.* New York: Bantam Books.

Bruffee, Kenneth. (1992, September/October). Science in a postmodern world. *Change, the Magazine of Higher Learning, 24,* 18–25.

Brush, Stephen. (1992). Women in science and engineering. *American Scientist, 79,* 404–419.

Buchwald, Caryl. (1992). Applying ideas from the AAAS project on liberal education and the sciences to geology. *Journal of Geological Education, 40,* 306–307.

Chickering, Arthur, & Gamson, Zelda. (1987). Seven principles for good practice in undergraduate education. *The Wingspread Journal, 9,* 1–8.

Claxton, Guy. (1992, January 18). Why science education is failing. *New Scientist,* 49–50.

Coates, Mary Sue. (1986, November). Women geologists work toward equality. *Geotimes, 31,* 11–14.

Crawford, Mary, Moody, Judith, & Tullis, J. (1977). Women in academia: Students and professors. *Geology, 5,* 502–503.

Crichton, Michael. (1990). *Jurassic park.* New York: Knopf.

Hall, Roberta, & Sandler, Bernice. (1982). *The classroom climate: A chilly one for women?* Project on the Status and Education of Women. Washington, DC: Association of American Colleges.

Hartwig, M. (1992). Scientific literacy in America. *Currents in Science, Technology, & Society, 1,* 1–5.

Horner, John R. (1988). *Digging dinosaurs.* New York: Workman.

Johnson, David, Johnson, Robert, & Smith, Karl. (1991). *Active learning: Cooperation in the college classroom.* Edina, MN: Interaction Book.

Keller, Walter. (1992, September). The most valuable thing we can teach in geology courses. *Journal of Geological Education, 40,* 307–309.

McPhee, John A. (1981). *Basin and range.* New York: Farrar, Straus, Giroux.

McPhee, John A. (1989). *The control of nature.* New York: Farrar, Straus, Giroux.

Mara, Susan. (1977). Alternative career opportunities for women geoscientists. *Geology, 5,* 504.

Matyas, Marsha L. (1985). Obstacles and constraints on women in science. In J. B. Kahle (Ed.), *Women in science.* Philadelphia: Falmer Press.

Merchant, Carolyn. (1980). *The death of nature.* New York: Harper & Row.

Merritts, Dorothy & Shane, Edward. (1992, September). Effective use of hands-on activities, state-of-the-art technology, and computers in introductory environmental geology. *Journal of Geological Education, 40,* 272–278.

Montgomery, Sy. (1991). *Walking with the great apes*. Boston: Houghton Mifflin.
Palmer, Allison. (1991, March). What should my neighbor (and thus every high-school graduate) know about the geosciences. *Journal of Geological Education, 39*, 142–145.
Richardson, Darlene. (1990). *IUP women science majors vs. national statistics*. A presentation at the 10th annual PA State System of Higher Education Women's Consortium Conference, East Stroudsburg, PA.
Richardson, Darlene. (1992). Women in science: 5000 years of obstacles and achievements. *Bulletin of Science, Technology, & Society, 12*, 187–191.
Richardson, Darlene, & Sutton, Connie. (1993). *Extraordinary and ordinary women in science*. A presentation at the eighth annual Technological Literacy Conference, Arlington, VA.
Rosser, Sue. (1986). *Teaching science and health from a feminist perspective*. Elmsford, NY: Pergamon Press.
Rosser, Sue. (1990). *Female-friendly science*. Elmsford, NY: Pergamon Press.
Schneiderman, Jill. (1992). Growth and development of a woman scientist and educator. *Earth Sciences History, 11*, 37–39.
Sigma Xi. (1989, January). *An exploration of the nature and quality of undergraduate education in science, mathematics and engineering*. Sigma Xi, Wingspread Press.
Suiter, Marilyn. (1992, January). Women in geoscience: A resource to develop. *Geotimes, 37*, 15–17.
Sutton, Connie. (1988). *Project to encourage female student participation in math/science courses and careers*. Technical report to ARIN Intermediate Unit 28, western PA.
Sutton, Connie, & Richardson, Darlene. (1993). *Which is square, the peg or the hole? Changing science curricula*. A presentation at the state spring symposium, Future Directions for College Science Curricula, Clarion, PA.
Tobias, Sheila. (1990). *They're not dumb, they're different: Stalking the second tier*. Tucson, AZ: Research Corporation.
White, Patricia, & Lewis, Laurie. (1992). *Survey on undergraduate education in geology* (Higher Education Surveys Report, Survey No. 15-Geology). Washington, DC: National Science Foundation.
Yoon, C. K. (1993, March 30). Biologists deny life gets more complex. *The New York Times*, pp. C1, C11.

CHAPTER 11

Female-Friendly Environmental Science

Building Connections and Life Skills

Sara L. Webb

Like most scientific subjects, environmental science has little obvious gendered content. Thus at first glance it is unclear what relevance feminism and women's studies have to the teaching of this discipline. In history, literature, and the arts, the exclusion of women's lives and works produces glaringly incomplete curricula (MacIntosh, 1983; Spanier, Bloom, & Boroviak, 1984). In biology and psychology, stereotypes and repression are perpetuated by biased studies (Bleier, 1984; Fausto-Sterling, 1985; Golub & Freedman, 1987; Gould, 1981; Lowe & Hubbard, 1983; Tavris, 1992). But how should environmental science, with its objective geological and botanical underpinnings, be transformed in the classroom?

The answer is that a course experience is much more than primary informational content. Pedagogy and secondary content are valuable tools for gender integration in science courses (Quina, 1986; Rosser, 1990; Schuster & Van Dyne, 1985). Transforming science courses in this way is important work toward attracting and retaining women, who continue to avoid science careers and drop out of the science pipeline at every level (Alper, 1993; Rosser, 1990; Tobias, 1990). As teachers, we have the opportunity to encourage all students through our choices of approach and material.

To transform science courses toward the goal of recruiting and retaining women scientists, we must do at least three things:

1. We must make science engaging.
2. We must provide role models and language that unequivocally include women in the world of science.
3. We must empower women with confidence-building skills for research, writing, and analysis.

There is room in every science course, I believe, to tackle these three needs with little sacrifice of primary informational content. In this chapter

I describe my college course, Advanced Environmental Science, and I explain those aspects of the syllabus designed with the three transformation objectives in mind: an engaging course, inclusiveness, and skills acquisition for all students. Some of my strategies can be employed in courses taught on other science subjects and to other audiences (secondary students, nonscience majors). Others can be expanded upon, especially in lab or field courses. I also discuss some alternative approaches to teaching about the environment; clearly mine is only one perspective, and I welcome suggestions and insights from fellow teachers.

Toward my first objective of an engaging course, in the absence of a laboratory component, I have three interrelated strategies. First, I urge students to make connections: connections to real-world problems, connections across disciplines, connections with environmental officials, and frequent connections with me as mentor and role model. Second, good pedagogy is essential to an inclusive course experience that does not discourage the "second tier" (Tobias, 1990)—those students not already committed to science. Third, principles of feminist theory are applied as we work to counter the fragmentation of knowledge, to explore the human face of environmental controversies, and to challenge the objectivity of science done under the funding of various players in environmental conflicts.

Toward inclusiveness, the second major objective of transformation, the course provides all students with a mentoring relationship with the professor and offers diverse role models through visiting lecturers as well as historical figures. Inclusive language is also ensured as we seek alternatives to the word *man* as proxy for the entire human race; even some textbooks cast environmental problems as a battle between "man and the environment," leaving women to feel distanced from and unempowered to tackle environmental problems.

Finally, the course builds scientific and life skills as an explicit component of its content. The course reaches out to women (but benefits all students) through activities consciously designed to build skills: public speaking, writing, calling officials for information, and searching the primary scientific literature. I believe that these and, in appropriate courses, quantitative skills should be woven into the fabric of all content-oriented science courses so that all students gain explicit training and confidence.

FORGING CONNECTIONS

Students truly learn when they forge connections: connections between fact and experience, connections between idea and observation, connections between fact and fact. All good teachers know this: When a student combines concepts, she or he begins to construct knowledge, moving beyond passively received information that is quickly lost from short-term memory after the next examination. In addition, when information is made relevant to the student's experience, we stimulate not only learning but also the enthusiasm that is so important for attracting uncommitted students to scientific study. Feminist scholarship suggests that women are especially responsive to pedagogy that places scientific information in a personal and social context (Harding, 1986; Rosser, 1990), although all students are likely to benefit from such an approach. Efforts to build connection into the classroom are worthwhile whether or not one believes that women learn differently from men in this regard (Belenky, Clinchy, Goldberger, & Tarule, 1986; Clinchy, Belenky, Goldberger, & Tarule, 1985).

Connection is a pedagogical theme in Advanced Environmental Science, woven into the course in three ways. First, students make interpersonal connections: All meet with me frequently (see Role Models and Mentoring, below), and all must contact environmental officials while researching their projects. Second, students are encouraged to connect academic and real-world problems through frequent reference to current newspaper items. Third, interdisciplinary perspectives are offered and reinforced through the requirement that both science and policy be treated in course writings.

The separation of knowledge from the polity has been criticized from a feminist perspective that argues for connecting academia with society's problems (Rosser, 1990). The increasing fragmentation of knowledge and the specialization of academic disciplines are related trends that should be actively countered in the classroom. Many disciplines experience deep divisions between academia and real-world applications, for example, in sociology (Adler, 1984), where the academy and social work are often out of step.

This separation is clearly seen in ecology, where scientists rarely enter the policy arena and where applied ecology is a low-status subfield. In fact, the highest prestige was attached to the most abstract and theoretical ecological work throughout the 1970s and 1980s (Kingsland, 1985). Meanwhile, the agencies that manage our natural resources are rarely staffed by ecologists (Chase, 1987). Through their own inquiry, students often discover for themselves the chasm between the state of our scientific knowledge and the policies in place for environmental protection.

GOOD PEDAGOGY

Students who are marginally committed to science are most in need of excellent teaching (Rosser, 1990; Tobias, 1990). As Quina (1986) points out, we must not forget the basics of good teaching as we broaden our epistemology and scrutinize our assignments for bias.

Teaching well requires institutional support because it takes an enormous amount of time on a per-student basis. Classes must be small and teaching loads manageable so that we can offer frequent and prompt feedback, be available for questions and mentoring, and teach by means of writing assignments and discussion. Other fundamentals include an organized course framework, explicit expectations of students, and clear explanations with examples, preferably drawn from students' experiences in the real world.

Good pedagogy also means breaking away from a traditional focus on memorizing information. Students are best served when we broaden our instructional goals beyond facts to the process and skills of learning: writing, discussing, and critical thinking. Several important movements in higher education acknowledge this need: the science-through-inquiry movement, the critical thinking movement, and efforts to teach writing across the curriculum. The trade-off between content and process is problematic in many science courses that must cover material more quickly than inquiry methods permit. Each of us must seek a comfortable balance. In Advanced Environmental Science, writing and research skills are taught and used as learning tools, with little sacrifice of informational content. The course retains its traditional lecture format, but each year the lecture component loses ground to other activities. Carefully crafted discussions and assignments can incorporate both content and process, and that is what good pedagogy is about.

FEMINIST PEDAGOGY AND SCIENTIFIC OBJECTIVITY

Feminist scholarship suggests other strategies for teaching well and engagingly (Rosser, 1986, 1990; Schuster & Van Dyne, 1985). Several concepts already mentioned have their roots in a feminist vision of inclusive, dynamic teaching: teaching through connection, forging interdisciplinary linkages, broadening the epistemology by teaching through student writings, and showing the human side of controversies. It is also essential to tend to classroom dynamics, where subtleties can lead women to disengage. Research has shown that male and female students still receive differential treatment from the podium (American Association of University Women [AAUW], 1992; Hall & Sandler, 1982; Rosser, 1990).

Feminist theory poses another, more controversial challenge to science teachers by calling into question the concept of scientific objectivity. Feminist philosophers and sociologists of science vary in the severity of their critiques but generally agree that scientific agendas and findings are grounded so firmly in social context that truly neutral objectivity is elusive or impossible (Bleier, 1984; Fee, 1983; Harding, 1991; Hubbard, 1979). The best studied cases of bias and subjectivity are found in the social and biological sciences (Fausto-Sterling, 1985; Hubbard, 1983; Tavris, 1992).

Even those convinced that science can be objective must agree that environmental issues have spawned an enormous body of biased science, much of it funded by pro-development organizations or government agencies that have an economic or political stake in downplaying environmental risk. Thus environmental science is an excellent discipline for teaching about bias and subjectivity in scientific research. We are obligated in the name of good teaching to help our students recognize how scientific findings often reflect the values of the funding sources behind them.

The acid-rain controversy is the example that I press into service in Advanced Environmental Science, but parallel scenarios have played out around many environmental issues. During the Reagan years, costly acid-rain reduction measures were postponed pending "more research": a 10-year $530 million government study that involved hundreds of scientists. The political agenda influenced this project in several ways. At scientific conferences I heard some scientists soft-pedaling their findings, reluctant to point the finger at acid rain lest they lose government research grants. Some final summary reports that reached the press and policy makers were misleading and clearly biased in their distillations of research findings (Loucks, 1992; Schindler, 1992; Webb & Glenn, 1993).

One way in which scientific findings are twisted is through a common line of illogic that antienvironment factions often follow: A failure to find causal linkages is treated as evidence that there is no causal linkage. For example, no studies proved that acid rain can degrade forest soils in a way that directly damages trees. This lack of proof resulted from a lack of investigation: Few soil studies were done. But those opposed to new pollution control seized upon this lack of proof of the problem as proof that there is no problem. Thence the unsupported conclusion: Soils are not being degraded. Peterman (1990) elaborates on the statistical mistake being made in such cases when inadequate evidence is treated as contrary evidence.

Pairs of opposing articles are valuable pedagogical tools for helping students sharpen their skills of weighing evidence and detecting bias. For example, see references on global warming in Figure 11.1. *Forbes* magazine and the *Wall Street Journal* are gold mines for articles with an antiregulatory angle, and *Amicus* is a pro-environment journal. Most environmental conflicts lend themselves to this sort of analysis.

ROLE MODELS AND MENTORING

Alongside a stimulating syllabus, we must provide women with examples of women scientists and with mentoring relationships if we hope to draw them into science careers. A paucity of female role models has traditionally been a major deterrent. We can look to historical figures such as Rachel Carson, who single-handedly brought the hazards of pesticides to public attention (Hynes, 1989). We can also bring in female guest speakers (Rosser, 1986) to break the stereotype of the scientist as male. With support from the Booth-Ferris Foundation, Drew University has invited visiting scientists for extended visits for both formal class presentations on science and informal discussions about careers, graduate school, and life; thus these visitors serve as temporary mentors in some cases. We can also use assignments to induce students to contact other scientists—women and men—and further broaden their exposure to diversity.

The importance of mentors to women in the sciences cannot be overstated (Fort, 1993; Primack & O'Leary, 1993; Sandler, 1993; Tobias, 1990). As Sandler (1993) points out, the mentoring relationship need not be lifelong but can be valuable under a variety of rubrics. During the semester-long course, I serve as mentor to all my students as I guide them through their projects, taking the opportunity to discuss with them their individual interests and aspirations. The one-on-one contact permitted by small class size is very valuable. In the many departments that lack women faculty members, men can obviously mentor women (Sandler, 1993), although the role model problem still needs to be addressed in these situations.

INCLUSIVE LANGUAGE

As anyone who teaches environmental science can attest, students love to blame the male of the species for all our ills ("man has destroyed the rain forest"). *Man* is a false generic; despite its second dictionary definition, the word does not evoke women along with men (Miller & Swift, 1980, 1991). This usage can have subtle and far-reaching impacts on women (Miller & Swift, 1991) and can be an obstacle to learning (Rosser, 1990). In my experience, in the environmental arena it distances women from environmental problems and weakens the sense of empowerment we all need for the resolution of these problems. Thus I insist that my class eliminate the word *man* from its overused position as proxy for the entire human race in writings and presentations. Texts should be carefully screened for this linguistic error. One school of ecofeminism finds it acceptable and appropriate to attribute our environmental problems to men alone. Ecofeminism is founded on an analogy between male subjugation of women and male subjugation of nature (Griffin, 1978; Merchant, 1980; King, 1983). From this perspective, ecological damage results from the traditional male drive for dominance and control. Although I understand the ecofeminist perspective, I believe that both men and women should feel included as creators and solvers of environmental problems.

BUILDING SKILLS

My third transformation objective toward attracting women to science is to build skills as an explicit component of the course. In environmental science, appropriate skills include writing, speaking, interviewing for information, and searching the scientific literature, including government documents. Other science courses can likewise incorporate quantitative, statistical, computer, and field or laboratory research techniques.

Such skills are a natural part of all science teaching. However, there is value in conceptually modifying the course's primary content to encompass skill building. Building skills is different from expecting students to acquire skills incidentally. For example, writing proficiency can be built by starting with small assignments and proceeding to larger papers, with plenty of feedback along the way. This differs from the common "sink or swim" approach that assigns a large term paper without previous groundwork.

Recent scholarship suggests that critical thinking skills are best learned in subject-matter context rather than in isolated courses on logic and problem solving (American Association for the Advancement of Science [AAAS], 1990; Meyers, 1986). I suspect that this holds true for other skills as well, from writing to library research. At the same time, students' comprehension of subject matter is deepened when learning is made active through writing, speaking, and seeking information.

It stands to reason that inexperienced and educationally disadvantaged students will benefit most from a structured program of skill development. Do women have special needs in this regard? The answer is yes for some skills, because women students tend to avoid courses with quantitative earmarks, such as computer science and statistics (Eccles & Jacobs, 1987; Pearson, Shavlick, & Touchton, 1989). Thus, hiding these skills in content-oriented courses should help ensure that women acquire this training. For skills of research and expression, the benefits are the same for men and women: increased confidence and competence. All will gain tools for success in both the practical and scholarly aspects of pursuing a life in science.

In Advanced Environmental Science, skills are built through three major activities: news analysis, short essays, and a major project. The news analysis assignments give students confidence speaking briefly and informally in front of the class. Through short essay assignments, students begin to hone their writing skills, including documentation, with detailed feedback from me. Only after much practice do students undertake a major project, which involves writing a longer paper and presenting a longer, more formal speech. Meanwhile, students also learn to pick up the phone and call officials for information, a life skill of value when seeking jobs, grants, and graduate school opportunities. Finally, library research techniques are explicitly taught through sessions with librarians and, for online literature searching, with me. Within an inclusive climate for connected learning, these activities convey confidence-building life skills in the hope that more women will enjoy science and succeed in its pursuit.

ALTERNATIVE PERSPECTIVES: DEEP ECOLOGY, ECOFEMINISM, AND ACTIVISM

Clearly my course takes only one of many possible approaches to teaching about the environment. Its perspective is influenced by my own training as a scientist and, probably more than I realize, by my own values, which call for environmental protection even when benefits to humans are not apparent. Because this course is explicitly about environmental science, it differs from environmental ethics and even from environmental studies (more emphasis on policy and planning). Although I focus on the scientific basis of environmental problems, I deal perhaps too little with environmental ethics and activism.

Two alternative perspectives are ecofeminism and deep ecology, unusual philosophical movements that call for a reexamination of both our spiritual relationship with nature and our exploitation of nature (Salleh, 1992; Zimmerman, 1987). Both relate only remotely to the science of ecology, which deep ecologists term "shallow ecology" (Devall & Sessions, 1985).

Ecofeminists attribute environmental problems to the same androcentric drive for exploitation that represses women (Griffin, 1978; King, 1983; Merchant, 1980; Plant, 1989). It may seem surprising that ecologists have generally ignored this movement, given that many of us are feminists. Our lack of comfort with ecofeminism stems from at least three concerns, in my view.

1. Philosophical and spiritual ways of knowing are very different from the scientific. Still fresh from battles over teaching creationism in the sci-

ence classroom, we resist mixing science with nonscience. In addition, our training does not equip us to teach philosophy or feminist theory, posing an impediment to cross-disciplinary teaching.
2. Feminists who have struggled for a place in the male-dominated scientific arena tend to disagree with the view that women are essentially different from men, a view that has served to repress women for decades. Ecofeminism asserts that women are more connected with nature than are men, and that women's nurturant perspective needs to replace our present patriarchal, exploitative approach to nature and people (Merchant, 1980; Plant, 1989; Salleh, 1984). This view seems to embody a regressive return to an essentialist "biology is destiny" view of gender differences (Prentice, 1988). Most ecofeminist writers consider these differences to be spiritually intrinsic, not socially constructed.
3. Ecologists fail to find resonance in the ecofeminist view of nature, which is generally at odds with what we know from our empirical observations of the natural world. It seems to us that an inaccurate vision of natural ecosystems underlies the ecofeminist paradigm. Contrary to assertions by Merchant (1980, 1985), it is not true that nature is a balanced, cyclical, stable system whose components are all equally essential to the proper functioning of the system. This appealing vision prevailed in ecology textbooks in the 1960s, but ecologists now know that nature is complex, extraordinarily dynamic, and often chaotic; that ecosystems are not finely tuned superorganisms but loose, delicate, vulnerable assemblages that change continually and unpredictably. This scientific picture of ecosystems does not provide an appealing metaphor for human social systems. The out-of-date science in ecofeminism is not essential to its major aims of empowering and validating the experience of women, but it does undermine the entire movement's credibility among scientists.

Deep ecology is a branch of environmental ethics that blames environmental problems on anthropocentrism. Deep ecologists call for a biocentric (or "ecocentric"; Fox, 1989) worldview in which humans are a fully connected part of nature and in which all life, from organisms to species to ecosystems, is equally important (Devall & Sessions, 1985). In my course, the biocentric perspective is presented when we discuss reasons for the preservation of species and biodiversity; the Miller (1990) textbook cogently distinguishes values that relate to human benefit from those that do not.

Controversial from the feminist perspective is the deep ecologists' call for control of human population growth, following from the belief that humans have no right to exploit nature for more than vital needs. Although population control is clearly essential to peaceful and long-term human

(text continues on page 206)

FIGURE 11.1. Annotated course syllabus.

TITLE: Advanced Environmental Science
DEPARTMENT: Biology
INSTITUTION: Drew University
AUDIENCE: Junior and senior college science majors
DIVERSITY: Typically 55%-70% female; less than 10% students of color
CLASS SIZE: 15-20 students
COURSE FORMAT: One semester, three 50-minute periods per week (no lab)
GRADING: Three essay-style exams count for half the grade; written and oral assignments constitute the other half (short essays, news analysis presentation, project outline, project presentation, written project report).
TEXTBOOK: Miller, G.T., Jr.(1990) Living in the Environment. Belmont CA: Wadsworth. Frequent new editions; avoids sexist language; treatment somewhat one-sided (pro-environment).
SUPPLEMENTARY READINGS:

1 McPhee, John. (1971) Encounters with the Archdruid. New York: Farrar, Straus & Giroux. This book reveals the complexity and human side of three environmental conflicts, in beautifully written essays "A Mountain," "A River," and "An Island."
2 Brief articles about current environmental controversies; specifics vary from year to year for up-to-date coverage. Recent topics and assignments:

Global Warming: Two diametrically opposed viewpoints are presented in:
Brookes, Warren T. (1989) "The Global Warming Panic." Forbes, 12/25/89, 96-102.
Schneider, Stephen H. (1989) "The Changing Climate." Scientific American, Sept. 1989, 70-79.
Pollution in Eastern Europe:
World Resources Institute (1992). World Resources 1992. Chapter 5. Central Europe. New York: Oxford University Press.
Ozone Depletion:
Kerr, Richard A. (1992) "New Assaults Seen on Earth's Ozone Shield." Science, 255, 797-798.
Appenzeller, Tim. (1991) "Ozone Loss Hits Us Where We Live." Science, 254, 645.
Wetland Preservation:
Apler, Joseph. (1992) "War Over the Wetlands: Ecologists vs. the White House." Science 257, 1043-1044.

ASSIGNMENTS:

News Analysis: Students take turns presenting current newspaper articles about environmental problems to the class. This activity accomplishes two things: it builds student comfort with speaking in front of a group, and it forges linkages between the course's academic content and real world problems. The news is often literally close to home and of personal concern. These news items then provide illustrations for later lectures and discussions, acting as connective tissue to engender interest while aiding the learning process.

Short Essays: Brief but fully referenced essays are assigned on controversial topics, with students required to present all sides of each issue. Recent topics: (1) Dams: Pro and Con, (2) Global Warming, (3) Wilderness Preservation. These assignments achieve three objectives: they induce students (1) to synthesize information from diverse sources, (2) to capture and review primary informational content in preparation for exams, and (3) to gain practice with writing and documentation in preparation for the larger written project; toward this end I provide prompt and very detailed feedback, identifying writing problems for each student to work on with subsequent assignments.

Major Project: Each student chooses an environmental problem to investigate. The steps of this project are built into the course, with sequential (and firmly enforced) deadlines for topic proposals, on-line literature searching, and detailed written outlines. This structure helps students produce wonderful work; it prevents procrastination and those terrible, last-minute papers that I once thought inevitable. The project culminates in both written and oral reports, and its content becomes part of the course content that all students are responsible for. This major project incorporates:

1. Required multidisciplinary investigation of both scientific and political aspects of the topic
2. Scheduled one-on-one progress meetings with the professor, for guidance and to head off procrastination which can result when students are overwhelmed by a large project
3. Required phone or personal contact with scientists or government officials, to connect the environmental problem to real people and to get students comfortable calling strangers (a life skill transferable to calling for information about graduate schools and jobs)
4. A library training session with a library faculty member, to introduce searching concepts and unfamiliar library resources such as government documents;
5. On-line literature searching with the professor at my computer, for awareness of the scientific literature and its structure
6. A written, fully documented research paper
7. Formal oral presentations to the class, after informal "news analysis" presentations have broken the ice

CLASS SESSIONS:

Lectures: Lectures are presented during 60%-70% of all class meetings, often illustrated with slides on topics such as biodiversity, extinctions, exotic species invasions, and acid rain. Guest lecturers are invited at least once or twice, recently with the support of the Booth-Ferris Foundation in a grant to Drew University designed to expose students to diverse role models.

Films: Films are utilized as much as possible; they are powerful visual learning aids. For maximum pedagogical value each film is best preceded by contextual remarks and followed by a review of major points. Screening and selecting films is a time consuming but important ongoing part of course preparation in this discipline; some films listed below will be out of date by the time this book is published. Environmental controversies and their scientific evidence are always changing; thus my choice of films varies from year to year. When possible I choose films that depict women in active roles. Also worth considering is the "Race to Save the Planet" series (CPB/Annenberg Project); Drew University utilizes this series elsewhere in our curriculum (in a more elementary nonmajors environmental science

(Continued)

FIGURE 11.1. *(Continued)*

course). Films shown in the most recent offering of Advanced Environmental Science appear in the course outline below.

Discussions: Discussions are held on occasional topics. For example, the first session is devoted in part to risk assessment. Students are given a list of environmental problems to designate as low, medium, or high risk to natural ecology and human welfare. Then groups of three students are created to reach consensus on which are the four highest-risk problems. The results are compared with a ranking prepared by the U.S. EPA's Science Advisory Board (1990). By starting the course in discussion motif I aim to create an open classroom atmosphere where students know that questions and comments are always welcome.

Student Presentations: Student presentations of "news analysis" punctuate one or two lectures out of three, and the final weeks of the course are devoted to projectpresentations by students as they take over the podium entirely.

TOPICS COVERED:

No single course in environmental science can give full justice to all relevant topics. Advanced Environmental Science has an ecology prerequisite, so we are freed from covering basics of energy flow, trophic interactions, biomes, and population growth. However, no geology is taught at my institution, so this subject needs more fundamental attention. I also emphasize current controversies and those topics that my own research pertains to.

COURSE OUTLINE, TOPICS, AND ASSIGNMENTS

1.	Environmental Risks; Water	Miller, Ch.13: Water Resources
2.	Water Conservation	McPhee, Part 3. "A River"
3.	Soil Conservation	Miller, Ch.12: Soil Resources
4.	Food Resources	Miller, Ch.14: Food Resources
5.	Film: "Will the World Starve?"[1]	Miller, Ch.13: Land Resources
6.	Forest and Rangelands, USA	ESSAY #1 DUE: DAMS/PRO AND CON
7.	Wilderness and Open Space	
8.	Deforestation: Tropical Forests	Miller, Ch.10: Deforestation
9.	Film: "Battle for Wilderness"[2]	
10.	EXAM #1	
11.	Endangered species	Miller, Ch.16: Plant/Animal Resources
12.	Biological invasions	Miller pp.161-162: Genetic Engineering PROJECT TOPIC DUE
13.	Bioremediation & risks	

14.	Air pollution	Miller, Ch.21: Air Pollution

MEET THIS WEEK WITH PROFESSOR TO DISCUSS YOUR PROJECT PLANS

15.	Greenhouse effect	Miller, Ch.11: Climate Change...
16.	Global warming: biotic effects	Brookes, 1989: Global warming panic Schneider, 1989: Changing climate
17.	Ozone depletion	ESSAY #2 DUE: GLOBAL WARMING
18.	Film: "Hole in the Sky"[1]	Appenzeller, 1991; Kerr, 1992: Ozone
19.	Acid rain: causes and effects	
20.	Acid rain: political case study	
21.	Energy and mineral resources	Miller, Ch.18: Nonrenewable Energy Miller, Ch.19: Mineral Resources
22.	Nuclear energy	McPhee, Part 1: "A Mountain"
23.	Renewable energy sources	Miller, Ch.17: Perpetual/renewable energy
24.	EXAM #2	
25.	Water pollution	Miller, Ch.22: Water Pollution
26.	Water pollution, continued	WRITTEN PROJECT OUTLINE DUE
27.	Pesticides	Miller, Ch.23: Pesticides
28.	Film: "The Insect Alternative"[1]	
29.	Hazardous waste	Miller, Ch.20: Risk, Human Health,..
30.	Pollution in central Europe	World Resources Institute (1992). Ch.5: Central Europe.
31.	Urbanization	Miller, Ch.9: Populations, urbanization.
32.	Land use planning	McPhee, Part 2: "An Island"; Miller, pp.132-143: Coastal Zone
33.	Environmental protection laws	Miller, Ch.25: Politics & environment
34-39.	Project presentations (Attendance required!)	
40.	EXAM #3 during finals week	

[1] NOVA Film Series
[2] American Experience Film Series

persistence on the planet, implementing such a program poses ethical implications for human rights, especially those of women (Salleh, 1984), which are well worth discussing in the classroom.

Ecofeminists have also criticized deep ecology for its lack of a social analysis and failure to incorporate the struggle for egalitarianism within the human race (Salleh, 1992). The deep ecology–ecofeminism debate makes for thought-provoking reading (Cheney, 1987; Fox, 1989; Salleh, 1984, 1992; Zimmerman, 1987).

Like ecofeminism, deep ecology is cynical about science, especially about its narrow oblivion to philosophical context and avoidance of real-world environmental conflicts. Golley (1987) found consistency between the major premises of deep ecology and the scientific principles of ecology, although my analysis reveals some naivete regarding recent discoveries about the dynamic, variable nature of real ecosystems.

Environmental activism is another related perspective from which to teach about the environment. Although ecofeminism and deep ecology are primarily concerned with changing our imperialist attitudes toward the environment, deep ecology also has a strong activist dimension. Earth First!, the environmental group known for its sometimes violent tactics, is loosely aligned with deep ecology. To cultivate activism, the class could immerse itself in a local environmental controversy as a sort of case study, going beyond "study" into involvement. By attending hearings, writing letters, and acquiring ecological data needed by environmental groups, students can acquire additional life skills while applying their book learning to real problems.

CONCLUSION

To summarize, environmental science courses can be transformed to encourage and train all students through attention to secondary content and pedagogy. My course for advanced undergraduates is only one model, itself imperfect and constantly changing as problems arise. I offer several strategies toward the goal of attracting and retaining women in science. I consciously strive to create an engaging experience for all students by forging connections to real-world problems, to real people, and across disciplinary boundaries. Feminist theory offers a framework from which to counter the fragmentation of knowledge and scrutinize scientific objectivity in the politicized environmental arena. It is imperative to ensure inclusive language, provide diverse role models, and offer mentoring opportunities. Advanced Environmental Science is also designed to build skills for success in the course and thereafter. With structured guidance and movement from modest to major assignments, students can make astounding progress with speaking and writing skills while simultaneously mastering subject matter more effectively through active learning. All students benefit when skills for communication and research are explicitly taught as part of course content, eliminating a "sink or swim" approach to student projects. Ongoing institutional support is needed to ensure small class sizes and manageable faculty workloads that permit the frequent feedback, learning through writing, and personal mentoring interactions that characterize a supportive learning environment for women and for all students.

REFERENCES

Adler, Emily S. (1984). A proposal for a course on the sociology of work and family (Working Paper No. 133). Wellesley, MA: Wellesley College Center for Research on Women.

Alper, Joe. (1992). War over the wetlands: Ecologists vs. the White House. *Science, 257*, 1043–1044.

Alper, Joe. (1993). The pipeline is leaking women all the way along. *Science, 260*, 409–410.

American Association for the Advancement of Science. (1990). The liberal art of science: Agenda for action. (Publication 90–135). Washington, DC: Author.

American Association of University Women. (1992). How schools shortchange girls. Washington, DC: AAUW Educational Foundation and National Education Association.

Appenzeller, T. (1991). Ozone loss hits us where we live. *Science, 254*, 645.

Belenky, Mary F., Clinchy, Blythe M., Goldberger, Nancy R., & Tarule, Jill M. (1986). *Women's ways of knowing*. New York: Basic Books.

Bleier, Ruth. (1984). *Science and gender: A critique of biology and its theories on women*. Elmsford, NY: Pergamon Press.

Brookes, W. T. (1989, December 25). The global warming panic. *Forbes*, pp. 96–102.

Chase, Alston. (1987, July). How to save our national parks. *Atlantic Monthly*, pp. 35–44.

Cheney, Jim. (1987). Ecofeminism and deep ecology. *Environmental Ethics, 9*, 115–145.

Clinchy, Blythe M., Belenky, Mary F., Goldberger, Nancy, & Tarule, Jill M. (1985). Connected education for women. *Journal of Education, 167*, 28–45.

Devall, Bill, & Sessions, George (Eds.). (1985). *Deep ecology: living as if nature mattered*. Salt Lake City, UT: Gibbs Smith.

Eccles, J. S., & Jacobs, J. E. (1987). Social forces shape math attitudes and performance. In M. R. Walsh (Ed.), *The psychology of women: Ongoing debates* (pp. 341–354). New Haven, CT: Yale University Press.

Fausto-Sterling, Anne. (1985). *Myths of gender: Biological theories about women and men*. New York: Basic Books.

Fee, Elizabeth. (1983). Women's nature and scientific objectivity. In Marian Lowe, & Ruth Hubbard (Eds.), *Women's nature: Rationalizations of inequality* (pp. 9–28). Elmsford, NY: Pergamon Press.

Fort, Deborah C. (Ed.). (1993). *A hand up: Women mentoring women in science*. Washington, D.C.: Association for Women in Science.

Fox, Warwick. (1989). The deep ecology-ecofeminism debate and its parallels. *Environmental Ethics, 11*, 5–25.

Golley, Frank B. (1987). Deep ecology from the perspective of ecological science. *Environmental Ethics, 9*, 45–55.

Golub, Sharon, & Freedman, Rita J. (1987). *Psychology of women: Resources for a core curriculum*. New York: Garland.

Gould, Stephen J. (1981). *The mismeasure of man*. New York: Norton.

Griffin, Susan. (1978). *Women and nature: The roaring inside her*. New York: Harper & Row.

Hall, Roberta M., & Sandler, Bernice R. (1982). *The classroom climate: A chilly one for women*? Washington, DC: Association of American Colleges.

Harding, Sandra. (1986). *The science question in feminism*. Ithaca, NY: Cornell University Press.

Harding, Sandra. (1991). *Whose science? Whose knowledge*? Ithaca, NY: Cornell University Press.

Hubbard, Ruth. (1979). Have only men evolved? In Ruth Hubbard, M. S. Henifin, & B. Fried (Eds.), *Women look at biology looking at women* (pp. 17–46). Cambridge, MA: Schenkman.

Hubbard, Ruth. (1983). Social effects of some contemporary myths about women. In Marian Lowe, & Ruth Hubbard (Eds.), *Women's nature: Rationalizations of inequality* (pp. 1–8). Elmsford, NY: Pergamon Press.

Hynes, H. Patricia. (1989). *The recurring silent spring*. Elmsford, NY: Pergamon Press.

Kerr, R. A. (1992). New assaults seen on earth's ozone shield. *Science, 255*, 797–798.

King, Ynestra. (1983). Toward an ecological feminism and a feminist ecology. In Joan Rothschild (Ed.). *Machina Ex Dea: Feminist perspectives on technology* (pp. 118–129). Elmsford, NY: Pergamon Press.

Kingsland, Sharon. (1985). *Modeling nature: Episodes in the history of population ecology*. Chicago: University of Chicago Press.

Lowe, Marian, & Hubbard, Ruth (Eds.). (1983). *Women's nature: Rationalizations of inequality*. Elmsford, NY: Pergamon Press.

Loucks, Orie L. (1992). Forest response research in NAPAP: Potentially successful linkage of policy and science. *Ecological Applications* 2, 117–223.

MacIntosh, Peggy. (1983). Interactive phases of curricular revision: A feminist perspective (Working Paper No. 124). Wellesley, MA: Wellesley College Center for Research on Women.

McPhee, John. (1971). *Encounters with the archdruid*. New York: Farrar, Straus, & Giroux.

Merchant, Carolyn. (1980). *The death of nature: Women, ecology, and the scientific revolution*. San Francisco: Harper San Francisco.

Merchant, Carolyn. (1985). Feminism and ecology. In Bill Devall, & George Sessions (Eds.), *Deep ecology: Living as if nature mattered* (pp. 229–231). Salt Lake City, UT: Gibbs Smith.

Meyers, Chet. (1986). *Teaching students to think critically*. San Francisco: Jossey-Bass.

Miller, Casey, & Swift, Kate. (1980). *The handbook of nonsexist writing*. New York: Harper & Row.

Miller, Casey, & Swift, Kate. (1991). *Words and women, updated*. New York: HarperCollins.

Miller, G. Tyler, Jr. (1990). *Living in the environment* (6th ed). Belmont, CA: Wadsworth.

Pearson, C., Shavlick, D., & Touchton, J. (1989). *Educating the majority: Women challenge tradition in higher education*. New York: Macmillan.

Peterman, Randall M. (1990). The importance of reporting statistical power: The forest decline and acidic deposition example. *Ecology, 71*, 2024–2027.

Plant, Judith (Ed.). (1989). *Healing the wounds: The promise of ecofeminism*. Philadelphia: New Society Publishers.

Prentice, Susan. (1988). Taking sides: What's wrong with ecofeminism? *Women and Environments, 10*, 9–10.

Primack, Richard B., & O'Leary, Virginia. (1993). Cumulative disadvantages in the careers of women ecologists. *BioScience, 43*, 158–165.

Quina, Kathryn. (1986). Teaching research methods: A multidimensional feminist curricular transformation plan (Working Paper No. 144). Wellesley, MA: Wellesley College Center for Research on Women.

Rosser, Sue V. (1986). *Teaching science and health from a feminist perspective: A practical guide*. Elmsford, NY: Pergamon.

Rosser, Sue V. (1990). *Female-friendly science*. Elmsford, NY: Pergamon.

Salleh, Ariel Kay. (1984). Deeper than deep ecology: The eco-feminist connection. *Environmental Ethics, 6*, 339–346.

Salleh, Ariel. (1992). The ecofeminism/deep ecology debate: A reply to patriarchal reason. *Environmental Ethics, 14*, 195–216.

Sandler, Bernice R. (1993). Mentoring: Myths and realities, dangers and responsibilities. In Deborah C. Fort, (Ed.), *A hand up: Women mentoring women in science* (pp. 271–279). Washington, DC: Association for Women in Science.

Schindler, David W. (1992). A view of NAPAP from north of the border. *Ecological Applications, 2*, 124–130.

Schneider, S. H. (1989, September). The changing climate. *Scientific America*, pp. 70–79.

Schuster, Marilyn, & Van Dyne, Susan. (1985). *Women's place in the academy: Transforming the liberal arts curriculum*. Totowa, NJ: Rowman and Allanheld.

Spanier, Bonnie, Bloom, Alexander, & Boroviak, Darlene (Eds). (1984). *Toward a balanced curriculum*. Cambridge, MA: Schenkman.

Tavris, Carol. (1992). *The mismeasure of woman*. New York: Touchstone.

Tobias, Sheila. (1990). *They're not dumb: They're different: Stalking the second tier*. Tucson, AZ: Research Corporation.

U.S. Environmental Protection Agency Science Advisory Board. (1990). Reducing risk: Setting priorities and strategies for environmental protection (Report SAB EC-90-021). Springfield, VA: National Technical Information Service.

Webb, Sara L., & Glenn, Marian G. (1993). Red spruce decline: A major role for acid deposition. *Ecology, 74,* 2170–2171.

World Resources Institute. (1992). *World Resources 1992.* New York: Oxford University Press.

Zimmerman, Michael E. (1987). Feminism, deep ecology, and environmental ethics. *Environmental Ethics, 9,* 21–44.

CHAPTER 12
No Classroom Is an Island

H. Patricia Hynes

No classroom is an island; it is a piece of the continent, a part of the mainland. Introducing feminist thought into university science and technology teaching, although singular and often solitary, is a highly charged undertaking—charged by the institution's culture of doing science and by its tradition of dealing with women. The stature of science and technology and the status of women at the Massachusetts Institute of Technology (MIT) were the continental backdrop for my course Environmental Pollution: Selected Problems, Solutions, and Policy, taught there from 1989 to 1993. I explore some of this figurative landscape briefly before introducing my course and pedagogy.

WOMEN ON THE MAINLAND

A thin thread of tradition can be traced back to MIT's first woman student and faculty member, Ellen Swallow, who is now honored and feted posthumously for pioneering environmental engineering and industrial ecology. In life, however, she was dismissed from MIT after 25 years of teaching and innovation. Caught in the middle of turf battles among the science departments during the latter part of the 19th century, she and her interdisciplinary curriculum of environmental science and human ecology were dismissed: "It was seen as an unpedigreed, mixed breed by the specialized science aristocracy—Swallow and most of her Ecology friends were women, and too few were scientists" (Clarke, 1973, pp. 152–153).

Her laboratory was closed; men she educated were named "father" of their respective disciplines; and she, in turn, was memorialized as the "mother of home economics." The fate of women faculty today at MIT who create their own agendas, be it feminism or another progressive worldview brought to a traditional discipline, is not unlike that of Swallow. Feminism applied to science, engineering, and environmental policy is envisaged—like home economics—as a small, domestic, unworldly endeavor that distracts from the hardcore, real world science, the clients for which are national and international government and industry.

Surprisingly, women students abound at MIT, with an average of 35% now entering at the undergraduate level. As more women students have entered, MIT has instituted, to its credit, a policy on pornography that prohibits the showing of pornographic films in common areas, including classrooms, lecture halls, corridors, and common spaces in dormitories. The policy cites the preponderance of female objectification and degradation in pornography as countervailing the institute's commitment to attract women students and build a climate of respect for women.

> Two factors give particular salience to the issue of pornography depicting the subjugation of women, and its effects on women at MIT. First, the preponderance of pornographic material focuses on women as the objects of degradation, abuse, and violence. Second, the Institute is committed to bringing large numbers of women into science and engineering. These recruitment efforts require a parallel commitment to maintain a suitable educational environment in which women and men can work as equals. (MIT Pornography Policy, 1990, p. 1)

Although the womanless past seems remote at MIT, male dominance is not; for gender change is apparent only at the bottom echelon, in what amounts to a trickle up model for "bringing larger numbers of women" into the institution. For example, in my years teaching environmental policy (1989–1993), in the Department of Urban Studies and Planning (DUSP), the status of women faculty in the department declined. In 1989 only 2 out of 20 tenured faculty in DUSP were women, and there were 3 women in the tenure-track category. By 1993, all of the women on a tenure-track line had been rejected for tenure. Thus, the number of tenure and tenure-track women faculty declined by 60% in a period of 4 years. During that same period women became a majority of the department's student population. Yet, in what has become an annual autumn ritual, male faculty rave at the quality of entering female students and remark tongue in cheek that the field is becoming a woman's field. The regressive movement of this department with regard to women faculty paralleled an erosion of intellectual vitality and political diversity in the department's offerings, made notable by several departures. Those who taught progressive labor theory, community economic development, and feminist theory on women and development left for more hospitable work environments, and a faculty member who spoke out consistently against racism and sexual harassment in the department took early retirement.

In tandem with the opening of doors to women students (while ceilings for women faculty stay solidly in place), MIT is undergoing a historical shift from being a defense-oriented technical institute to one with a well-coordinated environmental agenda in education and research. In the decades after World War II, "the Department of Defense," wrote historian of science Stuart Leslie, "became the single biggest patron of American science," particularly engineering and physical sciences, but also the natural and social sciences (quoted in Mitgang, 1993, p. C11). MIT has been widely known as a premier defense research and teaching institution, providing a steady stream of military research for the government and graduates for defense contractors. Electronics in labs and classrooms at MIT meant military electronics predominantly (Mitgang, 1993, p. C11). With the decline in defense contracts and the national transition to a more civilian economy, the Institute has launched ambitious environmental programs across the social, natural, and engineering sciences and the business school that range from global climate research and cleaner metallurgical processes to industrial ecology and pollution prevention.

However, there is no apparent shift in paradigm or pedagogy that parallels the shift in research and education. The major clients of research and teaching are still big industry and big government, whereas much of the national environmental agenda has been engendered by the studies, projects, and activism of nonprofit and community-based groups and coalitions. Like industrial processes, polluted natural systems are modeled mechanistically and will be salvaged in the classroom by top-down expert-designed technical fixes. This approach to environmental protection is solidly technocentric and avoids examining critically the role that an industrial worldview has in undermining ecological literacy, especially when applied to solve the very problems it has caused. Ultimately, MIT may play a substantial role in legitimating the ideology of neoclassical environmental economics in which natural resources are reified into natural capital and nature is commodified into a kind of gross natural product.

TEACHING THE MAJORITY

Within this MIT mainland, I taught a graduate course every spring semester entitled Environmental Pollution: Selected Problems, Solutions, and Policy. Class enrollment grew each year, with students coming from a wide variety of majors ranging from engineering, business, and government to environmental policy and design. The key learning objectives of the course included deepening both technical knowledge and a feminist analysis of specific topics such as pollution prevention, chemical pesticides and biotechnologies in agriculture, lead contamination in the urban environment, and the debates on environment and population. My explicit expectation for students was that they would fortify themselves with value-laden knowledge in order to challenge and transform the institutions in which they would work.

Having worked as a project engineer and then as a manager for the U.S. Environmental Protection Agency (EPA) and the Massachusetts Port Authority before teaching at MIT, I brought to the classroom experience-based insight into what professional qualities, in addition to technical expertise, help make women effective in the workplace. Consequently, I devised assignments that included group collaboration to teach skills of joint and equal decision making between men and women students; public speaking to teach voice projection and confidence on their feet; and short, persuasive memo writing and op-ed pieces as well as longer research papers. We discussed why women's voices are soft and often hesitant, who talks in class and who doesn't, and what in the classroom atmosphere frees and fetters their speech. To these discussions I added examples from my public-sector and consulting experience.

The pollution problems I selected for this course varied each year according to criteria such as timeliness of topic; significant national and international events, including the United Nations (U.N.) Conference on Environment and Development in Brazil and the U.N. Conference on Population and Development in Cairo; centrality of the issue in U.S. environmental policy and history; gravity of the issue for human health and environment; connections between urban policy and environmental policy; links with the environmental justice movement; and my expertise, current research, and writing. Feminist methods that I applied included raising questions of agency—for example, who does what to whom, who benefits, who pays?—about seemingly neutral pollution problems and posing questions about whose values and whose priorities have shaped particular research and policy agendas.

A key issue that meets many of the above-mentioned criteria and that has even more centrality in my course because of the recent U.N. conference on population is the subject commonly termed *environment and population*. With this issue, I illustrate the mix of technical and feminist analysis that I brought to the course.

ENVIRONMENT AND POPULATION

Debates in the United States about the impact of population growth on the environment emerged in the 1970s primarily among population-control groups. A formula published in 1974 by scientists Paul Ehrlich and John

Holdren, and then propounded by Paul and Anne Ehrlich in subsequent books, has framed the population-environment debate over the past 2 decades, so much so that advocates and critics alike have been locked into its parameters.

The impact of humans on the environment (I) is equal to the product of population (P), consumption of goods (A), and the pollution generated by manufacture and disposal of those goods (T). Thus:

$$\text{Environmental impact} = \text{Number of people} \times \frac{\text{Goods}}{\text{Person}} \times \frac{\text{Pollution}}{\text{Good}}$$

or I = PAT, where I is units of pollution.[1]

The rhetoric of "population bomb" and "population explosion" fortified the algebraic formula, gained it currency in environmental circles during the 1980s, and singularly weighted the P factor of IPAT. By 1990, environmental and population groups were consolidating a joint position that population was a major, if not the major, threat to the environment. Increased investment in international population control was the commonly held solution, with much more support for long-lasting hormonal methods such as Norplant for women than for barrier methods that would protect against both pregnancy and sexually transmitted diseases. Further, as the environment and population debate becomes more nuanced, the P of IPAT increasingly refers to the one fifth of humanity in Africa, Latin America, and southern Asia who are absolutely poor and have the highest fertility rates; the A and T are associated with the consumption and technology of the wealthiest and most industrialized fifth of the world's population. It is common now to read that the bottom billion and the top billion of the world—one by fertility rates, the other by lifestyle—pose equal threats to the planet. This facile adaptation of the IPAT equation obscures the differences in power, gender, race, and class between the poorest fifth of the world, who are mainly women and children of color, and the wealthiest fifth, the majority of whom are white men.

As preparations for the U.N. conference on population were getting under way, the growth curve of white papers, policy statements, and position papers calling for fertility control and demographic targets accelerated. Women's international health networks and organizations as well as feminist environmentalists rapidly recognized that unless feminists were central participants at the Cairo conference and unless feminists challenged the argot of IPAT, the conference could result in a setback for the reproductive rights of poor women. (As this book went to press, the Cairo conference was in progress.)

My initial assignment on the IPAT topic would be for students to discover the inconsistency and bias in its use. They would explore why, despite the lip service to consumption in the formula, concepts such as "consumption bomb" and "consumption explosion" have barely gotten a foothold in environmental policy, whereas demographically driven international population programs have a 20- to 30-year history of abuse of poor women of color. Students could do a content analysis of policy papers from national government, U.N. agencies, and environmental journals to document the discrepant emphasis on the roles of population and consumption in environmental degradation. Their findings could begin a discussion of bias, self-interest, and economic protectionism in U.S. and U.N. environmental policy and mainstream environmental research.

Next we would examine the elements of the equation, asking whether they are accurate and sufficient in modeling human impact on the environment. I would introduce the fact that key structural factors in environmental degradation—military pollution, the burden of debt in developing countries that has further impoverished the "bottom billion," and female subordination—are omitted from the algebraic model and subsequent public-policy analysis on the environment and population. In this discussion, we would examine the limitations of an equation that models only a particular biophysical reality—the fact that each human generates waste in his or her daily activities—but ignores complex social and political factors that are integral to the issue. The question then arises, Can the equation be corrected, or should it be jettisoned? I would suggest that we try to correct it.

My underlying pedagogical objectives are to place women's human rights and environmental justice at the core of the environment-population debate and to give students practice in working with and amending a controversial algebraic identity so that they gain intellectual competence and confidence with it. My method would be to reformulate the I=PAT equation in a participatory session with students by separating the survival activities of all people from the luxury ones of a minority, by adding factors that include the military impact on the environment and the environmental benefits of people as resource managers, and by employing an analysis of male and female agency in each factor of the equation. In the final discussion, we would devise a feminist public policy on population and environment.

The equation would ultimately be reformulated accordingly:

$$I = [PAT]_{survival} + [PAT]_{luxury} + MAT - C$$

where $[PAT]_{survival}$ is the aggregate of resources such as land, forests, and water used by all humans for survival.

$[PAT]_{luxury}$ is the aggregate impact of those humans consuming luxury goods and services that generate significant pollution, such as golf courses, speedboats, and private planes.

M is the military population, particularly those with authority over budget, arms technology, and defense policy.

A is the consumption of renewable and nonrenewable resources such as land, oil, metal, and solvents for manufacture of military hardware, testing, maneuvers, and war.

T is the pollution generated by research, weapons manufacture, testing, maneuvers, uranium and metals mining, and waste disposal.

C is the environmentally beneficial work of natural resource management, preservation, and restoration; indigenous dooryard gardens that preserve agricultural biodiversity; urban forests; gardens; and composting (Hynes, 1993, pp. 16, 26).

We would discuss the significance of factors such as MAT, drawing from environmental studies that estimate the pollution impact of the military. Working with unevenly reported data, researchers estimate, for example, that the military accounts for 5% to 10% of global air pollution, carbon dioxide, ozone depletion, and smog- and acid-rain–forming chemicals. The Research Institute for Peace Policy (Hynes, 1993, p. 20) in Starnberg, Germany, estimates that 20% of all global environmental degradation is due to military and related activities. These figures for a relatively small population of military personnel are contrasted with the lesser impact of the poorest billion people who are now the targets of international population-control policy.

Next I would point out that IPAT envisages humans as having only a negative impact on the environment, as parasites, predators, and polluters. Yet we have models of environmental stewardship in the Chipko forest-saving movement of India and the Green Belt movement of Africa, in the stable existence of indigenous peoples in rain forests for centuries. Feminist environmentalists, geographers, and development experts have documented that the majority of environmental stewards and resource managers in developing countries are women (Seager, 1993). By adding the factor C to IPAT to account for the positive environmental impact of some humans, we could also discuss the difference between what Winona LaDuke (cited in Hynes, 1993, p. 23) calls the "industrial mind" and the "indigenous mind" in order to identify the cultural roots of this equation.

Taking the reformulated equation, I would pose a series of questions that encourage students to look at human agency and responsibility in the factors of the equation.

- How often do women choose to become pregnant?
- How free are women to avoid pregnancy?
- What are the links between male subordination of girls and women—through rape, unavailability of safe birth control and abortion, refusal to use or allow birth control, feminization of poverty, and compulsory heterosexuality—and population rates?
- Why are the hormonal and chemically altering birth-control technologies that carry risk of cancer, infection, and death developed for use on women while indigenous methods are ignored and low-tech methods for men are underutilized?
- Why don't men love women enough to use condoms or undergo vasectomies and collectively demand more research on male birth-control methods?
- If a country spends two times more on military armaments than on health and education, who is responsible for high fertility rates in that country if infant and child mortality is high, if contraceptives are not available when people want them, and if girls drop out of school sooner to help with household work?
- Do men and women spend and consume differently, both in quantity and in kinds of goods, in developed and developing countries? What implications do these differences have for environmental policy on reducing consumption?
- If women have been systematically barred and discouraged from the physical sciences and engineering, who is primarily responsible for the T of IPAT, that is, the global climate change–inducing and other polluting technology?
- What is ecological literacy, and what would be the science and technology priorities of an ecologically literate people?

We would conclude the session on this topic with the class creating a feminist policy on population and environment. Although this is an open-ended, collaborative project, the recommendations year-to-year have had many common themes. They include moving away from demographic targets and toward overall reproductive health programs, educating men as well as women in sexuality and reproduction, reducing military budgets and forgiving international debt, investing in ecological literacy and environmental stewardship projects, and having industrial countries commit to reducing their consumption of global resources.[2]

AFTERWORD

The students who enrolled in this course were genuinely hungry for a feminist and humanist study of environment that takes on the limitations of a technocentric model but does not jettison the technical. However, the mental mainland of environmental science, engineering, and policy is deeply estranged from and hostile to analysis of the sexual politics of pollution. No classroom is an island—even if it is an oasis from the dominant pedagogy and methods. The crucible for me is no longer feminist pedagogy and feminist content in the classroom—this is trusted terrain. It is, rather, the not yet female-friendly continent and mainland.

NOTES

1. The IPAT formula was first published in Paul Ehrlich and John Holdren (1974). Impact of population growth. *Science*, Vol. 171, 1212–1217. In 1977 the two co-authored *Ecoscience* with Anne Ehrlich, in which they propounded the same formulaic approach to population. See also Paul Ehrlich and Anne Ehrlich. (1990). *The Population Explosion*, New York: Simon & Schuster.

2. A complete analysis of the IPAT equation is available as a 64 page report entitled *Taking Population Out of the Equation: Reformulating I=PAT*. It is published and sold for $7.00 by the Institute on Women and Technology, P.O. Box 9338, North Amherst, MA 01059–9338.

REFERENCES

Clarke, Robert. (1973). *Ellen Swallow: The Women Who Founded Ecology*. Chicago: Follett.

Hynes, H. Patricia. (1993). *Taking Population Out of the Equation: Reformulating I=PAT*. North Amherst, MA: Institute on Women and Technology.

MIT Pornography Policy. (1990). Cambridge, MA: MIT.

Mitgang, Herbert. (1993, June 1). Review of Leslie Stuart. *The Cold War and American Science. The New York Times* p. C11.

Seager, Joni. (1993). *Earth Follies*. New York: Routledge.

CONCLUSION

Changing Curriculum and Pedagogy to Reach the Majority Results in a Positive Upward Spiral

Sue V. Rosser

The transformed curricula, expanded problem sets and laboratory exercises, and successful pedagogical techniques presented by the authors of *Teaching the Majority* were contributed to aid others in breaking the gender barrier in science and technology. The authors hope to encourage faculty members at colleges, universities, and institutes of technology who teach courses in geology, chemistry, physics, mathematics, computer science, environmental science, and engineering on both the undergraduate and graduate levels to undertake similar initiatives in the courses they teach. Deans, department chairs, and other administrators may use *Teaching the Majority* as a foundation for faculty development workshops designed to integrate the new scholarship on women into the physical sciences, mathematics, and engineering. Many professionals outside of academia, such as managers in industry and government who give on-the-job training to engineers, scientists, and technicians, will find new models and ideas to use with their employees.

The authors of *Teaching the Majority* have explored changing curricula and teaching techniques in the hope of producing a different composition in the pool of scientists—scientists who hold a slightly modified theoretical perspective. This perspective may in turn be reflected in further transformation of curricula and teaching techniques to make science more attractive to women and to people of color. The ultimate end of this up-

A different version of parts of this chapter appeared under the title "Diversity among students—Inclusive curriculum—Improved science: An upward spiral," by Sue V. Rosser (1993) in *Initiatives, 55*(2): 11–19.

ward spiral would be the creation of a community of scientists that proportionately represents the diversity of the population as a whole with regard to gender, race, class, and sexual orientation.

A spiral implies continuity and linkage among the steps or stages leading from one part to the next—leading from lack of diversity in science to diversity within the community of scientists proportional to the population as a whole. Seven steps are used to describe this positive upward spiral in this concluding chapter. Each step includes four interacting factors: composition of the pool of scientists, curricular content, theoretical underpinnings, and pedagogical techniques. Each factor interacts and links with other factors at its step and with factors at other steps. The seven-step spiral describes a scenario for breaking the gender and race barriers in science and technology to teach the majority.

STEP 1

At this stage, the community of scientists consists of white middle- to upper-class men from relatively homogeneous ethnic backgrounds rooted in the Judeo-Christian tradition who either are heterosexual or assume a heterosexual norm. Although they think little about the philosophical or historical underpinnings of their approach to science (most have never taken a course in the history or philosophy of science), they are logical positivists. They believe that science can be both objective and value-free (Jaggar, 1983).

Their beliefs in objectivity and the value-free nature of scientific inquiry are reflected in their approaches to pedagogy and curriculum, and they have not noticed the absence of women. Since science and its presentation through textbooks, laboratory exercises, and other curricular materials are objective, they are assumed to be free from any bias, including those of race, class, or gender. In teaching this nonbiased curriculum, the scientist puts considerable emphasis on the distance between the scientist as observer and the object or subject he or she is observing, as a mechanism for maintaining objectivity. Although the scientist-teacher recognizes that some students enter the course better prepared than others, such differences are assumed to be the result of differential innate abilities or motivations to take advantage of educational opportunities. A uniform background of hands-on experiences and previous equitable treatment in the classroom is not questioned. Competition among peers is fostered through techniques such as working problems at the board, taking timed tests, and working individually to solve problems, complete experiments, or write laboratory reports.

STEP 2

A few women receive undergraduate and graduate degrees in science. They are part of the community of scientists, and in their roles as technicians, research associates, and high school science teachers, they perform much of the actual work of science. However, none of them holds a theoretical or decision-making position within the scientific establishment or has direct power within the scientific hierarchy. Although these women are logical positivists who accept the objective and value-free nature of science, some occasionally reflect that the science produced by men represents a masculine approach to the physical and natural world (Keller, 1982, 1985). They note that they occasionally jar their male superiors when they suggest a different approach to solving a problem. When this occurs, both the woman scientist and the male head of the laboratory note that it was an event from her experiences growing up as a female that led her to that different approach to the solution.

At step 2, the scientist-teacher makes no changes in the curricular content from step 1, except to note that most scientists have been and continue to be men, and perhaps to discuss this with the students and to wonder privately whether curricular content based on science created predominantly by women scientists would differ from current curriculum. Although continuing to use traditional techniques for teaching science, the scientist-teacher notes that the female students seem particularly turned off by problems in which bombs, rocket trajectories, or other military terminology is used. In contrast to the male students, the female students are particularly eager to solve similar problems when they are embedded in a social context that might help another person (J. Harding, 1985). The scientist-teacher also notes that male students seem enthusiastic about solving problems on a reduced, limited scale—problems that have clear-cut solutions. The female students seem restive with reductionistic approaches and want to know how the small question resolved by this particular experiment relates to a problem on a more global scale that cannot be resolved either by this experiment or by using only the methods of science (Rosser, 1990). The scientist-teacher wonders whether these observations about male and female students are unique to his or her population of students and whether they might have contributed to the fact that there are more men than women seeking careers in science.

STEP 3

More women enter science and are able to make their livings through careers in science. Most work in industry, where they may receive minor contract grants or work under the supervision of male senior scientists. Some teach in community colleges or 4-year liberal arts colleges; none holds a theoretical or decision-making position in a prestigious educational institution or economically powerful company. When these women scientists become aware that they can't reach higher-level positions within the establishment, they begin to explore specific barriers (Matyas, 1985; National Science Foundation [NSF], 1992; Vetter, 1992) and to research obstacles evident from the history of women in science (Keller, 1983; Rossiter, 1982; Sayre, 1975) that may have contributed to the problem. Some brave women scientists discuss the barriers and obstacles with their male colleagues and superiors.

At this stage in their teaching, women scientists and their enlightened male colleagues begin to raise questions about whether the objectivity of science may in fact harbor a hidden androcentric bias. Since virtually all scientists in decision-making positions are men, how will any bias that reflects a male perspective on the world be winnowed out when the male scientific community scrutinizes the hypothesis? At some level, the scientist-teacher recognizes that he or she is moving away from the acceptance of the objective, value-free nature of scientific knowledge toward the acceptance of the social construction of all knowledge, including scientific knowledge (Kuhn, 1970; Longino, 1990).

Based on these new perspectives on science and science curriculum, the scientist-teacher begins to try new techniques. Recognizing that sex-role socialization and different extracurricular activities (Kahle, 1985) may be responsible for the data from the National Assessment of Educational Progress (NSF, 1992) indicating that females have significantly fewer science experiences than males of comparable ages, the scientist-teacher considers alternative structures for the laboratory. He or she expands the numbers and kinds of observations and permits the students more time for the observational stage in the laboratory, understanding that girls and young women who lack hands-on experience with laboratory equipment are apt to feel apprehensive about using it to gather data (Daniels & LeBold, 1982). Incorporating and validating personal experiences that women are likely to have had as part of class discussions or laboratory exercises also allows females to feel more comfortable in an environment in which many phenomena may be unfamiliar.

The scientist-teacher wonders whether work done by women scientists has often differed from that done by male scientists. She or he questions whether women scientists' work serves as a corrective to biased science or whether it represents isolated examples.

STEP 4

More women become scientists, but most find positions in science-related fields. Those in science research usually work in the less prestigious institutions or companies. The few who work in more prestigious institutions and companies do not reach the top levels of the scientific hierarchy.

Aware of their marginalized position and of the barriers keeping them from the higher positions, they begin to search for the missing women who must have been shunted to the periphery in the past. Historians of science have shown that although women have always been in science, their work was often defined as nonscience (Hynes, 1989; Mozans, 1974), misunderstood (Sayre, 1975), ignored (Keller, 1983), or attributed to the husband, brother, or father with whom they worked (Schiebinger, 1989).

When they see that women scientists and their work have been excluded from the mainstream of scientific thought, scientists begin to question the flaws in science that may have resulted from this. Feminist historians and philosophers of science (Fee, 1982, 1986; Haraway, 1978, 1990; S. Harding, 1986; Longino, 1990) and feminist scientists (Birke, 1986; Bleier, 1984, 1986; Fausto-Sterling, 1992; Keller, 1983, 1985; Rosser, 1988) have pointed out a source of bias and absence of value-neutrality in science, particularly biology.

By excluding females as experimental subjects, focusing on problems of primary interest to males, using faulty experimental designs, and interpreting data based on language or ideas constricted by patriarchal parameters, scientists obtained experimental results in several areas of biology that were biased or flawed. These flaws and biases were permitted to become part of the mainstream of scientific thought and were perpetuated in the scientific literature for decades, because most scientists were men. Since most, if not all, scientists were men, values held by them as males were not distinguished as biasing. Values held by male scientists were congruent with values of all scientists and became synonymous with the "objective" view of the world (Keller, 1982, 1985).

The scientist-teacher uses information from the search for missing women scientists and its potential biasing efects in making pedagogical changes to include and name famous women scientists in discussions of material whenever possible. In addition to including the nine women who have won the Nobel Prize in physiology or medicine, she or he uses the first and last names of all experimenters. In selecting problems or examples for illustration, she or he looks to fields such as home economics (Hynes, 1989) and nursing—traditionally defined as nonscience, partially because they are dominated by women—as possible sources for material and corrects laboratory exercises to include females as subjects, pointing out to students the previous flaw in the experiment.

In drawing theories and conclusions from the data, the scientist-teacher encourages students to describe their results in precise gender-neutral language. When teaching how to write a laboratory report, he or she prods the students to examine problems associated with extrapolating beyond what the data warrant (for example, when results from an experiment run on only males are applied to both males and females of the species). He or she also invites students to question to what extent the required use of the passive voice in scientific writing reinforces notions of objectivity and distance between observer and object of study and hides biases such as gender, race, and class, which might be more readily apparent if the scientist wrote in the active voice.

STEP 5

More women enter science. A select few reach leadership positions after more years and more outstanding contributions than white male scientists of their generation. Impressed by the work of their female colleagues and by women's contributions to the history of science, a few women use the lens of gender to compare and contrast the work done by women with that done by men. The theoretical question that shapes their comparisons and contrasts is What would be the parameters of a feminist or woman-centered science? They suspect that such a science might focus on problems of particular concern to women such as pregnancy, childbirth, menstruation, and menopause in the arena of health. It might consider the social values and significance of research for human beings in determining whether the research should be funded. The anatomy, physiology, and life-cycle changes of the female might become the norm against which variations are measured. Approaches that shorten the distance between the experimenter and the subject of study are explored, and feelings for the organism under study are permitted.

Consideration of the parameters of a woman-centered science leads the scientist-teacher to incorporate pedagogical techniques that are more in tune with female life cycles and experiences. Exploration of socialization processes and theories of female developmental psychology (Chodorow, 1978; Belenky, Clinchy, Goldberger, & Tarule, 1986) leads the scientist-teacher to evolve less competitive models to teach science. Avoiding timed tests and competitions to see who can solve the problem first at the blackboard and encouraging cooperative problem solving where everyone "wins" may be more attractive to women students. A consideration of differences in the life cycles of men and women leads the scientist-teacher to consider research demonstrating that many potential women scientists drop out of science because of their perception that being a scientist is incompatible with having a relationship or a family (Arnold, 1987). They discuss the role of scientist as only one facet that must be smoothly integrated with other aspects of women's lives. They provide the class with role models of practicing women scientists who demonstrate that a successful career in science can be combined with a variety of lifestyle options.

STEP 6

More people of color and individuals of different classes, ethnicities, and sexual orientations, as well as more women, become scientists. Despite the increased diversity in this larger pool of scientists, white middle- to upper-class heterosexual men continue to dominate the leadership positions in the scientific establishment. The exclusion of men because of race, class, or sexual orientation leads women to recognize the intersection of gender with race, class, and sexual orientation to determine in part the position of individual scientists within the scientific hierarchy.

A realization that factors in addition to gender strongly influence who becomes a leader in science causes women to recognize that the androcentric bias in science research may be compounded by ethnocentric, class, and homophobic bias. The scientist-teacher encourages students to uncover all biases and to explore similarities and differences in the critiques written by individuals based on class, race, and gender. For example, reading *Black Apollo of Science: The Life of Ernest Everett Just* (Manning, 1983) helps sensitize students to the discrimination and alienation felt by African American male scientists. Comparing Manning's work and other African American critiques of science with feminist critiques helps elucidate the separate but overlapping biases contributed by race and gender (Fee, 1986; S. Harding, 1986).

STEP 7

At this final stage of the upward spiral, the diversity of race, class, gender, and sexual orientation within the pool of scientists is proportional to the diversity within the population as a whole. That diversity is also represented proportionally within the scientific leadership. Diversity within the pool of scientists has produced an inclusive curriculum in which flaws in research from androcentric and other biases due to race, class, and sexual orientation have been corrected. Hypotheses held up for scrutiny to the scientific community are refined by a continuing dialogue between a diverse community of scientists and laypeople.

In the classroom and laboratory, the scientist-teacher demonstrates and encourages students to use interdisciplinary approaches to problem solving that combine qualitative and quantitative methods where appropriate (Rosser, 1990). She or he encourages the development of theories and hypotheses that are relational, interdependent, and multicausal; discusses the practical uses of scientific discoveries to help students place science in its social context; and communicates with nonscientists to eliminate any barriers that continue to separate the scientist from the layperson (Bentley, 1985).

Laypeople also work to communicate with scientists and eliminate any remaining barriers. Since the people who are scientists represent the diversity of individuals within the broader population, the work scientists do is perceived as being in the best interests of the population. More people are eager to become scientists because science is no longer seen as the province of white, middle- to upper-class, heterosexual men. Because the necessity of having a diverse pool of scientists to produce an improved science that is not biased by the perspective of only one group is recognized, more people seek to become scientists to maintain that diversity. As more people from different races, classes, ethnic backgrounds, and genders become scientists, the science they develop is more accessible, varied, and humane. The authors of *Teaching the Majority* hope that this volume provides a step toward such diversity and improved science.

REFERENCES

Arnold, Karen. (1987). *Retaining high achieving women in science and engineering.* Paper presented at Women in Science and Engineering: Changing Vision to Reality conference, University of Michigan, Ann Arbor, sponsored by the American Association for the Advancement of Science.

Belenky, Mary Field, Clinchy, Blythe McVicker, Goldberger, Nancy R., & Tarule, Jill Mattuck. (1986). *Women's ways of knowing.* New York: Basic Books.

Bentley, Diana. (1985). Men may understand the words, but do they know the music? Some cries de coeur in science education. In *Supplementary Contributions to the Third GASAT Conference* (pp. 160–168). London: Chelsea College, University of London.

Birke, Lynda. (1986). *Women, feminism, and biology: The feminist challenge.* New York: Methuen.

Bleier, Ruth. (1984). *Science and gender: A critique of biology and its theories on women.* Elmsford, NY: Pergamon Press.

Bleier, Ruth. (1986). Sex differences research: Science or belief? In Ruth Bleier (Ed.), *Feminist approaches to science* (pp. 147–164). Elmsford, NY: Pergamon Press.
Chodorow, Nancy. (1978). *The reproduction of mothering: Psychoanalysis and the sociology of gender*. Berkeley, CA: University of California Press.
Daniels, Jane, & LeBold, William. (1982). Women in engineering: A dynamic approach. In Sheila Humphreys (Ed.), *Women and minorities in science* (pp. 139–163). AAAS Selected Symposia Series. Boulder, CO: Westview.
Fausto-Sterling, Anne. (1992). *Myths of gender*. New York: Basic Books.
Fee, Elizabeth. (1982). A feminist critique of scientific objectivity. *Science for the People, 14*(4), 8.
Fee, Elizabeth. (1986). Critiques of modern science: The relationship of feminism to other radical epistemologies. In Ruth Bleier (Ed.), *Feminist approaches to science* (pp. 42–56). Elmsford, NY: Pergamon Press.
Haraway, Donna. (1978). Animal sociology and a natural economy of the body politic. *Signs, 4*(1), 21–60.
Haraway, Donna. (1990). *Primate visions*. New York: Routledge.
Harding, Jan. (1985). Values, cognitive style and the curriculum. In *Contributions to the Third Girls and Science and Technology Conference* (pp. 159–166). London: Chelsea College, University of London.
Harding, Sandra. (1986). *The science question in feminism*. Ithaca, NY: Cornell University Press.
Hynes, Patricia. (1989). *The recurring silent spring*. Elmsford, NY: Pergamon Press.
Jaggar, Alison. (1983). *Feminist politics and human nature*. Totowa, NJ: Rowman & Allanheld.
Kahle, Jane B. (1985). *Women in science*. Philadelphia: Falmer Press.
Keller, Evelyn F. (1982). Feminism and science. *Signs, 7*(3), 589–602.
Keller, Evelyn F. (1983). *A feeling for the organism*. San Francisco: Freeman.
Keller, Evelyn F. (1985). *Reflections on gender and science*. New Haven, CT: Yale University Press.
Kuhn, Thomas. (1970). *The structure of scientific revolutions*. Chicago: University of Chicago Press.
Longino, Helen. (1990). *Science as social knowledge*. Princeton, NJ: Princeton University Press.
Manning, Kenneth. (1983). *Black Apollo of science: The Life of Ernest Everett Just*. Oxford: Oxford University Press.
Matyas, Marsha L. (1985). Obstacles and constraints on women in science. In Jane B. Kahle (Ed.), *Women in science* (pp. 77–101). Philadelphia: Falmer Press.
Mozans, H.J. (1974). *Women in science*. Cambridge, MA: MIT Press. (Original work published 1913)
National Science Foundation. (1992). *Women and minorities in science and engineering: An update* (NSF 92-303). Washington, DC: Author.
Rosser, Sue V. (1988). *Feminism within the science and health care professions: Overcoming resistance*. Elmsford, NY: Pergamon Press.
Rosser, Sue V. (1990). *Female friendly science*. Elmsford, NY: Pergamon Press.
Rossiter, Margaret. (1982). *Women scientists in America: Struggles and strategies to 1940*. Baltimore: Johns Hopkins University Press.

Sayre, Anne. (1975). *Rosalind Franklin and DNA: A vivid view of what it is like to be a gifted woman in an especially male profession.* New York: Norton.
Schiebinger, Londa. (1989). *The mind has no sex? Women in the origins of modern science.* Cambridge, MA: Harvard University Press.
Vetter, Betty M. (1992). *What is holding up the glass ceiling? Barriers to women in the science and engineering workforce* (Occasional Paper 92-3). Washington, DC: Commission on Professionals in Science and Technology.

Bibliography

Faye A. Chadwell

This bibliography emphasizes the feminist transformation of the science classroom through curricular and pedagogical changes. The major section has a broad focus covering science, engineering, and mathematics. The individual sections that follow pinpoint particular areas: astronomy, chemistry, computer science, engineering, geological sciences, mathematics, physics, and technology.

GENERAL

Adamu, Abdalla U. (1990, June). Balancing the equation—girls, tradition, and science education in northern Nigeria. *AFHAD Journal, 7*, 14–31.

Aldrich, Michele L., & Hall, Paula Quick. (Compilers with the assistance of K. L. Ehrlich, R. Long, & R. Warner). (1980). *Programs in science, mathematics, and engineering for women in the United States: 1966–1978*. Washington, DC: American Association for the Advancement of Science. (ERIC Document Reproduction Service No. ED 199 049)

Alic, Margaret. (1979). Discovering the history of women in science: A course outline. *Science for the People, 11*(6), 27–28.

Alic, Margaret. (1982). The history of women in science: A women's studies course. *Women's Studies International Forum, 5*(1), 75–82.

Allen, Nessy. (1992). A proposed course on women in science in an Australian university. *Feminist Teacher, 6*(3), 40–44.

Alper, Joe, & Gibbons, Ann. (1993, April 16). The pipeline is leaking women all the way along. *Science, 260*(5106), 409–411.

Balka, Ellen. (1986, November). Calculus and coffee cups—learning science on your own. *Resources for Feminist Research, 15*, 11–12.

Banziger, George. (1992). Women-in-the-sciences program at Marietta College: Focusing on math to keep women in science. *Journal of College Science Teaching, 21*(5), 279–281.

Barba, Roberta H., Pang, Valerie O., & Tran, Myluong T. (1992). Who really discovered aspirin? *Science Teacher, 59*(5), 26–27.

Barinaga, Marcia, & Gibbons, Ann. (1993, April 16). Feminists find gender everywhere in science. *Science, 260*(5106), 392–393.

Bartlett, Diana. (1989, May 20). A suitable job for a woman? *New Scientist, 122*(1665), 64–65.

Beauchamp, Rachelle S. (Ed.). (1991). Women in science: Options and intolerance [Special issue]. *Women's Education Des Femmes, 9*(2).

Birchmore, Sue. (1989, August 26). How to get your woman. *New Scientist, 123*(1679), 64–65.

Black achievers in science: Teacher's guide. (1988). Chicago: Museum of Science and Industry.

Bleier, Ruth (Ed.). (1986). *Feminist approaches to science.* New York: Pergamon Press.

Blosser, Patricia E. (1990). *Procedures to increase the entry of women into science-related careers.* Washington, DC: Office of Educational Research and Improvement.

Borman, Stu. (1991, November 4). College science studies: Women, minority recruitment lags. *Chemical & Engineering News, 69*(44), 6–7.

Brennan, Mairin B. (1993, February 8). Women scientists, engineers seek more equitable industrial environment. *Chemical & Engineering News, 71*(6), 13–16.

Brennan, Mairin B. (1993, June 14). Programs seek to draw more women into engineering and science. *Chemical & Engineering News, 71*(24), 43–44, 46, 47.

Briscoe, Anne M., & Pffaflin, Sheila M. (Eds.). (1979). *Expanding the role of women in science.* New York: New York Academy of Sciences.

Brodsky, Stanley M. (1989). *Staff development to improve recruitment & retention of women & minorities in associate degree science & engineering technology programs. Final report.* New York: City University of New York, Institute for Research and Development in Occupational Education. (ERIC Document Reproduction Service No. ED 323 082)

Brodsky, Stanley M. (1990). *Campus seminars/workshops to improve recruitment and retention of women and minorities in associate degree science and engineering technology programs. Final report.* Albany, NY: New York State Education Department. (ERIC Document Reproduction Service No. ED 325 197)

Brodsky, Stanley M. (1991). *Campus seminars/workshops on strategies for retention of women & minorities in associate degree science & engineering-related programs.* Albany, NY: New York State Education Department. (ERIC Document Reproduction Service No. ED 338 158)

Brush, Stephen G. (1991). Women in science and engineering. *American Scientist, 79*(5), 404–419.

Campbell, Patricia B. (1992a). *Math, science, and your daughter: What can parents do? Encouraging girls in math and science series.* Washington, DC: Women's Educational Equity Program. (ERIC Document Reproduction Service No. ED 350 172)

Campbell, Patricia B. (1992b). *Nothing can stop us now: Designing effective programs for girls in math, science, and engineering. Encouraging girls in math and science series.* Washington, DC: Women's Educational Equity Program. (ERIC Document Reproduction Service No. ED 350 173)

Campbell, Patricia B. (1992c). *What works and what doesn't? Ways to evaluate programs for girls in math, science, and engineering. Encouraging girls in math and science series*. Washington, DC: Women's Educational Equity Program. (ERIC Document Reproduction Service No. ED 350 171)

Campbell, Patricia B. (1992d). *Working together, making changes: Working in and out of school to encourage girls in math and science. Encouraging girls in math and science series*. Washington, DC: Women's Educational Equity Program. (ERIC Document Reproduction Service No. ED 350 170)

Carter, Carol J. (1987). Strategies for recruiting and retaining minorities and women in nontraditional programs. *New Directions for Higher Education, 15*(1), 75–82.

Cassidy, Robert. (1989). What do women want? A chance to be scientists. *R&D, 31*(4), 11.

Chinn, Phyllis Zweig. (Comp.) (1988). *Women in science and mathematics: Bibliography*. Arcata, CA: Humboldt State University Foundation. (ERIC Document Reproduction Service No. ED 316 435)

Chomicka, Debra, Truchan, Leona, & Gurria, George. (1992). The "Women in Science Day" at Alverno College: Collaboration that leads to success. *Journal of College Science Teaching, 21*(5), 306–309.

Clark, Julia V. (1988, March/April). Black women in science: Implications for improved participation. *Journal of College Science Teaching, 17*, 348–352.

Clewell, Beatriz C., & Anderson, Bernice. (1991). *Women of color in mathematics, science & engineering: A review of the literature*. Washington, DC: Center for Women Policy Studies. (ERIC Document Reproduction Service No. ED 347 222)

Cole, Michael, & Griffin, Peg. (Eds.). (1987). *Contextual factors in education: improving science and mathematics education for minorities and women*. Madison, WI: Wisconsin Center for Education Research. (ERIC Document Reproduction Service No. ED 288 947)

Collea, Francis P. (1990). Increasing minorities in science and engineering: A critical look at two programs. *Journal of College Science Teaching, 20*(1), 31–34, 41.

Cooper, Bruce S. (1987). Retooling teachers: The New York experience. *Phi Delta Kappan, 68*(8), 606–609.

Cordes, Colleen. (1988, November 16). Colleges try to attract women and minority students to the sciences. *Chronicle of Higher Education, 35*(12), A33–A34.

Culotta, Elizabetta, Kahn, Patricia, Koppel, Toomas, & Gibbons, Ann. (1993, April 16). Women struggle to crack the code of corporate culture. *Science, 260*(5106), 398–404.

Damarin, Suzanne K. (1991). Rethinking science and mathematics curriculum and instruction: Feminist perspectives in the computer era. *Journal of Education, 173*(1), 107–23.

Davis, Barbara G., & Humphreys, Sheila M. (1985). *Evaluating intervention programs: Applications from women's studies programs in math and science*. New York: Teachers College Press.

Didion, Catherine J. (1993, May). Attracting graduate and undergraduate women as science majors. *Journal of College Science Teaching, 22*(6), 336, 368.

Didion, Catherine J. (1993, September). Letter of reference: An often-deciding factor in women's academic or career advancement. *Journal of College Science Teaching, 23*(1), 9–10.

Dix, Linda S., Matyas, M. L., & Dresselhaus, Mildred S. (Eds.). (1992). *Science and engineering programs: On target for women?* Washington, DC: National Academy Press.

Dobson, Henry D., & Hranitz, John R. (1992). *Adapting the thinking processes to enhance science skills in females and minorities.* Paper presented at the annual conference of the Institute for Critical Thinking (Montclair, NJ, 1990). (ERIC Document Reproduction Service No. ED 350 288)

Dresselhaus, Mildred S. (1983). *Current crisis in science education? Women in science and problems for the behavioral scientists. Some perspectives of a physicist.* Paper presented at the 91st annual convention of the American Psychological Association, Anaheim, CA. (ERIC Document Reproduction Service No. ED 241 870)

Dresselhaus, Mildred S. (Ed.). (1991). *Women in science and engineering: Increasing their numbers in the 1990s; A statement on policy and strategy.* Washington, DC: National Academy Press.

Eldredge, Mary. (1990). Gender, science, and technology: A selected annotated bibliography. *Behavioral & Social Sciences Librarian, 9*(1), 77–134.

Ember, Lois R. (1989, July 24). Luce Foundation program helps women develop science careers. *Chemical & Engineering News, 67*(30), 23–25.

Fabricant, Mona, & Adner, Haya. (1989). *Women in science and technology.* Paper presented at the 15th annual convention of the American Mathematical Association of Two-Year Colleges, Baltimore. (ERIC Document Reproduction Service No. ED 325 143)

Falconer, Etta Z. (1989). A story of success—the sciences at Spelman College. *Sage, 6*(2) 36–38.

Fausto-Sterling, Anne, & English, Lydia L. (1985). *Women and minorities in science: An interdisciplinary course.* Wellesley, MA: Wellesley College Center for Research on Women.

Fausto-Sterling, Anne, & English, Lydia L. (1987, January). Women and minorities in science: An interdisciplinary course. *Radical Teacher,* 16–20.

Feminism as an analytic tool for the study of science. (1983, September–October). *Academe,* 15–21.

Freundlich, Naomi. (1989, August 28). Making science more seductive to women on campus. *Business Week* [Industrial/Technology ed.], p. 89.

Giese, Patsy A. (1992). Women in science: 5000 years of obstacles and achievements. *Appraisal: Science Books for Young People, 25*(2), 1–20.

Hall, Paula Quick. (1981). *Problems and solutions in the education, employment and personal choices of minority women in science.* Washington, DC: American Association for the Advancement of Science. (ERIC Document Reproduction Service No. ED 221 328)

Hammonds, Evelynn M. (1991, August 23). Underrepresentations. *Science, 253* (5022), 919.

Harding, Jan. (1983a). How the world attracts girls to science. *New Scientist, 99,* 754–755.

Harding, Jan. (1983b). *Switched off: The science education of girls.* York, England: Longman Resources Unit.

Harding, Jan. (1985). Girls and women in secondary and higher education: Science for only a few. *Prospects: Quarterly Review of Education, 15*(4), 553–564.
Harding, Jan. (Ed.). (1986). *Perspectives on gender and science*. London: Falmer Press.
Hinton, Kate. (1983). Women in science [course outline]. *Bulletin of Science, Technology and Society, 3*, 313–401, 435–487.
Holden, Constance. (1989, March 3). Radical reform for science education. *Science, 243*(4895), 1133.
Holden, Constance. (1989, June 30). Wanted: 675,000 future scientists and engineers. *Science, 244*(4912), 1536–1537.
Hornig, Lilli S. (1984, November/December). Women in science and engineering: Why so few? *Technology Review, 87*(8), 31–41.
Hughes, Donna M. (1991, August). Transforming science and technology: Has the elephant yet flicked its trunk? NWSA *Journal, 3*, 382–401.
Humphreys, Sheila. (Ed.). (1982). *Women and minorities in science: Strategies for increasing participation*. Boulder, CO: Westview Press.
Hussey, Sharon Woods. (1987). *Leading girls to mathematics, science, and technology: Into the world of today and tomorrow*. Tacoma, WA: Weyerhauser Company Foundation. (ERIC Document Reproduction Service No. ED 309 087)
Illman, Deborah. (1993, August 2). Research for women, minority undergrads. *Chemical & Engineering News, 71*(31), 31.
Ivey, Elizabeth S. (1987). Recruiting more women into science and engineering. *Issues in Science and Technology, 4*(1), 83–87.
Ivey, Elizabeth S. (1988). Recruiting more women into engineering and science. *Engineering Education, 78*(8), 762–765.
Jump, Teresa, Heid, Camilla, & Harris, John J. (1985). Science and math careers for women. *Feminist Teacher, 1*(3), 18–20.
Kahle, Jane Butler. (1983a). *The disadvantaged majority: Science education for women*. Burlington, NC: Carolina Biological Supply.
Kahle, Jane Butler. (1983b). *Factors affecting the retention of girls in science courses & careers: Case studies of selected secondary schools*. Washington, DC: National Science Foundation. (ERIC Document Reproduction Service No. ED 244 781)
Kahle, Jane Butler. (1983c). *Girls in school: Women in science*. Washington, DC: National Association of Biology Teachers. (ERIC Document Reproduction Service No. ED 258 812)
Kahle, Jane Butler, & Lakes, Marsha K. (1983). The myth of equality in science classrooms. *Journal of Research in Science Teaching, 20*(2), 131–140.
Keller, Evelyn Fox. (1988 Summer/Fall). Feminist perspectives on science studies. *Science, Technology, and Human Values, 13*(3/4), 235–249.
Keller, Evelyn Fox. (1992). *Secrets of life, secrets of death: Essays on language, gender, and science*. New York: Routledge.
Kelly, Alison, Whyte, Judith, & Smail, Barbara. (1984). *Girls into science and technology. Final report*. Manchester, England: GIST, Department of Sociology. (ERIC Document Reproduction Service No. ED 250 203)
Kien, Jenny, & Cassidy, David. (1984). The history of women in science, a seminar at the University of Regensburg, F.R.G. *Women's Studies International Forum, 7*(4), 313–317.

Kirkup, Gill, & Keller, Laurie Smith (Eds.). (1992). *Inventing women: Science, technology, and gender*. Cambridge, England: Polity Press/Open University.

Kleinfeld, Judith, & Yerian, Sue. (1991). *Preparing prospective teachers to develop the mathematical and scientific abilities of young women: The development of teaching cases. Final report*. Fairbanks, AK: Alaska University. (ERIC Document Reproduction Service No. ED 346 025)

Koritz, Helen (Ed.). (1992, March/April). Women and science [Special issue]. *Journal of College Science Teaching 21*,(5).

Koshland, Daniel E., Jr. (1992, November 15). Minorities in science. *Science, 258* (5085), 1067.

Kramarae, Cheris, & Spender, Dale (Eds.). (1992). *The knowledge explosion: Generations of feminist scholarship*. New York: Teachers College Press.

Kreinberg, Nancy. (1981). *Ideas for developing and conducting a women in science career workshop*. Washington, DC: National Science Foundation. (ERIC Document Reproduction Service No. ED 210 965)

Kreinberg, Nancy. (1982). *The math and science education of women and minorities: The California perspective*. Davis, CA: University of California–Davis. (ERIC Document Reproduction Service No. ED 218 114)

Labossière, Diane. (1986, December/1987, January). Les filles et les matières scientifiques au niveau secondaire [Girls and scientific subjects on the secondary level]. *Resources for Feminist Research, 15*, 56–57.

Lantz, Alma. (1979). Strategies to increase the number of women in science. *Signs, 5*(1), 186–189.

Lee, Lesley. (1986, November). The scientific exclusion of women from science. *Resources for Feminist Research, 15*, 21–22.

Levine, Dana. (1984). An innovative approach to attract young women to careers in engineering and science. *Engineering Education, 75*(3), 162–164.

Levine, Dana. (1985). Adding a woman's touch. *Science Teacher, 52*(6), 25–29.

Malcolm, Shirley M. (1983). *Equity and excellence: An assessment of programs that facilitate increased access and achievement of females and minorities in K–12 mathematics and science education*. Washington, DC: American Association for the Advancement of Science, Office of Opportunities in Science. (ERIC Document Reproduction Service No. ED 419 420)

Malcolm, Shirley M. (1989). Increasing the participation of black women in science and technology. *Sage, 6*(2), 15–17.

Malcolm, Shirley M. (1990). Essay. *Scientific American, 262*(2), 112.

Mallow, Jeffry. V. (1981). *Science anxiety: Fear of science and how to overcome it*. New York: Van Nostrand Reinhold.

Mappen, Ellen F. (1989). Guest comment: Creating a support system for women in science—combining co-curricular programming and student life at Douglass College. *American Journal of Physics, 59*(12), 1065.

Matthews, Christine M. (1990). *Underrepresented minorities and women in science, mathematics, and engineering: Problems and issues for the 1990s. CRS report for Congress*. Washington, DC: Library of Congress. (ERIC Document Reproduction Service No. ED 337 525)

McCartney, Andra. (1991). The science and technology careers workshop—integrating feminist approaches in residential science education. *Resources for Feminist Research, 20*(1/2), 50–51.

McMillen, Liz. (1987, August 12). Step up recruitment of women into science or risk U.S. competitive edge in field, colleges are warned. *Chronicle of Higher Education, 33*(48), 9, 12.

McMillen, Liz. (1989, July 5). Clare Boothe Luce Fund to spend $3.5-million a year to encourage women to study and teach science. *Chronicle of Higher Education, 35*(43), A23–A24.

Melnick, Susan L., Wheeler, Christopher W., & Gunnings, Barbara B. (1986). Can science teachers promote gender equity in their classrooms? How two teachers do it. *Journal of Educational Equity & Leadership, 6*(1), 5–25.

Meschel, S. V. (1992). Teacher Keng's heritage: A survey of Chinese women scientists. *Journal of Chemical Education, 69*(9), 723–730.

Messing, Karen. (1986, November). What would a feminist approach to science be? *Resources for Feminist Research, 15*, 65–66.

Misra, K. S. (1985, November). Scientific creativity among girls: Impact of school environment. *Journal of Indian Education, 11*, 53–57.

Mitchell, R. (1984, Fall). Coping with science anxiety. *Feminist Teacher, 1*, 14–17.

Morgan, Carolyn S. (1992). College students' perceptions of barriers to women in science and engineering. *Youth & Society, 24*(2), 228–236.

Nulty, Peter. (1989, July 31). The hot demand for new scientists. *Fortune, 120*(3), 155–163.

Oakes, Jeannie. (1990). *Lost talent: The underparticipation of women, minorities, and disabled persons in science*. Washington, DC: National Science Foundation. (ERIC Document Reproduction Service No. ED 318 640)

Otto, Paul B. (1991). One science, one sex? *School Science & Mathematics, 91*(8), 367–372.

Peltz, William H. (1990). Can girls + science – stereotypes = success? *Science Teacher, 57*(9), 44–49.

Pfafflin, Sheila M. (1984, October). Women, science, and technology. *American Psychologist, 39*, 1183–1186.

Price, Jill S. (1993). Guest comment: Gender bias in the sciences—some up-to-date information on the subject. *American Journal of Physics, 61*(7), 589–590.

Quimbita, Grace. (1991). *Preparing women and minorities for careers in math and science: The role of community colleges*. Los Angeles: ERIC Clearinghouse for Junior Colleges. (ERIC Document Reproduction Service No. ED 333 943)

Raat, Jan H., Harding, Jan, & Mottier, I. (1981). *Girls and science and technology* (*GASAT*). *Vol. 1*. Proceedings of the first GASAT conference, Eindhoven, the Netherlands. (ERIC Document Reproduction Service No. ED 262 995)

Raat, Jan H., Harding, Jan, & Mottier, I. (1981). *Girls and science and technology* (*GASAT*). *Vol.* 2. Proceedings of the first GASAT conference, Eindhoven, the Netherlands. (ERIC Document Reproduction Service No. ED 262 996)

Raloff, Janet. (1990, December 14). Science: Recruiting nontraditional players. *Science News, 140*(24), 396–398.

Ramsden, Judith M. (1990). All quiet on the gender front? *School Science Review, 72*(259), 49–55.

Raymond, Chris. (1991, December 11). Continuing shortage of women in science decried: Many drop out. *Chronicle of Higher Education, 38*(16), A31–A32.

Rosser, Sue V. (1985). *The feminist perspective on science: Is reconceptualization possible?* (ERIC Document Reproduction Service No. ED 266 985)

Rosser, Sue V. (1986). *Teaching science and health from a feminist perspective: A practical guide.* Elmsford, NY: Pergamon Press.

Rosser, Sue V. (1987). Science and health-related women's studies course: A report after 10 years in the academy. *Feminist Teacher, 2*(2), 30–34.

Rosser, Sue V. (1989). Teaching techniques to attract women to science. *Women's Studies International Forum, 12*(3), 363–377.

Rosser, Sue V. (1990). *Female-friendly science: Applying women's studies methods and theories to attract students.* Elmsford, NY: Pergamon Press.

Scheinin, Rose. (1981). The rearing of women for science, engineering, and technology. *International Journal of Women's Studies, 4*(4), 339–347.

Scheinin, Rose. (1989). Women as scientists: Their rights and obligations. *Journal of Business Ethics, 8*(2–3), 131–155.

Science and Technology [Thematic issue]. (1984). *Canadian Women Studies/Les Cahiers de la Femme, 5.*

Science and Technology [Special issue]. (1989). *Sage, 6*(2).

Science in the U.S.—with one hand tied behind us. (1988–1989). *Hood on the Issues,* 3–14.

Science lives: Women and minorities in the sciences. (1991). Minneapolis, MN: Minnesota University. (ERIC Document Reproduction Service No. ED 348 421)

Scott, Linda U., & Heller, Patricia. (1991). Team work works! Strategies for integrating women and minorities into the physical sciences. *Science Teacher, 58*(1), 24–28.

Searing, Sue, & Shult, Linda. (Comps). (1985). *Women and science: Issues and resources [and] women and information technology: A selective bibliography.* Madison, WI: Wisconsin University Systems Women's Studies Librarian at Large. (ERIC Document Reproduction Service No. ED 256 657)

Shepherd, Linda Jean. (1993). *Lifting the veil: The feminine face of science.* Boston: Shambhala.

Shult, Linda, Searing, Sue, & Lester-Massman, E. (Eds.). (1991). *Women, race, and ethnicity: A bibliography.* Madison, WI: Wisconsin University Systems Women's Studies Librarian at Large.

Siebert, Eleanor. (1992). Women in science? *Journal of College Science Teaching, 21*(5), 269–271.

Siegel, Mary Ellen. (1984). *Her way: A guide to biographies of women for young people* (Rev. and expanded ed.). Chicago: American Library Association.

Skolnick, Joan, Langbort, Carol, & Day, Lucille. (1982). *How to encourage girls in math and science: Strategies for parents and educators.* Englewood Cliffs, NJ: Prentice-Hall.

Sloat, Barbara Furin. (1990). Perspectives on women and the sciences. *LSA Magazine, 13*(2), 13–17.

Smail, Barbara. (1981, December). Girls into science and technology: The first two years. *School Science Review, 63*(225), 620–630.

Smail, Barbara. (1983). Getting science right for girls. *Contributions to the Second Girls and Science and Technology Conference* (pp. 30–40). Oslo, Norway: University of Oslo, Institute of Physics.

Stallings, Jane. (1980). *Comparisons of men's and women's behaviors in high school classes.* Washington, DC: National Institute of Education.

Steiger, Arlene, & Davis, Fran. (1992). *Feminist pedagogy and the teaching of science: An experiential workshop.* Description of a workshop conducted at the annual conference of the Association of Canadian Community Colleges, Montreal, Canada. (ERIC Document Reproduction Service No. ED 348 116)

Stolte-Heiskanen, Veronica, & First-Dilic, Ruza. (1991). *Women in science: Token women or gender equality?* New York: Oxford.

Stoney, Sheila M., & Reid, Margaret I. (1981). *Balancing the equation: A study of women and science and technology within further education. Project report.* London: Further Educational Curriculum Review and Development Unit. (ERIC Document Reproduction Service No. ED 219 534)

Strauss, Mary Jo. (1983, Fall). Feminist education in science, mathematics, and technology. *Women's Studies Quarterly, 11,* 23–25.

Tilghman, Shirley. (1993). The status of science: Male versus female scientists. *WIN [Women's International Network] News, 19*(2), 73–74.

Tobias, Sheila. (1992). Women and science. *Journal of College Science Teaching, 21*(5), 276–278.

Travis, John. (1993 April 16). Making room for women in the culture of science. *Science, 260*(5106), 412–415.

Tsuji, Gerry, & Ziegler, Suzanne. (1990). *What research says about increasing the numbers of female students taking math and science in secondary school.* Toronto, Canada: Toronto Board of Education. (ERIC Document Reproduction Service No. ED 317 417)

Vetter, Betty. (1992). Ferment: yes-progress: maybe-change: slow. *Mosaic, 23*(3), 34–41.

Warren, Karen J. (1989, Fall). Rewriting the future: The feminist challenge to the malestream curriculum. *Feminist Teacher, 4,* 46–52.

Whyte, Judith. (1986). *Girls into science and technology: The story of a project.* Boston: Routledge & Kegan Paul.

Whyte, Karen. (1988, June). "Can we learn this? We're just girls"—Feminists and science: Visions and strategy. *Resources for Feminist Research, 17,* 6–9.

Wilson, Meg, & Snapp, Elizabeth. (1992). *Options for girls: A door to the future: An anthology on science and math education.* Austin, TX: Pro-Ed.

Woodhull, Amy M., Lowry, Nancy, & Henifin, Mary Sue. (1985). Teaching for change: Feminism and the sciences. *Journal of Thought, 20*(3), 162–173.

Yentsch, Clarice M., & Sindermann, Carl J. (1992). *The woman scientist: Meeting the challenges for a successful career.* New York: Plenum Press.

Zuckerman, Harriet, Cole, Jonathan R., & Bruer, John. (1991). *The outer circle: Women in the scientific community.* New York: Norton.

ASTRONOMY

Couper, Heather. (1988). Where are all the women amateur astronomers? *Sky & Telescope, 75*(1), 4.

Flam, Faye. (1991, June 21). Still a "chilly climate" for women? *Science, 252*(5013), 1604–1606.

Fraknoi, Andrew, & Freitag, R. (1992, January/February). Astronomical resources —women in astronomy: A bibliography. *Mercury, 21*, 46–47.

Grinstein, Louise S. (1980 May/June). Women in physics and astronomy: A selected bibliography. *Social Science and Mathematics, 80*(5), 384–398.

Kistiakowsky, Vera. (1979). Women in physics and astronomy. In Anne Briscoe, & Sheila Pfafflin (Eds.), *Expanding the role of women in the sciences* (pp. 35–47). New York: New York Academy of Sciences.

Lankford, John, & Slavings, Rickey L. (1990, March). Gender and science: Women in American astronomy, 1859–1940. *Physics Today, 43*(3), 58–65. Commentary in: Giving women astronomers their due. (1990, August). *Physics Today, 43* (pt. 1), 91–92.

Mack, Pamela E. (1990a, February 1). Strategies and compromises: Women in astronomy at Harvard College Observatory, 1870–1920. *Journal for the History of Astronomy, 21*(1), 65–76.

Mack, Pamela E. (1990b). Straying from their orbits: Women in astronomy in America. In G. Kass-Simon & Patricia Farnes (Eds.), *Women of science: Righting the record* (pp. 72–116). Bloomington, IN: Indiana University Press.

McDonald, Kim A. (1991, February 13). Many female astronomers say they face sex harassment and bias. *Chronicle of Higher Education, 37*(22), A11, A15.

Spradley, Joseph L. (1990, September). Women and the stars. *Physics Teacher, 28*(6), 372–377.

Women in astronomy: A sampler of issues and ideas. (1992, January). *Mercury, 21*(1), 27–37.

CHEMISTRY

Amato, Ivan. (1992). Profile of a field: Chemistry. *Science, 255*(5050), 1372–1373.

Benfey, Theodor. (1985, February). The chemistry professor—where is she? *Journal of College Science Teaching, 14*, 229.

Brickhouse, Nancy W., Carter, Carolyn S., & Scantlebury, K. C. (1990). Women and chemistry: Shifting the equilibrium toward success. *Journal of Chemical Education, 67*(2), 116–118.

Briscoe, Anne M. (1984). Scientific sexism: The world of chemistry. In Violet B. Haas & Carolyn C. Perrucci (Eds.), *Women in scientific and engineering professions* (pp. 147–159). Ann Arbor, MI: University of Michigan Press.

Creese, Mary R. S. (1991). British women of the nineteenth and early twentieth centuries who contributed to research in the chemical sciences. *British Journal for the History of Science* (*pt.* 3), 24(82), 275–305.

Everett, Kenneth G., & Deloach, Will S. (1991). Chemistry doctorates awarded to women in the United States—a historical perspective. *Journal of Chemical Education, 68*(7), 545–547.

Grinstein, Louise S., Rose, Rose K., & Rafailovich, Miriam H. (Eds.). (1993). *Women in chemistry and physics: A bio-bibliographic sourcebook.* Westport, CT: Greenwood.

Handler, Bonnie S., & Shmurak, Carole B. (1991). Rigor, resolve, religion: Mary Lyon and science education. *Teaching Education, 3*(2), 137–142.

Hessley, Rita K. (1992). Women and careers in chemistry! Why not? *Journal of College Science Teaching, 21*(6), 373–376.

Heylin, Michael. (1987). Women, minorities, and chemistry. *Chemical & Engineering News, 65*(37), 3.

Heylin, Michael. (1989). Female chemistry faculty numbers remain low. *Chemical & Engineering News, 67*(19), 34.

Levine, Dana. (1985). Encouraging young women to pursue science and engineering careers through chemistry. *Journal of Chemical Education, 62*(10), 837–839.

Mason, Joan. (1991). A forty years' war. *Chemistry in Britain, 27*, 233–238.

Miller, Jane. A. (1990). Women in chemistry. In G. Kass-Simon, & Patricia Farnes (Eds.), *Women of science: Righting the record* (pp. 300–334). Bloomington, IN: Indiana University Press.

Nixon, Alan C. (1979). Changing attitudes toward women in the profession of chemistry. In Anne Briscoe, & Sheila Pfafflin (Eds.), *Expanding the role of women in the sciences* (pp. 146–172). New York: New York Academy of Sciences.

Rayner-Canham, Geoffrey W., & Frenette, H. (1985). Some French women chemists. *Education in Chemistry, 22*(6), 176–178.

Roscher, Nina M. (1976). Women chemists. *CHEMTECH, 6*(12), 738–743.

Roscher, Nina M., & Ammons, Phillip L. (1981). Early women chemists of the Northeast. *Journal of the Washington Academy of Sciences, 71*(4), 177–182.

Roscher, Nina M., & Cavanaugh, Margaret A. (1987, October). Academic women chemists in the 20th century: Past, present, projections. *Journal of Chemical Education, 64*, 823–827. Discussion in *Journal of Chemical Education, 66*(1989, May), 447–448; Pt. II: *69*(1992, November), 870–873.

Warner, Mary D. (1985). Women in analytical chemistry—equality at last? *Analytical Chemistry, 57*(13), 1358A-1360A, 1362A, 1364A.

COMPUTER SCIENCE

Clewell, Beatriz C., Anderson, Bernice T., & Thorpe, Margaret E. (1992). The prevalence and nature of mathematics, science, and computer science intervention programs serving minority and female students in grades four through eight. *Equity & Excellence, 25*(2–4), 209–215.

Dain, J. (1991). Women and computing—some responses to falling numbers in higher education. *Women's Studies International Forum, 14*(3), 217–225.

Gibbons, Ann. (1992). Creative solutions: Electronic mentoring. *Science, 255*(5050), 1369.

Hafner, Katie. (1993, August 29). Woman, computer nerd—and proud. *New York Times*, section 3, p. 1.

Hawkins, Jan. (1985). Computers and girls: Rethinking the issues. *Sex Roles, 13*, (3–4), 165–180.

Martin, C. Diane, & Murchie-Beyma, Eric (Eds.). (1992). *In search of gender free paradigms for computer science education*. Eugene, OR: International Society for Technology in Education. (ERIC Document Reproduction Service No. ED 349 941)

NSF grant to fund mentoring project for women & minorities. (1992, January). *Communications of the ACM, 35* (Suppl. 1), 2.

Pearl, Amy, Pollack, Martha E., Riskin, Eve, Thomas, Becky, Wolf, Elizabeth, & Wu, Alice. (1990). Becoming a computer scientist. *Communications of the ACM, 33*(11), 47–57.

Perry, Ruth, & Greber, Lisa. (1990). Women and computers: An introduction. *Signs, 16*(1), 74–101.

Rasmussen, Bente, & Hapnes, Tove. (1991). Excluding women from the technologies of the future? A case study of the culture of computer science. *Futures, 23*(10), 1107–1119.

Sanders, Jo, & McGinnis, Mary. (1991). *What is computer equity? A trainer's workshop guide*. Metuchen, NJ: Scarecrow.

Stalker, Sylvia. (1983). *Computers in the classroom: A feminist issue*. Paper presented at the National Women's Studies Association Conference, Columbus, OH. (ERIC Document Reproduction Service No. ED 240 015)

Turkle, Sherry. (1984). Women and computer programming: A different approach. *Technology Review, 87*(8), 48–50.

Women of computer history: Forgotten pioneers. (1989). Wilmington, DE: World Information Institute.

ENGINEERING

Baum, Eleanor. (1989, August 9). The anticipated shortage of engineers can be avoided if the profession gets serious about recruiting women. *Chronicle of Higher Education, 35*(48), B1, B3.

Beardsley, Charles W. (1988). A matter of bias. *Mechanical Engineering, 110*(5), 2.

Benedetti, Marti. (1990, February 26). Opportunities far exceed supply of women engineers. *Automotive News*, 8i.

Bradby, Marie. (1989). Hispanic women at the Johnson Space Center. *Hispanic Engineer, 5*(3), 28–31.

Carter, Ruth, & Kirkup, Gill. (1990). *Women in engineering: A good place to be?* Houndmills, Basingstoke, Hampshire, UK: Macmillan.

Christensen, Lawrence O. (1988). Being special: Women students at the Missouri School of Mines and Metallurgy. *Missouri Historical Review, 83*(1), 17–35.

Cromwell, Robert A. (1986). The effective recruitment of women students in engineering technology. *Engineering Education, 76*(8), 755–757.

Daniels, Jane Z. (1988). Women in engineering: A program administrator's perspective. *Engineering Education, 78*(8), 766–768.

Daniels, Jane Z., & LeBold, Willliam K. (1982). Women in engineering: A dynamic approach. In Sheila Humphreys (Ed.), *Women and minorities in science: Strategies for increasing participation* (pp. 139–163). Boulder, CO: Westview Press.

Emmett, Arielle. (1992). A women's institute of technology? *Technology Review, 95*(3), 16–18.

Florman, Samuel C. (1984). Will women engineers make a difference? *Technology Review, 87*(8), 51–52.

Haas, Violet B., & Perrucci, Carolyn C. (Eds.). (1984). *Women in scientific and engineering professions.* Ann Arbor, MI: University of Michigan Press.

Hacker, Sally. (1989). *Pleasure, power and technology: Some tales of gender, engineering and the cooperative workplace.* Boston: Unwin Hyman.

Hayles, N. Katherine. (1992). Gender encoding in fluid mechanics: Masculine channels and feminine flows. *Differences: A Journal of Feminist Cultural Studies, 4*(2), 16–44.

Herzenberg, Caroline L., & Howes, Ruth Hege. (1993). Women of the Manhattan Project. *Technology Review, 96*(8), 32–40.

Hynes, H. Patricia. (1992). Feminism and engineering: The inroads. In Cheris Kramarae & Dale Spender (Eds.), *The knowledge explosion: Generations of feminist scholarship* (pp. 133–140). New York: Teachers College Press.

Kozloski, Lillian, & Mackowski, Maura J. (1990, May/June). The wrong stuff. *Final Frontiers,* 20–23, 52–55.

Lytle, Vicky. (1990, March 7). From Marie Curie . . . to Sally Ride . . . to. . . . *NEA Today, 8*(7), 4–5.

McIlwee, Judith S., & Robinson, J. Gregg. (1992). *Women in engineering: Gender, power and work place culture.* Albany, NY: State University of New York.

McNutt, Anne B. (1983). Message to women: Break out of the mold! *Engineering Education, 73*(8), 805–807.

National Action Council for Minorities in Engineering. (1992). *The gender gap in minority engineering education. Research Letter,* 3(1). New York: National Action Council for Minorities in Engineering. (ERIC Document Reproduction Service No. ED 356 951)

Parrish, John B. (1988). Women continue in the professions. *Chemical Engineering Progress, 84*(1), 50–56.

Powell, Doug. (1992, May 1). Women in engineering: Canadian panel calls for more. *Science, 256*(5057), 607.

Pursell, Carroll W., Jr. (1993). "Am I a lady or an engineer?" The origins of the women's engineering society in Britain, 1918–1940. *Technology and Culture, 34*(1), 78–97.

Riggs, Carol R. (1993). Women industrial designers make a difference. *D&B Reports, 42*(2), 20–23.

Robinson, Gail, Drummey, Deirdre, & Myers, Signe. (1989, August 15). Women engineers: A very rare breed. *Design News, 45*(15), 62–79.

Robinson, J. Gregg, & McIlwee, Judith S. (1989). Women in engineering: A promise unfulfilled? *Social Problems, 36*(5), 455–472.

Robinson, J. Gregg, & McIlwee, Judith S. (1991). Men, women, and the culture of engineering. *Sociological Quarterly, 32*(3), 403–421.

Saigal, Anil. (1988). Women engineers: An insight into their problems. *U. S. Woman Engineer, 34*(4), 42–43.

Schoenberger, Ann K. (1988). *College women's persistence in engineering and physical science: A further study*. Paper presented at the annual meeting of the American Educational Research Association, New Orleans, LA. (ERIC Document Reproduction Service No. ED 296 889)

Trescott, Martha M. (1979). A history of women engineers in the United States, 1850–1975: A progress report. In *Proceedings of the Society of Women Engineers 1979 National Conference* (pp. 1–14). New York: Society of Women Engineers.

Trescott, Martha M. (1981). Women engineers in history: Profiles in holism and persistence. In Violet B. Haas, & Carolyn C. Perrucci (Eds.), *Women in scientific and engineering professions* (pp. 181–204). Ann Arbor, MI: University of Michigan Press.

Trescott, Martha M. (1988). Women and engineering education: Historical sketches. In *Women and engineering education: Report on a conference of the California State University, 20 and 21 March 1987, Los Angeles, CA* (pp. II1–II16). Northridge, CA: Women in Science and Engineering Programs, School of Engineering and Computer Science, California State University.

Trescott, Martha M. (1990). Women in the intellectual development of engineering: A study in persistence and systems thought. In G. Kass-Simon, & P. Farnes (Eds.), *Women of science: Righting the record* (pp. 147–187). Bloomington, IN: Indiana University Press.

Ward, Daniel. (1990, May). Not just a man's world: Women engineers are finally finding acceptance in Britain's male-dominated automotive industry. *Automotive News*, 10.

Werman, Jill, & Baum, Eleanor. (1990). Engineering change. *Working Woman, 15*(6), 40.

Wilson, Robin. (1991, June 12). Colleges start programs to encourage women who are interested in engineering careers. *Chronicle of Higher Education, 37*(39), A27, A29.

Women in engineering. [Special issue]. (1985). *IEEE Transactions on Education, E-28*,(4).

Wood, Rose M., & Schaer, Barbara B. (1991). *Race and gender effects on persistence, barriers to engineering and life goals by middle school children*. Paper presented to Mid-South Educational Research Association, Lexington, KY. (ERIC Document Reproduction Service No. ED 350 146)

GEOLOGICAL SCIENCES

Aldrich, Michele L. (1982). Women in paleontology in the United States, 1840–1960. *Earth Sciences History, 1*, 14–22.

Aldrich, Michele L. (1990). Women in geology. In G. Kass-Simon, & P. Farnes

(Eds.), *Women of science: Righting the record* (pp. 42–71). Bloomington, IN: Indiana University Press.
Coates, Mary Sue. (1986). Women geologists work toward equality. *Geotimes, 31*(11), 11–14.
Elder, Eleanor S. (1982). Women in early geology. *Journal of Geological Education, 30*(5), 287–293.
LeMone, Margaret A., Frisch, J. V., & Julian, L. T. (1984, August). Tracking women and the weather: Their growing role in meteorology. *Weatherwise, 37*, 176–181.
Rongguang, Shang, & Meini, Guo. (1990, July 23). The path less traveled: A woman geologist. *Beijing Review, 33*, 30–32.
Rossiter, Margaret W. (1981). Geology in nineteenth century women's education in the United States. *Journal of Geological Education, 29*(5), 228–232.
Schwarzer, Theresa F. (1979). The changing status of women in the geosciences. In Anne Briscoe, & Sheila Pfafflin (Eds.), *Expanding the role of women in the sciences* (pp. 48–64). New York: New York Academy of the Sciences.
Suiter, Marilyn J. (1991a). Tomorrow's geoscientists: Recruiting and keeping them. *Geotimes, 36*(1), 12–14.
Suiter, Marilyn J. (1991b). Women and minorities in the geosciences. *Geotimes, 36*(2), 58–59.
Suiter, Marilyn J. (1992a). 1991—the geosciences in review: Women and minorities in the geosciences. *Geotimes, 37*(2), 44.
Suiter, Marilyn J. (1992b). Women in geoscience: A resource to develop. *Geotimes, 37*(1), 14–17.
Survey of women geoscientists: Results. (1985, December 24). *Eos: Transactions, American Geophysical Union, 66*, 1358–1359.
Wallace, Jane. H. (1979). Women in the survey. *Geotimes, 24*(3), 34.

MATHEMATICS

Anderson, Margo. (1992). The history of women and the history of statistics. *Journal of Women's History, 4*(1), 14–36.
Arianrhod, Robyn. (1992). Physics and mathematics, reality and language: Dilemmas for feminists. In Cheris Kramarae, & Dale Spender (Eds.), *The knowledge explosion: Generations of feminist scholarship* (pp. 41–53). New York: Teachers College Press.
Ayers-Nachamkin, Beverly. (1992). A feminist approach to the introductory statistics course. *Women's Studies Quarterly, 20*(1–2), 86–94.
Bernstein, Peg. (1992). *Math without fear: A concrete approach to mathematics.* Philadelphia: Lutheran Social Mission Society, Lutheran Settlement House. (ERIC Document Reproduction Service No. ED 352 529)
Blum, Lenore, & Givant, Steven. (1982). Increasing the participation of college women in mathematics-related fields. In Sheila Humphreys (Ed.), *Women and minorites in science* (pp. 119–138). Boulder, CO: Westview Press.
Burton, Leone. (Ed.). (1986). *Girls into maths can go.* London: Holt, Rinehart & Winston.

Burton, Leone. (Ed.). (1990). *Gender and mathematics: An international perspective.* London: Cassell Educational Limited. (ERIC Document Reproduction Service No. ED 337 349)

Campbell, Patricia B. (1986, March). What's a nice girl like you doing in a math class? *Phi Delta Kappan,* 516–520.

Campbell, Paul J., & Grinstein, Louise S. (1976/77). Women and mathematics: A preliminary selected bibliography. *Philosophia Mathematica, 13/14,* 171–203.

Chinn, Phyllis Zweig. (1979). *Women in science and mathematics: Bibliography.* Arcata, CA: Humboldt State University Foundation. (ERIC Document Reproduction Service No. ED 316 435)

Chipman, Susan F., Brush, Lorelei R., & Wilson, Donna M. (Eds.). (1985). *Women and mathematics: Balancing the equation.* Hillsdale, NJ: Erlbaum.

Clewell, Beatriz C., Anderson, Bernice T., & Thorpe, Margaret E. (1992). *Breaking the barriers: Helping female and minority students succeed in mathematics.* San Francisco: Jossey-Bass.

Confrey, Jere. (1983). *SummerMath: Research into practice.* Paper presented at the 67th annual meeting of the American Educational Research Association, Montreal, Canada. (ERIC Document Reproduction Service No. ED 242 549)

Cronkite, Ruth C., & Perl, Teri Hoch. (1982). A short-term intervention program: Math science conferences. In Sheila Humphreys (Ed.), *Women and minorities in science: Strategies for increasing participation* (pp. 65–86). Boulder, CO: Westview Press.

Dunham, Penelope H. (1990). *Procedures to increase the entry of women in mathematics-related careers.* Washington, DC: Office of Educational Research and Improvement. (ERIC Document Reproduction Service No. ED 324 195)

Eriksson, Inger V., Kitchenham, Barbara A., & Tijdens, Kea G. (Eds.). (1991). *Women, work, and computerization: Understanding and overcoming bias in work and education: Proceedings of the IFIP TC9/WG 9.1 Conference on Women, Work, and Computerization.* New York: North-Holland/Elsevier Science.

Farquhar, Diane, & Mary-Rose, Lynn. (1989). *Women sum it up: Biographical sketches of women mathematicians.* Christchurch, New Zealand: Hazard Press.

Fennema Elizabeth, & Leder, Gilah C. (Eds.). (1990). *Mathematics and gender: Influences on teachers and students.* New York: Teachers College Press.

Franklin, Margaret. (Project director). (1990a). *Add-ventures for girls: Building math confidence, elementary teacher's guide.* Reno, NV: Nevada University, Research and Educational Planning Center. (ERIC Document Reproduction Service No. ED 323 096)

Franklin, Margaret. (Project director). (1990b). *Add-ventures for girls: Building math confidence, junior high teacher's guide.* Reno, NV: Nevada University, Research and Educational Planning Center. (ERIC Document Reproduction Service No. ED 323 097)

Friedman, Batya. (1990). Bringing knowledge of women mathematicians into the mathematics classroom. *Mathematics and Computer Education, 24*(3), 250–253.

Gray, Mary W. (1991). The association for women in mathematics—a personal view. *Mathematical Intelligencer, 13*(4), 6–11.

Green, Judy, & LaDuke, Jeanne. (1987). Women in the American mathematical community: The pre-1940 Ph.D's. *Mathematical Intelligencer, 9*(1), 11–23.

Green, Judy, & LaDuke, Jeanne. (1990). Contributions to American mathematics: An overview and selection. In G. Kass-Simon & Patricia Farnes (Eds.), *Women of science: Righting the record* (pp. 117–146). Bloomington, IN: Indiana University Press.

Green, Judy, LaDuke, Jeanne, & Perl, Teri Hoch. (1985). Women in mathematics. In Joseph W. Dauben (Ed.), *The history of mathematics: From antiquity to the present: A selected bibliography* (pp. 428–434). New York: Garland.

Grinstein, Louise S., & Campbell, Paul J. (Eds.). (1987). *Women of mathematics: A biobibliographic sourcebook.* Westport, CT: Greenwood.

Gwizdala, Joyce, & Steinback, Myriam. (1990). High school females' mathematics attitudes: An interim report. *School Science & Mathematics, 90*(3), 215–222.

Hensel, Robin A. M. (1989). Mathematical achievement: Equating the sexes. *School Science & Mathematics, 89*(8), 646–653.

Keith, Sandra. (1989). *Women and communication in mathematics: One woman's viewpoint.* Paper presented at the 10th annual meeting of the National Women's Studies Association, Minneapolis, MN. (ERIC Document Reproduction Service No. ED 298 583)

Kenschaft, Patricia C. (1981, October). Black women in mathematics in the United States. *American Mathematical Monthly, 88*(8), 592–604. (Also in *Journal of African Civilizations, 4*(1), 63–83)

Kimball, Meredith M. (1989, March). A new perspective on women's math achievement. *Psychological Bulletin, 105*(2), 198–214.

Kroll, Diana. (1985). Evidence from the *Mathematics Teacher* (1908–1920) on women and mathematics. *For the Learning of Mathematics, 5*(2), 7–10.

Perl, Teri Hoch. (1993). *Women and numbers: Lives of women mathematicians plus discovery activities.* San Carlos, CA: Wide World Publishing.

Sells, Lucy W. (1982). Leverage for equal opportunity through mastery of mathematics. In Sheila Humphreys (Ed.), *Women and minorities in science: Strategies for increasing participation* (pp. 7–26). Boulder, CO: Westview Press.

Selvin, Paul. (1992, March 13). Profile of a field: Mathematics. *Science, 255*(5050), 1382–1383.

Stinnett, Sandra. (1990, May). Women in statistics: Sesquicentennial activities [Part of a Special Issue on: American Statistical Association History]. *The American Statistician, 44*(2), 74–80.

Stinson, Stephen. (1990, February 19). Dorm for women science, math majors opens on Rutgers campus. *Chemical & Engineering News, 68*(8), 26–27.

Tracy, Dyanne M., & Davis, Susan M. (1989, December). Females in mathematics: Erasing a gender-related math myth. *Arithmetic Teacher, 37*(4), 8–11.

Turner, Judith A. (1989a, February 15). In math ability, differences between sexes disappearing. *Chronicle of Higher Education, 35*(23), A10.

Turner, Judith A. (1989b, December 6). More women are earning doctorates in mathematics, but few are being hired by top universities. *Chronicle of Higher Education, 36*(14), A13–A15.

Wallis, Ruth, & Wallis, Peter. (1980, February). Female philomaths. *Historia Mathematica, 7*(1), 57–64.

Whitman, Betsey S. (1983, September/October). Women in the American Mathematical Society before 1900. *Association for Women in Mathematics Newsletter, 13*(5), 7–9.

Women as mathematicians. A course to reduce math anxiety and sex-role stereotyping in elementary education. (1984). Washington, DC: Women's Educational Equity Act Program. (ERIC Document Reproduction Service No. ED 259 917)

Women mathematicians before 1950. (1979, July/August). *Association for Women in Mathematics Newsletter, 9*(4), 9–11.

Women, mathematics, and careers. A course to reduce math anxiety and sex-role stereotyping in elementary education. (1984). Washington, DC: Women's Educational Equity Act Program. (ERIC Document Reproduction Service No. ED 259 924)

Women not good in math? Don't you believe it! (1993, January). *Teaching PreK–8, 23*(4), 44–47

PHYSICS

Ancker-Johnson, Betsy. (1974). Physicist. In Ruth B. Kundsin (Ed.), *Successful women in the sciences: An analysis of determinants* (pp. 23–28). New York: Morrow.

Arianrhod, Robyn. (1992). Physics and mathematics, reality and language: Dilemmas for feminists. In Cheris Kramarae, & Dale Spender (Eds.), *The knowledge explosion: Generations of feminist scholarship* (pp. 41–53). New York: Teachers College Press.

Blin-Stoyle, Roger. (1983). Girls and physics. *Physics Education, 18*(5), 225–228.

Brush, Stephen G. (1985, January). Women in physical science: From drudges to discoverers. *Physics Teacher, 23*, 11–19.

Couture-Cherki, Monique. (1980). Women in physics. In Hilary Rose, & Steven P. R. Rose (Eds.), *Ideology of/in the natural sciences* (pp. 206–216). Boston: G. K. Hall.

Duxbury, John. (1984). Girls and physics: The role of a head of physics. *School Science Review, 65*(233), 648–654.

Fava, Sylvia F., & Deierlein, Kathy. (1988). Women physicists in the U.S.: The career influence of marital status. CSWP *Gazette: Newsletter of the Committee on the Status of Women in Physics, 8*(2), 1–3.

Fehrs, Mary, & Czujko, Roman. (1992). Women in physics: Reversing the exclusion. *Physics Today, Pt. 1, 45*(8), 33–40.

Franz, Judy. (1990, February). Has anything changed? *Physics Teacher, 28*, 71.

Freeman, Joan. (1991). *A passion for physics: The story of a woman physicist*. Philadelphia: A. Hilger.

Hall, N. (1990). Physics appeal. *New Scientist, 127*(1728), 64–65.

Heller, Renee. (1993). I am still combining physics with women's studies. *Women's Studies International Forum, 16*(4), 391–392.

Jackson, Shirley A. (1979). From clerk-typist to research physicist. In Anne Briscoe & Sheila Pfaflin (Eds.), *Expanding the role of women in the sciences* (pp. 296–299). New York: New York Academy of the Sciences.

Jones, L. M. (1990). Intellectual contributions of women to physics. In G. Kass-

Simon, & Patricia Farnes (Eds.), *Women of science: Righting the record* (pp. 188–214). Bloomington, IN: Indiana University Press.
Julian, Maureen M. (1990). Women in crystallography. In G. Kass-Simon, & Patricia Farnes (Eds.), *Women of science: Righting the record* (pp. 335–384). Bloomington, IN: Indiana University Press.
Keller, Evelyn F. (1977). The anomaly of a woman in physics. In Sara Ruddick, & Pamela Daniels (Eds.), *Working It Out* (pp. 77–91). New York: Pantheon Books.
Kistiakowsky, Vera. (1979). Women in physics and astronomy. In Anne Briscoe, & Sheila Pfaflin (Eds.), *Expanding the role of women in the sciences* (pp. 35–47). New York: New York Academy of the Sciences.
Kistiakowsky, Vera. (1980). Women in physics: Unnecessary, injurious and out of place? *Physics Today, 33*(2), 32–40.
Koballa, Thomas R., Jr. (1988). Persuading girls to take elective physical science courses in high school: Who are the credible communicators? *Journal of Research in Science Teaching, 25*(6), 465–478.
Krane, Kenneth S. (1993). Guest comment: Women in physics: A male department chair's perspective. *American Journal of Physics, 61*(5), 393–394.
Kumagai, Jean. (1990). AIP survey finds more women majoring in physics. *Physics Today, 43*(7), 64.
Lotze, Barbara. (Ed.). (1984). *Making contributions: An historical overview of women's role in physics*. College Park, MD: American Association of Physics Teachers.
Max, Claire E. (1982). Career paths for women in physics. In Sheila Humphreys (Ed.), *Women and minorities in science: Strategies for increasing participation* (pp. 99–118). Boulder, CO: Westview Press.
Menard, Albert, & Uzun, Ali. (1993). Educating women for success in physics: Lessons from Turkey. *American Journal of Physics, 61*(7), 611–615.
Roth, Laura M., & O'Fallon, Nancy M. (1981). *Women in physics*. New York: American Physical Society. (ERIC Document Reproduction Service No. ED 237 335)
Schoenberger, Ann K. (1988). *College women's persistence in engineering and physical science: A further study*. Paper presented at the annual meeting of the American Educational Research Association, New Orleans, LA. (ERIC Document Reproduction Service No. ED 296 889)
Smith, Stuart E., & Walker, William J. (1985). *High school physics: A male domain?* (ERIC Document Reproduction Service No. ED 262 972)
Taber, K. S. (1991). Girl-friendly physics in the national curriculum. *Physics Education, 26*(4), 221–226.
Traweek, Sharon. (1984). High energy physics: A male preserve. *Technology Review, 87*(8), 42–43.

TECHNOLOGY

Alic, Margaret. (1981). Women and technology in ancient Alexandria: Maria and Hypatia. *Women's Studies International Quarterly, 4*(3), 305–312.
Bindocci, Cynthia G. (1993). *Women and technology: An annotated bibliography*. New York: Garland.

Bose, Christine. (1981). Teaching women and technology at the University of Washington. *Women's Studies International Quarterly, 4*(3), 374–377.

Cummins, Helene, McDaniel, Susan A., & Beauchamp, Rachelle S. (1990, Spring). Becoming inventors: Women who inspire to invent. *Atlantis, 15*, 90–93.

Hacker, Sally, Smith, Dorothy, & Turner, Susan M. (Eds.). (1990). *Doing it the hard way: Investigations of gender and technology*. Boston: Unwin Hyman.

Herzenberg, Caroline L., & Howes, Ruth H. (1993). Women of the Manhattan Project. *Technology Review, 96*(8), 32–40.

Howes, Ruth H., & Herzenberg, Caroline L. (1993). Women in weapons development: The Manhattan Project. In Ruth H. Howes, & M. R. Stevenson (Eds.), *Women and the use of military force* (pp. 95–110). Boulder, CO: Lynne Riener.

Kelly, Jan Wallace. (1984). *The culture of high technology: Is it "female friendly?"* (ERIC Document Reproduction Service No. ED 246 498)

King, Ynestra. (1981). Feminist pedagogy and technology—reflections on the Goddard Feminism and Ecology Summer Program. *Women's Studies International Quarterly, 4*(3), 370–372.

Leach, Juliette D., & Roberts, Shirley L. (1988). A soft technology: Recruiting and retaining women and minorities in high tech programs. *Community, Technical, and Junior College Journal, 59*(2), 34–37.

McDaniel, Susan A., Cummins, Helene, & Beauchamp, Rachelle S. (1988). Mothers of invention? Meshing the roles of inventor, mother, and worker. *Women's Studies International Forum, 11*(1), 1–12.

Miller, James A. (1991). Recruitment and support for women students in technology teacher education. *Journal of Epsilon Pi Tau, 17*(2), 27–30.

Reynolds, Terry S. (Comp). (1987). *The machine in the university: Sample course syllabi for the history of technology and technology studies* (2nd ed.). Bethlehem, PA: Lehigh University, Society for the History of Technology.

Rothschild, Joan. (Ed.). (1983). *Machina ex dea: Feminist perspectives on technology*. Elmsford, NY: Pergamon Press.

Rothschild, Joan. (1987). *Teaching technology from a feminist perspective: A practical guide*. Elmsford, NY: Pergamon Press.

Rothschild, Joan. (1989). Technology and education: A feminist perspective. *American Behavioral Scientist, 32*(6), 708–718.

Sluby, Patricia C. (1989). Black women and inventions. *Sage, 6*(2), 33–35.

Stanley, A. (1992). Once and future power—women as inventors. *Women's Studies International Forum, 15*(2), 193–203.

Swarbrick, Ailsa. (1981). Women in technology—a role for the open university? *Physics Education, 16*(5), 266–270.

Vare, Ethlie A., & Ptacek, Greg. (1989). *Mothers of invention: From the bra to the bomb: Forgotten women and their unforgettable ideas*. New York: Quill.

Wajcman, Judy. (1991). *Feminism confronts technology*. University Park, PA: Pennsylvania State University Press.

Wheeler, Roger, & Snowdon, Philip. (1987). American women in space. *Journal of the British Interplanetary Society, 40*, 81–88.

Wilson, Jane S., & Serber, Charlotte. (Eds.). (1988). *Standing by and making do: Women of wartime Los Alamos*. Los Alamos, NM: Los Alamos Historical Society.

Women in technology. (1991). El Paso, TX: El Paso Community College. (ERIC Document Reproduction Service No. ED 344 014)
Women, technology, and innovation [Thematic issue]. (1981). *Women's Studies International Quarterly, 4*.
Zientara, Marguerite. (1987). *Women, technology, and power: Ten stars and the history they made*. New York: AMACOM.

About the Editor and the Contributors

Sue V. Rosser, a PhD in zoology, is director of women's studies at the University of South Carolina, where she is also professor of family and preventive medicine in the medical school. She has edited collections and written approximately 60 journal articles on the theoretical and applied problems of women in science and is the author of five books on women, science, and health. She is also the principal investigator of a National Science Foundation grant to attract and retain women in science.

Karen Barad is associate professor of physics at Pomona College. She is a theoretical particle physicist and does research on quantum chromodynamics and other aspects of theoretical physics. She teaches jointly in the Departments of Physics and Women's Studies and has been instrumental in setting up joint concentrations in the sciences and women's studies. She co-organized two major conferences that brought women's studies scholars and scientists together to talk about gender and science issues. She has published articles in both theoretical physics and feminist science studies. Her research has been supported by the National Science Foundation and the Irvine Foundation, among others. She is currently working on a book tentatively titled *Meeting the Universe Halfway: Discontinuous Interactions in Quantum Physics, Feminist Epistemologies, and the Politics of Scientific Knowledge Construction.*

Noni McCullough Bohonak received a BS in zoology from North Carolina State University, an MS in education from the University of Tennessee at Martin, and an MS in computer science from Shippensburg University of Pennsylvania. She is a candidate for a PhD in computer science at Nova University and is an associate professor of computer science at the University of South Carolina at Lancaster, where she is actively involved in finding ways to increase the number of women and minorities in the sciences.

Mary Anne Campbell is a doctoral candidate in English at Purdue University. She has taught college writing and has done research in feminist theory.

Randall K. Campbell-Wright is an assistant professor of mathematics at the University of Tampa (Florida). He recently spent 2 years as co-chair of the university's Diversity Project, which sponsors programs that explore varying points of view. His mathematical research is in the area of operator theory.

Karen R. Cercone earned her PhD in geology from the University of Michigan. She has been at Indiana University of Pennsylvania since 1986. Her research interests include hydrogeology, geochemistry, and the uses of science fiction in teaching science.

Faye A. Chadwell received her MA in English from Appalachian State University in Boone, North Carolina, and her master's in library science from the University of Illinois at Urbana-Champaign. She is the social sciences bibliographer at the University of South Carolina at Columbia.

Caroline M. Eastman is a professor in the Department of Computer Science at the University of South Carolina at Columbia. Previous employers include Florida State University, Southern Methodist University, and the National Science Foundation. She received her BA in applied mathematics from Radcliffe College and her MS and PhD in computer science from the University of North Carolina at Chapel Hill. She has taught a wide variety of computer science courses at both introductory and advanced levels. Her primary research interests are in information systems, and she has published papers in the areas of information retrieval, database management systems, and computer science education. She is currently working on a book on information retrieval, to be published by Oxford University Press.

Holly Harris received her PhD in theoretical inorganic chemistry from the University of Wisconsin–Madison in 1988. She is currently the Clare Boothe Luce Professor for Women in Science and assistant professor of chemistry at Creighton University. She has published several articles on molecular electronic structure in major professional journals. Her current research involves studying electron transfer mechanisms at transition metal sites in enzymes. She is also interested in the history of women in science, particularly during the medieval period.

H. Patricia Hynes is visiting associate professor of environmental policy at Tufts University and director of the Institute on Women and Technology. An environmental engineer, she served as section chief in the EPA's hazardous waste program and chief of environmental management at the Massachusetts Port Authority. She is the author of *The Recurring Silent Spring*, *EarthRight*, and *Taking Population Out of the Equation: Reformulating I=PAT*. Currently she is completing a book on community gardens in inner cities.

Bonnie Kelly received her master of science in mathematics in 1992 and is studying part time for her PhD in the same subject. She is currently a mathematics instructor for TRIO Programs at the University of South Carolina. These programs provide access to education for students who are socioeconomically disadvantaged and are the first generation in their family to go to college.

Sara Majetich is a professor of physics at Carnegie-Mellon University. She received her education and training at Princeton, Columbia, the University of Georgia, and Cornell. Her current research interests focus on the synthesis and properties of nanocrystalline materials, and she received a National Young Investigator Award from the National Science Foundation. She has also been active in promoting women in science and in encouraging the participation of undergraduates in research.

Catherine Hurt Middlecamp graduated Phi Beta Kappa from Cornell University in 1972 and received a Danforth Fellowship to pursue a career in teaching at the college level. At the University of Wisconsin–Madison, she earned both a PhD in chemistry and a masters degree in counseling. Currently, at UW–Madison, she is the director of the Chemistry Learning Center, which is designed to provide a supportive, multicultural environment for students enrolled in general chemistry courses. In 1992, based on her teaching experiences both at the center and in large undergraduate courses, she initiated a graduate seminar course entitled Culturally Inclusive Chemistry. Middlecamp is coauthor of several resources for students, including CHEMPROF, an artificial intelligence–based computer tutor for general chemistry, and the book *How to Survive (and Even Excel) in General Chemistry*.

Indira Nair is associate professor and associate department head in the Department of Engineering and Public Policy at Carnegie Mellon University in Pittsburgh. After receiving her PhD in physics from Northwestern University, she taught high school physics for several years. At Carnegie-Mellon, her research areas include health risk analysis, particularly of electromagnetic radiation and fields; environmentally conscious design; public education; and the ethics of science and technology. Her teaching philosophy is based on understanding the diverse learning analysis of students and teaching science and engineering in their social and ethical contexts.

Darlene S. Richardson earned her PhD in geology from Columbia University. She taught abroad but she has been at Indiana University of Pennsylvania since 1981. Her research interests include sedimentary petrology, women's science education, and women scientists in the 18th and 19th centuries.

Jo Sanders is principal investigator of the Teacher Education Equity Project at the Center for Advanced Study in Education, City University of New York. This is a 3-year nationwide project to improve the teaching of gender equity to preservice teachers in science, mathematics, and computers. She has carried out many school-based action research projects since 1979, including the Computer Equity Expert Project, a nationwide project that trained 200 educators to achieve gender equity in their schools. She has written and spoken widely on gender equity in the United States and abroad.

Connie J. Sutton earned her MEd in science education from Indiana University of Pennsylvania and is a doctoral candidate in science education at the University of Pittsburgh. She has been at Indiana University of Pennsylvania since 1968. Her research interests include astronomy, math anxiety in grades K–12, women's science education, and women astronomers.

Sara L. Webb is associate professor of biology at Drew University, where she teaches ecology and botany as well as environmental science. She received her PhD (1986) and MS (1983) in ecology at the University of Minnesota and her BA (1976) in geography and environmental studies at Macalester College. Her research explores the dynamics of northern forests. Recent projects have examined forest responses to natural disturbance by windstorms, to ancient climate change as recorded in paleoecological records, and to human influences, including acid rain, introduction of invasive exotic plants, and forest fragmentation.

Index